Changing Offending Behaviour

A Handbook of Practical Exercises and Photcopiable Resources for Promoting Positive Change

Clark Baim and Lydia Guthrie

Illustrations by Jessica Mikhail
Foreword by Fergus McNeill

Jessica Kingsley *Publishers*
London and Philadelphia

First published in 2014
by Jessica Kingsley Publishers
73 Collier Street
London N1 9BE, UK
and
400 Market Street, Suite 400
Philadelphia, PA 19106, USA

www.jkp.com

Copyright © Clark Baim and Lydia Guthrie 2014
Illustrations copyright © Jessica Mikhail 2014
Foreword copyright © Fergus McNeill 2014

Library of Congress Cataloging in Publication Data

Baim, Clark.

Changing offending behaviour : a handbook of practical exercises and photocopiable resources for promoting positive change / Clark Baim and Lydia Guthrie ; foreword by Fergus McNeill.

pages cm

Includes bibliographical references.

ISBN 978-0-85700-928-9 (alk. paper)

1. Criminals--Rehabilitation. 2. Behavior modification. 3. Criminal psychology. I. Guthrie, Lydia. II. Title.

HV9275.B35 2014

364.4'8--dc23

2014007798

British Library Cataloguing in Publication Data

A CIP catalogue record for this book is available from the British Library

ISBN 978 1 84905 511 6
eISBN 978 0 85700 928 9

Printed and bound in Great Britain

Contents

Foreword

Twenty years ago, one of the hardest parts of my working day was figuring out exactly what to do with the people coming to see me in a criminal justice social work office in northeast Glasgow. My social work training had done a great deal to help me understand and even explain why people ended up under my supervision on probation or parole, and it had honed the skills that helped us build relationships and work together. It had also equipped me with a range of practice theories or intervention approaches, whether 'task-centred', 'solution-focused', 'problem-solving', 'crisis intervention' or 'cognitive behavioural'. What it didn't really do was actually give me 'stuff' to do; useful stuff that might not just help me and my clients to understand the issues, but also to develop new skills and find new solutions to complex problems.

That is exactly what this book aims to do, and succeeds in doing. It provides criminal and youth justice practitioners with lots of useful, practical 'stuff'. Drawing on the extensive practice and training experience of the authors (much greater experience than mine), the book is a repository of both 'practice wisdom' and practice tools. If I were still a practitioner and came across this book, I'd see it immediately for what it is – a godsend.

But I suspect I'd also appreciate the fact that this book doesn't aim to tell its readers what to do. It is most definitely not an instruction manual. Rather, in keeping with its function as a repository, it invites the reader to jump into a respectful professional dialogue; you (the reader) and your clients have to work out what is relevant and what is not; you and your clients have to work out what might work and what might not – and then you have to experiment, reflect and evaluate. In my view, it is exactly this sort of reflexive engagement that ultimately enriches rehabilitative practice and produces results.

In sorting out those questions of relevance and effectiveness, the opening two chapters provide useful orientation points. Neither of them offers an elaborated synthesis of the theories and perspectives they introduce – again that job is left for the professional reader. But just as much as in the later sections with the practical tasks and tools, so in these chapters the reader is invited into dialogue. You will have to figure out which of these theories and perspectives is going to be most valuable to you and the people you meet and support. But like all great books, this one will help you by encouraging you to ask intelligent and provocative questions – and if you use it wisely, it will support positive changes in your practice and therefore positive changes in others.

Fergus McNeill

Professor of Criminology and Social Work

Acknowledgements

In writing this book, we have drawn upon our experiences over several decades working with adults and young people in prisons, young offender institutions, probation hostels, community supervision settings, secure hospitals, shelters, drug and alcohol rehabilitation centres, services for victims and survivors, services for families, children and vulnerable adults, and voluntary services. We thank the many thousands of people with whom we have worked, and we honour their brave engagement in the complex process of personal change.

We have also been inspired by many colleagues. We are keen advocates of co-working, and much of our best work has been done in collaboration with others. We offer our thanks and appreciation to colleagues, past and present, from HM Prison Grendon Underwood, HM Young Offender Institution Aylesbury, the National Offender Management Service, the Probation Service for England and Wales, the Midlands Training Consortium, the Thames Valley Unit, Cheswold Park Hospital, the Lucy Faithfull Foundation and the Wolvercote Clinic, Circles of Support and Accountability, the Nelson Trust, the Make a Change team, Geese Theatre Company, the Victoria Department of Corrections (Australia), Berry Street (Melbourne), the State Probation Service of Latvia, Pollsmoor Prison in Cape Town, South Africa, the Irish Prison Service and Probation Service, the Probation Board for Northern Ireland, Criminal Justice Social Work Services in Scotland, Start360, Hertfordshire Constabulary, the Facilitator Agency, the National Organisation for the Treatment of Abusers (NOTA), the British Psychodrama Association (BPA), Mentor Forensics, Barnardo's, the NSPCC, Birmingham University School of Psychology (forensic programme), Wilcox Psychological Associates, South London and Maudsley NHS Foundation Trust, Oxfordshire Youth Offending Service, Richmond Youth Offending Service, LAURUS Development, Oxfordshire Domestic Abuse Unit, Domestic Violence Intervention Project (DVIP), Ashworth Special Hospital, Rape Crisis, Victim Support and Escaping Victimhood. In addition, we have each had a long involvement, as lead national trainers, programme authors, supervisors and group workers, with the community-based sexual offending groupwork programmes in the UK and Northern Ireland. This work has been a cornerstone of our professional lives, and we extend our thanks and profound respect to all those colleagues who we worked alongside in this endeavour. Most particularly, we thank Mary Leyland, David Middleton, Elizabeth Hayes, Anita McLeod, David Cook, Mark Farmer, Phil Jarvis, Ian Macnair, Sarah Winwin-Sein, John Richards and Joanna Bell for their support and liaison during these crucial years of programme development in the UK.

During our work as trainers and supervisors, we have had the privilege of listening to stories about moments of good practice and moments of challenge. We offer deepest thanks to everyone who has attended our courses, shared their insights and helped us to translate their experiences into useful practice knowledge to share with others.

We also owe a huge debt to those who have taught us on professional development and academic courses, covering themes such as criminology, neuro-development, self-compassion, psychodrama, psychotherapy, sociodrama, sociometry, systemic therapy, resilience, mindfulness, mentalisation, applied theatre, dramatherapy and attachment theory. In particular, we thank Dr Patricia Crittenden, whose observations about attachment theory, psychopathology and the role of the professional helper are rigorously researched, insightful and profoundly humane.

We have enjoyed working alongside the team at Jessica Kingsley Publishers, including Stephen Jones, Sarah Minty, Kitty Walker, Sarah Evans and Victoria Nicholas. We thank them for their guidance and professionalism. We also thank Professor Fergus McNeill for his generous and heartfelt foreword to the book, and Jess Mikhail for her insightful illustrations that perfectly capture a range of concepts. Finally, we thank our families and friends, who have offered crucial support and encouragement during the writing of this book.

Clark Baim and Lydia Guthrie

May 2014

Introduction

This handbook is our contribution to the growing knowledge about effective and culturally aware interventions with people who have committed offences of all types. It offers a wide range of exercises and structured activities. The overall purpose of the exercises is to help people lead productive, fulfilling and offence-free lives. The book is meant as a resource for use in criminal justice and forensic hospital settings, and in charitable and voluntary sector settings that work alongside the criminal justice system. It is our hope that this handbook will bring theory and practice alive in a conceptually clear but dynamic, engaging and hands-on manner that helps you to practise effectively with your clients.

We work from the premise that most people are capable of personal change when motivated, given the opportunity to express themselves differently and the opportunity to try out new ways of dealing with life's challenges. There is good evidence that the integrative, strengths-based approach taken in this book can help people work towards a more positive future for themselves and their community. We hope this handbook will encourage the further development of effective, humane, creative and responsive criminal justice interventions internationally.

A Broad, Accessible Approach

Most resources available for criminal justice practitioners come in four types:

- textbooks that summarise research and/or describe programmes and approaches

- offence-specific manuals and programmes (e.g. domestic violence, sexual offending, or drink-drive programmes)

- texts focusing on assessment, policies and processes for managing offenders

- academic journals.

This book offers a different approach, namely a practical, hands-on book with a range of photocopiable exercises that can be used with anyone who has committed offences.

In addition, this handbook deliberately moves away from the idea that each type of offence and each type of offender must have a custom-designed approach with a range of constituent manuals and programme guides. On the contrary, we offer the view that people who commit offences are first and foremost people, rather than simply 'criminals'. As human beings, people who commit offences will have much more in common with every other human being than they will have differences. This approach is reflected in our choice to use the word 'client' as opposed to 'offender' throughout this book.

In our experience of delivering offending behaviour programmes and training for criminal justice professionals in rehabilitative approaches across the range of offence types, we can see that the broad trend of programme design is leading steadily towards the same common themes. Myriad programmes have been developed for all manner of special groups, with significant overlaps between them. Therefore, in this handbook, we have tried to capture what is essential to most offence-specific programmes in order to offer what might be seen as a common underlying framework of exercises that, when delivered well and in an appropriate setting, will help people who have committed offences to live a fulfilling and offence-free life. Where needed, you can add to and supplement these exercises with more offence-specific exercises, but these exercise are designed to encompass the broadest possible cross-section of potential clients. Indeed, almost all of the exercises in this handbook could be adapted for use with any adult engaged in a personal change process, even those with no criminal history.

Origins of this book

The origins of this book lie in our shared commitment to developing effective practice-based resources for frontline practitioners. Together we have, to date, written more than 15 manuals describing and supporting offending behaviour programmes of all types. The impetus for writing this book lies in the development and successful road testing of these ideas across professions, sectors and jurisdictions, and in our desire to make these ideas more accessible to practitioners. We have seen first-hand, through thousands of sessions with clients and also in hundreds of training sessions for criminal justice professionals, how clear the need is for interactive and practice-orientated forms of learning that engage not only the intellects but the full range of senses and emotional and cognitive learning capacities of our clients, and thus make learning richer, deeper and more brain-friendly.

Who is this book for?

This book is relevant to a wide range of professionals working across the criminal justice, youth justice, social care, voluntary and health sectors. These include social workers, psychologists, psychiatrists, youth workers and youth justice workers, voluntary sector workers, probation and prison officers and criminal justice professionals of all types, psychotherapists, counsellors and education professionals. In addition, this handbook is relevant to those providing pre- and post-qualifying training for practitioners, and those providing supervision, support, coaching and mentoring for frontline practitioners. By extension, the guide will also be informative for those in a leadership position who are concerned about the role of enduring and purposeful relationships in social and mental well-being within organisations and across society. Finally, although this book has been written in the context of our work in the UK, Ireland, several other countries in Europe, the USA, South Africa and Australia, it will be relevant to professionals in other countries, although its application will require consideration of local cultural, organisational and service delivery variations.

What are the aims of this book?

Thinking about the needs and interests of such potential readers, we drew up the following list of what this book should offer:

- a practical, theoretically coherent and user-friendly workbook for busy frontline practitioners

- tools and other resources to assist practitioners who want to use a relationship-based approach

- a work-based resource that can be used by individuals, teams, co-workers, supervisors, teachers and trainers to reflect on and improve the preparation, use and support of exercises aimed at promoting positive change

- specific but flexible strategies to build practitioner confidence in working in a varied and responsive way

- an approach to the application of varied methods that complements rather than competes with existing frameworks

- an approach that speaks to diverse professions and modalities, and which can be used in a multidisciplinary environment

- a guide that increases the confidence of practitioners to act as change agents with their clients.

What this book cannot provide

Space does not allow us to provide a comprehensive account of rehabilitation theory. Instead, this guide describes the key theory necessary for busy practitioners to understand and use. If you are interested in reading more deeply into the theory behind this work, we provide a wide range of references at the end of the book.

Furthermore, this handbook cannot train you to be a therapist. What it can offer is wide-ranging and practical guidance that will help you to deliver relationship-based practice that is highly adaptable and responsive to the needs, aspirations, interests, risks and challenges posed by each individual you work with.

Finally, this guide cannot be a substitute for training, supervision and continuing professional development, which are so crucial to every practitioner's effectiveness and professional growth. It is essential that facilitators have sufficient training and skill to undertake the exercises in this workbook, and that they are properly supervised, insured and working to established principles of safety and ethics within the social care, criminal justice, health and related professions.

In preparing this book, we were guided by some simple but deeply held beliefs

Intentions behind the book

- The intended outcome of working with people who have committed offences must be a balance of reducing re-offending while at the same time promoting their social inclusion and ability to lead a fulfilling life.

- This book is not a manualised programme. It is intended more as a menu for reflective practitioners to choose from and use with creativity and skill, taking into account the needs, strengths, resources and preferences of the client.

The systems perspective

- People exist within small and large systems and these systems can have a very powerful influence on the onset of offending behaviour, the continuation of the behaviour or, indeed, the ability of the person to desist from crime.

- We recognise the inequalities which are inherent in our society. Our clients may face challenges and discrimination based upon culture, race, gender, sexuality, religion, disability, age, class, criminal history, etc. We, as workers, cannot fix these problems on our own, but we can listen to and validate our clients' experiences, while encouraging them to use their strengths and the resources around them to find coping strategies and positive solutions.

The process of change

- People can choose to change the ways in which they think about themselves, others and the world in general. These changes can range from the subtle to the very significant.

- A person decides to change for their own reasons, which will be unique to them.

- The constructive approach is one that starts where the client is and builds from there. Many clients will start their work with us while they are still pre-contemplative – in other words, they do not see that there is a problem or that they have a role to play in the problem. Many will see their future as a life of crime or being a gang member. This needs to be acknowledged and validated. Only then can we begin to move forward and help the client see and develop new possibilities for their life.

- The brain is an organ of adaptation and change, with the potential for change across the lifespan. No one is too set in their ways to make changes if given the right incentives (although some people might face significant obstacles to change).

- Change is difficult, and can be frightening, and there are often setbacks. Change is a process, not a one-off event.

Relationship-based practice

- Our most precious resource in helping other people is how we use ourselves. Relationships are the main tool for promoting and sustaining change.

- Frontline practitioners must be empowered and liberated to use all of their skills, creative powers, flexibility, humanity and intellect to help clients to access theirs.

- Working with people who have committed offences requires particular skills and qualities from the facilitator. Facilitators who work with people who have committed offences have to combine a delicate balance of roles including facilitator of change, assessor of risks/needs/strengths, advocate, case manager, social connector and other roles.

- Everyone has the capacity for change, but we cannot change anyone else. It is work that we do *with* people, not *to* them. The exercises in the book are meant to be facilitated as a *co-production* with the client, not as something they receive passively.

- Genuine praise and encouragement are far more effective at promoting change than criticism, threat and sanction. The worker needs to be alert for even the smallest word or action on the part of the client that hints at positive change, so that it can be held up to the light and reinforced.

- One of the most difficult skills to learn is knowing when *not* to challenge an unhelpful thought or attitude. Insufficient challenge can promote collusion, but too much challenge will damage rapport and motivation. There is a difference between reinforcing an offence supportive statement and hearing it, acknowledging it, but responding neutrally.

Balancing care, control and public protection

- In some agencies, workers will also have a formal role of assessing risk and reporting to public protection meetings. This is sometimes known as the care versus control dilemma. It is often difficult to negotiate, but a mutually respectful and boundaried relationship is the key to managing this potential role conflict (Masters 1994).

- Public protection demands that we hold in mind an objective assessment of the risk posed by a client, whilst at the same time developing a respectful and attuned relationship with the client.

- Public protection – indeed the general public – requires that we are clear about our roles. We are not the judge, nor the jury, nor an advocate for the victim or for society at large. Our role is to prevent harm to potential victims in the future by helping the client to develop and maintain a positive and offence-free lifestyle.

Tips for different readers

General tips

How you use this book will depend on your learning style, prior knowledge, work context and occupational role. However, we would strongly advise that, in order to make good use of Part II (Chapters 3–6), you will need to be familiar with the concepts in Part I (the first two chapters). You may want to return to Part I after working through Part II, as theory often makes more sense once it is linked to practice.

Tips for individual practitioners and co-workers

Learning is often easier and more memorable if shared with others. Think about a colleague, co-worker, mentor or supervisor with whom you would like to share your exploration. For instance, by working together you could:

- reflect on your current knowledge about theory and practice of working constructively with people who have committed offences

- reflect on your current strategies and working practices

- consider how to implement these exercises within the context of the agency in which you work

- co-deliver or share ideas about delivering the exercises in this book

- develop ideas for new approaches to working with your clients

- identify other people, opportunities, resources, training or literature to develop your practice

- share together your experience of doing these exercises for yourselves. It is strongly recommended that you complete the exercises for yourself before facilitating them with a client. Then, with colleagues, you can share what the experience was like for you and what learning you gained. (This does not mean you need to discuss everything that you wrote or thought about, as this might be too personal to share with a colleague.)

Tips for supervisors

Good supervision is crucial for practitioners who work with troubled and troubling people. Good supervision helps workers to be clear on their purpose and tasks and helps them to reflect on the emotions, dynamics and meaning of their work. Supervision should offer a predictable, focused, containing and reflective opportunity for workers to explore and improve their work. This is a deeply rewarding but challenging role for supervisors. This book offers the opportunity for supervisors to:

- reflect on your current knowledge about theory and practice of working constructively with people who have committed offences

- use a common reference point for exercises aimed at reducing re-offending and helping people to lead offence-free lives

- help frontline workers to integrate a wide range of relevant theories into a highly practical approach to working with people who have committed offences

- become actively involved in developing each worker's skills through shared use of the exercises in this book.

Tips for teachers, trainers, mentors and tutors

This book can be used as a resource for a range of disciplines to engage students and qualified staff in developing both a practice-based understanding of rehabilitation and its relevance to their roles. Here are some issues to consider:

- What is your current knowledge about the theory and practice of working constructively with people who have committed offences? How are you currently using this as a teacher, trainer, mentor or tutor?

- What place does relationship-based practice and reflective practice currently have in your organisation's practice knowledge and skills framework?

- How might the approaches used in this book enhance your teaching, training, mentoring or tutoring programme?

- How can you use the material in Chapters 3 to 6 for group learning or one-to-one learning?

Tips for your organisation

If you work with people who may pose a risk to themselves or others, you need to work within a clear policy and practice framework – in other words, your own 'secure base'. You need to be clear about:

- your roles and responsibilities, and in particular any statutory responsibilities regarding assessment, planning, intervention, sharing information, collaboration, report writing and review processes

- the organisation's framework for case assessment, planning and intervention

- working with other agencies or disciplines with regards to referrals, assessment, planning, intervention and review, particularly in statutory or risk-management situations

- the supervision available to you and how you are accountable for your practice
- the knowledge, skills and values you require to practise competently and how the organisation will support you in developing these.

How the book is organised

The book is divided into two parts. Part I consists of two chapters focusing on essential theory and skills. Part II consists of four chapters of practical exercises and activities, arranged by theme and in a suggested sequence from start to finish.

Part I: Essential theory, principles and skills

CHAPTER 1: ESSENTIAL THEORY AND PRINCIPLES OF PRACTICE

This chapter describes the essential theories we draw upon and integrate in the exercises in this book. This includes the model of change and also the integrated model we use to conceptualise the etiology of offending. The chapter also outlines what we consider to be essential tasks for preparation and principles of practice for workers.

CHAPTER 2: ESSENTIAL SKILLS AND FRAMEWORKS FOR PRACTITIONERS

This chapter covers topics including assessment, planning and evaluation; working constructively with clients who deny their offence; the skills and qualities of the facilitator; the art of asking questions; adaptations that can be used with all of the exercises; and several handy techniques that can be used at any time.

Part II: Exercises to promote positive change

CHAPTER 3: BUILDING ON STRENGTHS AND MOTIVATING CHANGE

This chapter has ten exercises aimed at helping the client to think about their life, how they have arrived at this point, and what directions they want their life to go. The exercises help the person to locate their strengths, their values, their sense of self-worth, and their understanding of the challenges they face. By addressing issues such as family and social networks, life experiences and values, the facilitator has an opportunity to engage constructively with the client, build a basis of trust and provide a realistic opportunity for successful engagement. The exercises will also help the person to understand their role in the process of change, and what is involved in the process of change. They will be helped to begin to set in place changes they can begin immediately.

CHAPTER 4: LOOKING INWARD: UNDERSTANDING MYSELF AND MY PATTERNS OF BEHAVIOUR

This chapter contains ten exercises that help the client to look at some of the significant highs and lows they have experienced in their life, how they have coped, and the strategies they use for regulating and expressing their emotions when they are in stressful or threatening situations. This includes an exercise focusing on the impact of perceived danger upon the brain, and how the limbic system can become activated by real or perceived danger.

The chapter contains several autobiographical exercises aimed at helping the client to understand their patterns of behaviour at key points in their life, and to find meaning in their responses. This includes an exercise designed to promote better understanding of the offence, and alternative decisions they could have made. The client is encouraged to talk through their understanding of why they responded as they did, and how they want things to be different (or similar) in the future. Several exercises specifically look at experiences during childhood, and how these experiences may have influenced the development of their later responses and strategies.

The chapter also contains exercises aimed at promoting improved self-regulation, for example through practising the skills of mindfulness, self-compassion, internal dialogue and reflection, and other self-regulation skills.

CHAPTER 5: LOOKING OUTWARD: ME IN RELATION TO OTHER PEOPLE

This chapter contains 10 exercises aimed at helping the client to understand how they relate to other people and how their behaviour affects other people. The chapter begins with an autobiographical exercise looking at the person's history of relationships of all types. There are exercises aimed at helping to improve self-esteem and the ability to recognise and communicate about emotions. Other exercises look more broadly at perspective-taking and developing empathy and compassion for other people. One of the exercises encourages the client to understand the impact of their behaviour on the victim(s) of their crime(s) and the people related to the victim. There are also exercises aimed at helping the client to develop their interpersonal/social skills, and becoming more integrated in their emotional, social and psychological functioning.

CHAPTER 6: LOOKING FORWARD: SETTING GOALS, PREPARING FOR CHALLENGES AHEAD AND MOVING FORWARD WITH MY LIFE

This chapter contains four exercises that help the client to think about important life goals and aspirations, and then to anticipate, plan and prepare for their future life. An important aim in these sessions will be to look ahead to possible high-risk scenarios and situations that can elicit old responses. This can then lead to skills practice of positive ways to deal with challenging situations. During these sessions the client is encouraged to develop more links with the community and to develop more of a stake in society. The exercises encourage the client to link with other people in their support network, for example family, friends, people in the community, volunteers, para-professionals and professionals. This will reflect the important notion of 'social capital', which is a cornerstone of contemporary desistance theory. The exercises are aimed at helping the client to become more confident that they can maintain changes and also ask for help when they need it. The last exercise encourages the client to look back over their progress and look to the future.

The advantages of a learning-by-doing approach

In this book we have tried to emphasise the importance of making the exercises active and immediately relevant to the person you are working with. Wherever possible, try to get the person you are working with actively involved. This does not necessarily mean up on their feet and moving around (although it might); it may simply mean that you get them involved in a focused way in an activity or trying to solve a problem. These methods have significant advantages over presentation-based or instructional approaches.

Frequently asked questions

Can these exercises be applied to one-to-one work and groups?

Yes, they can. Although we mainly describe the exercises in relation to one-to-one work, they can also be used in groupwork situations.

Do these exercises apply to people who have committed all types of offence?

Yes they do. While most offending behaviour programmes are designed to address a particular type of crime (e.g. violence, property crime, sexual abuse, domestic abuse), this book is designed to apply across the spectrum. The exercises have been used with people convicted of all types of offences. This includes work with males and females, both adults and young people aged 14 and older.

You should be able to adapt the exercises and methods in this book to any population or offence type, providing you have knowledge and experience in working with their particular needs.

Can these exercises be adapted for use with other groups and individuals?

Yes. The majority of the exercises outlined in this book share much in common with work done in fields as wide-ranging as counselling and psychotherapy, education, adventure therapy, mental health, work with refugees, human relations training and corporate team development. The exercises, with appropriate modifications, apply to almost any group of people.

Is it necessary to use all of the exercises or to use them in the published sequence?

Typically, the client will undertake some of the exercises but not necessarily all of them, depending on their needs. Some people may not need to do some of the exercises, particularly if they have successfully completed a similar exercise in an offence-focused programme or if the topic is not relevant to them. For example, some people may not need to do the exercises on resolving trauma and loss, and others may not need to work on interpersonal/social skills.

Similarly, you and the client may choose to do the exercises in a different sequence. There may be any number of reasons for this, and this is left to your professional judgement. The published order is meant only as a suggested sequence and is not meant to be prescriptive. There are some limits, however. For example, the preliminary and motivational exercises in Chapter 3 should be completed before engaging with offence-focused work.

Can this material be used in work with young people?

We have applied many of the exercises to work with people as young as 14. However, if you are working with people below age 18 it is important to understand the particular needs and vulnerabilities of this age group, which will mean making adjustments to the level of intensity and focus of the work.

How does this type of work take into account cultural differences and socio-economic constraints?

In our descriptions of the exercises, you will see that we suggest many different ways of delivering the sessions. We encourage you to use story-telling, music, art, role play, and multi-sensory ways of working in order to fully engage with your clients and find the mode of expression and learning that works best for them. For many clients, particularly that high proportion who have had a troubled history in school, it would be highly counter-productive to take a 'chalk and talk' approach to the sessions. By using a wide variety of ideas and approaches to learning, combining talk-based approaches with experiential and creative modes of working, you can be far more responsive to the learning styles and cultural differences of participants from different cultural, ethnic and socio-economic backgrounds.

We also need to be aware of the socio-economic constraints that influence trends in offending, and this includes the potentially debilitating effects of poverty, social exclusion, social stigma and limited expectations that affect whole sections of the population. We must acknowledge these systemic forces without encouraging a sense of hopelessness or the view that an individual's circumstances are completely beyond their control. The task is to treat all participants individually within their social/historical context, emphasising individual responsibility while acknowledging external influences.

Can these exercises be used with people diagnosed with mental health conditions or personality disorders?

The exercises have been designed to be adaptable for all people who have committed offences, including men and women who have been diagnosed with personality disorders or mental illness. As long as you have a solid grounding in the work with your particular client group, you should be able to adapt and structure the material in this book appropriately.

For many clients, particularly those who are highly symptomatic (e.g. hearing voices, delusional, clinically depressed), it would not be appropriate to begin these sessions until the person has been psychologically stable for at least six months, particularly if they are taking medication for their psychological condition. Clients who are emotionally fragile may need extra support from staff, family, friends, volunteers and others in order to make the most use of the sessions, particularly when the topics become emotionally charged or complex.

Can these exercises be used with people with intellectual disabilities?

Yes, indeed. The exercises can be adapted in a very wide variety of ways to suit the learning needs and intellectual capacities of clients. Many of the exercises, for example, can be made mainly experiential, using live situations, role play, practice and concrete examples. These can be repeated and modified as often as needed. Such experiential methods are often uniquely advantageous when used with people who have intellectual disabilities, and you are encouraged to adapt the exercises to suit the client. Chapter 2 describes a wide variety of adaptations that can be used with any exercise in the book, and many of the descriptions of individual exercises also contain suggested adaptations and variations.

Who can facilitate this type of work?

The exercises in this book should only be delivered by staff members who are adequately trained, supported and supervised. Due to the nature of the content of the exercises, the potential impact issues that affect delivery and staff performance, and the interpersonal dynamics that can result from addressing the material in this book, there must be adequate supervision, training and support in place before the exercises are started. This includes risk assessments for health and safety. While the exercises are 'tried and tested' and the principles of working are well established, the exercises will only be as good as the worker

delivering them and the context in which the work is done. We are firm believers in 'who works' just as much as 'what works' (Vennard, Hedderman and Sugg 1997).

On a related point, the exercises in this book should be delivered only in coordination with and within the requirements of the governing agencies, laws, ethical guidelines, policies and procedures pertaining to the organisation where they are used.

Is there a suggested format for each session?

For one-to-one sessions, each session is designed to last from 45 to 90 minutes. The session length should be agreed with the client in advance of the sessions. Occasionally, sessions may run longer than 90 minutes, for example, where a particularly sensitive piece of work needs to be completed. In any event, sessions should not run longer than one hour and 45 minutes. If you offer groupwork, sessions will normally be 1½ to 2 hours in length. One-to-one and groupwork sessions can have the following suggested format:

1. Mood check and noting anything significant that has happened since last session.

2. Setting agenda for the session.

3. Collecting/discussing any out-of-session work or tasks.

4. An optional short exercise or question to warm up to the day's theme.

5. The exercise for that session.

6. Agreeing and preparing for out-of-session task.

7. Check out feelings, key learning, feedback for facilitator, and closure (relaxation exercise where needed).

Now you are ready to start

We hope that you will find this book thought-provoking, engaging and most of all, of real practical use.

PART I
Essential Theory, Principles and Skills

CHAPTER 1

Essential Theory and Principles of Practice

In this chapter, you will learn about:

- the multi-factor, integrated etiological model of offending behaviour that we use
- the theories that underpin the exercises in this book
- essential preparation and principles of practice for workers.

Introduction

The exercises in this book have been designed with maximum flexibility in mind (McNeill 2012) while also retaining the principles of consistency and what are generally known as 'Risk, Needs and Responsivity' (RNR) principles (Andrews, Bonta and Wormwith 2006; Andrews and Dowden 2007). The exercises place emphasis on trying to match intervention to the needs of the individual person, responding to their particular strengths and aspirations while taking into account cultural diversity and the social/systemic factors that have influenced their offending and which can affect their change process. On the whole, the exercises emphasise the importance of helping all people to believe that their life and their situation can improve, and that they have a crucial role to play in improving their life (Gorman *et al.* 2006). With such an emphasis, the exercises also seek to improve the individual's sense of agency and self-determination – the sense that they can have a positive influence on their own 'life script'. With this emphasis in mind, the exercises should be seen as a collaborative endeavour between the client, the worker and the agency, rather than being something 'done to' the client. The principle here is that of 'collaborative enquiry' as opposed to treatment that is imposed and passively received.

Etiological theory

Etiology is the study of the causes of things, for instance, a disease, a malfunction, or – in the context of this book – offending behaviour. Single factor theories which attribute the cause of offending to a single trait or developmental experience are insufficiently flexible to account for the diversity of offending and the diversity of people who commit offences. Single factor theories offer a partial explanation of the predominant causal pathways towards offending but cannot explain why a majority of those who have experienced developmental obstacles do not go on to commit offences in adulthood. For these important reasons, multi-factorial approaches may be more helpful in explaining the routes towards offending behaviour (Andrews and Bonta 2006; Marshall *et al.* 2006; Thornton 2002; Ward and Maruna 2007).

The integrative, multi-factorial approach we use in this book incorporates micro- and macro- factors that influence the development of criminal behaviour, such as social, economic, environmental and cultural influences, including poverty and experiences of discrimination and social exclusion; insecure parent-child attachment; childhood abuse, including neglect and sexual, physical, emotional and verbal abuse; unresolved trauma and loss; peer/family influences; cultural messages, including media-driven and politically driven messages; witnessing domestic violence and parental rape; inconsistent discipline; disrupted early attachments, for instance, being taken into state care, or living with non-parental relatives; problems in emotional and behavioral coping; insecure attachment in adulthood (e.g. fear of abandonment, fear of rejection, fear of closeness, ambivalence towards relationships); failure to successfully negotiate the challenges of adolescent peer relationships and sexual relationships; and failure to achieve satisfactory goals in life.

Among this wide range of potential factors contributing to the development of offending behaviour, the integrated model holds that with certain individuals, a combination of these factors during childhood and/or adolescence, *in combination with insufficient protective factors*, will contribute to the onset of offending behaviour. It is also possible that the factors mentioned will lead to a low sense of self-worth and a poor ability to meet one's needs legally. In such circumstances, a person may feel like it is a better short term solution to offend, rather than to try to achieve life goals, satisfaction or comfort through law-abiding means (Ward *et al.* 2004). This book acknowledges this as a starting place for looking at potential new routes to living a fulfilling and meaningful life without resorting to offending behaviour.

Underpinning theory and models of change: An integrative approach

The fields of criminology, sociology, clinical psychology, forensic psychology and psychotherapy offer a wide range of theories, models and approaches that have been shown to be effective as constructive ways of engaging with offenders and helping them to reduce their risk of re-offending (Craig, Dixon and Gannon 2013). In this book, we use an integrative approach to treatment and intervention, drawing on a wide range of theories and models in order to promote a flexible approach that is best able to meet the needs of each person while also adhering to well-established principles of safe and effective practice.

The integrated model underpinning the approach we take in this book is informed by 20 theories and methods. We see a large overlap between and among these approaches, adding up to a comprehensive combination that is holistic, evidence-based and powerfully motivational. Desistance theory (Maruna and LeBel 2010; McNeill *et al.* 2012), the Good Lives Model (Ward and Gannon 2006), cognitive-behavioural theory (Beck 1976; Beck, Freeman and Davis 2003), attachment theory (Bowlby 1969; Crittenden 2008; Marshall, Serran and Cortoni 2000), social learning theory (Bandura 1977), motivational interviewing (Miller and Rollnick 2002), the cycle of change (Prochaska and DiClemente 1982; Prochaska, DiClemente and Norcross 1992) and the Risk-Needs-Responsivity Model (Andrews and Dowden 2007; Andrews *et al.* 2006) have all been shown to be important underlying theories and approaches used in offending behaviour programmes. These are the central organising theories used to underpin the integrated approach we take in this book.

In addition, there are a number of other theories and approaches that we use in order to provide maximum flexibility to meet a range of needs and learning styles among the clients. The supplementary theories and approaches include systems theory (Bateson 1972, 1979), the invitational approach (Jenkins 1997), role theory (Moreno 1946, 1993), person-centred therapy (Rogers 1967), positive psychology (Seligman *et al.* 2005), narrative therapy (Dallos 2006; White and Epston 1990), the ecological-transactional model (Cicchetti and Valentino

2006), mentalisation (Fonagy *et al.* 2004) the Therapeutic Spiral Model (Hudgins 2002), psychodynamic theory (Bateman, Brown and Pedder 2010), the theory of spontaneity-creativity (Blatner 2000; Moreno 1946) and labelling theory (Becker 1963; Goffman 1959; Mead 1934; Tannenbaum 1938).

What follows is a summary of these key theories and approaches, described in the order listed above. The theories selected are not meant as an exhaustive list; there are many other theories we are aware of which have been used successfully with a wide variety of clients, including offenders. If you are trained in a modality not mentioned here, we strongly encourage you to bring that knowledge and expertise into play as you deliver the exercises in this book.

Desistance theory

The theory that we and many others have found to be the most promising and inspirational recent development in the sphere of offender rehabilitation is desistance theory, which has a quickly expanding literature and research base (Maruna 2001; Maruna and LeBel 2010; McNeill 2012; McNeill *et al.* 2012; McNeill and Weaver 2010). Desistance theory is a branch of criminological theory which seeks to analyse and explain the change processes which are associated with individuals ceasing to offend. Desistance theorists emphasise that desistance is not a one-off event, but rather a process which may involve lapses, relapses and uncertainty (Laub and Sampson 2001; Laws and Ward 2011; Maruna 2001).

Desistance theorists often explore the question of how individuals who have committed offences construct alternative pro-social identities for themselves by the creation of self-narratives that hold the promise of redemption (Maruna 2001). For example, many ex-offenders may develop a self-narrative that accounts for their previous offending as being uncharacteristic of them, as in 'I lost my head', 'It was the drugs talking', or, 'I was just a teenager and wasn't thinking'. Such a self-narrative allows the person to acknowledge their offending while also being able to hold out an image of themselves as being better than their worst deeds, and able to move forward into a non-offending lifestyle.

By interviewing and examining in detail the lives of people who have 'made good' and 'gone straight', desistance researchers are making great strides in helping us to identify the factors that help this process, the factors that are neutral in their effects, and the factors that weaken individual resolve and lead people back to crime. The theory considers these processes in the context of the family, social, work, statutory and other systems which impact on the individual.

Some of the findings of the desistance research are common sense. For example, it is not surprising that having a stable job, a stake in society, a supportive family and a fulfilling relationship with a partner should be highly correlated with desistance. Yet the desistance research goes further and helps us to see that constructive work can be even more effective when we build on the person's strengths and promote positive ways of living. Laws and Ward (2011) propose that those involved in the treatment of individuals who have offended should view their clients not as individuals who are primarily characterised by an absence of strengths or resources, or as a collection of risk factors to be managed. Rather, we should view individuals who have offended first and foremost as 'people like us'. We should emphasise and promote the person's pro-social identity and facilitate their social connections. Furthermore, desistance theory focuses on the importance of helping the individual to exercise their autonomy and to construct a personal identity which is incompatible with further offending. The phrase used for this is 'assisted desistance' – an elegant re-frame of what rehabilitative programmes can accomplish. Porporino neatly summarises this point when he writes:

> Perhaps we may be more successful, offenders and our communities may be better served, if we get past our programme fetishism, casework managerialism, and our

compliance-on-demand syndromes when working with offenders. The desistance paradigm suggests that we might be better off if we allowed offenders to *guide us* instead, listened to what they think might best fit their individual struggles out of crime, rather than insist that our solutions are their salvation.' (Emphasis is the author's)

(Porporino 2010, p.80)

This is in contrast to some views of offender rehabilitation which foreground issues of risk, control and management of offenders. While assessing and managing risk is central to public protection, and we would never want to minimise its importance, when we are focused on rehabilitation and promoting positive change, our approach should also emphasise positive incentives of leading a fulfilling and law-abiding life. This means we see the client as far more than a collection of risks and dangers to be managed, or a 'subject' that must be fixed. We focus mainly on the positive aims and aspirations of the intervention as opposed to the problems that came before. The approach becomes one where we collaboratively discuss the client's life, goals and incentives, and then work together with them to tackle risks and obstacles by developing their internal and social strengths (Gorman *et al.* 2006).

Farrall (2002) offers a very useful quote from a probation client, responding to a question about what he found helpful in preventing him from re-offending. He offers a concise argument in favour of the desistance paradigm:

It's finding people's abilities and nourishing and making them work for those things… why not go forward into something… For instance, you might be good at writing – push that forward, progress that, rather than saying 'well look, why did you kick that bloke's head in? Do you think we should go back into anger management courses?' when all you want to do is be a writer. Does that make any sense to you at all? Yeah, yeah. To sum it up, you're saying you should look forwards not back. Yeah. I know that you have to look back to a certain extent to make sure that you don't end up like that [again]. The whole order seems to be about going back and back and back. There doesn't seem to be much 'forward.'

(Farrall 2002, p.225)

The Good Lives Model

The Good Lives Model (Ward and Gannon 2006; Ward and Maruna 2007) is a holistic and strengths-based way of conceptualising healthy human functioning and what it means to live a pro-social and meaningful life. It is a model deeply grounded in the ethical concept of human dignity and universal human rights. It also places a strong emphasis on human agency – that is, the ability of human beings to determine their own values and goals in life and to strive towards meeting those goals in positive and pro-social ways. The model can be applied to any offender or client base, and indeed it is relevant to every human being. As Ward and colleagues have developed the model in recent years and researched its applications, the model has increasingly moved to the centre of offender rehabilitation thinking.

The Good Lives Model suggests that in order to help people reduce their risk of re-offending, we need to help them build their capabilities and strengths. The Good Lives Model also offers a view of human nature as striving towards human 'goods' – that is, aspects of life that are sought for their own intrinsic value to the individual. The model divides these into 11 areas:

- healthy living
- knowledge
- leisure/ recreational pursuits
- work
- autonomy
- inner peace
- relatedness
- community/connection with social groups

- spirituality/meaning and purpose in life
- pleasure/enjoyment
- creativity/expression.

Although all human beings tend to pursue the same primary goals to one extent or another, personal identity is derived from our individual conception of how we value the goods and the means we choose in order to achieve them. According to the Good Lives Model, offending behaviour represents a maladaptive attempt to meet a normal and natural human 'good' – in other words, an outcome that most people value. However, because of a wide variety of obstacles faced by the individual, the desire for a human good results in offending behaviour. Ward argues that, through a lack of internal skills and external conditions or resources, offenders sometimes seek to achieve their primary goods through anti-social means. Offending, therefore, reflects harmful, socially unacceptable and often personally frustrating attempts to pursue primary goods (Ward and Gannon 2006; Ward and Maruna 2007).

Using the Good Lives Model, we are helped to shape interventions that encourage the person to develop pro-social and sustainable ways to meet their needs and goals in life. Our interventions can then be individually tailored to help the person implement their plan while also addressing any weaknesses or needs that may get in the way of success. By assisting clients to achieve their desired goals, their criminogenic needs will be modified, and their risk of re-offending will be reduced. Ward and Maruna offer the view that this approach to relapse prevention is more motivational than one based on avoidance goals (i.e. things which an individual must not do): 'By proceeding in this manner, individuals do not need to abandon those things that are important to them – only to learn to acquire them differently' (Ward and Maruna 2007, p.108). Please see *The Wheel of Life* exercise in Chapter 3 (p.78) for a practical exercise that is based on and adapted from the Good Lives Model. The Good Lives Model informs many other aspects of the exercises in the book.

Cognitive-behavioural therapy

Cognitive-behavioural therapy (CBT) (Beck 1976; Beck *et al.* 2003) is among the most well-established approaches in offending behaviour programmes (McGuire 2000). Indeed, it is a very widely used approach in many areas of mental health, counselling and psychotherapy. CBT provides a framework for understanding how our beliefs and attitudes – and most particularly our core fears and self-doubts – affect our thinking, our feeling and ultimately, our behaviour. Changes in these core beliefs are likely to produce a profound effect on behaviour, and much of the focus of cognitive-behavioural therapy – as it applies to offenders – is on addressing and modifying beliefs and habitual thinking and feeling cycles which prove self-defeating and which can lead to offending behaviour.

Cognitive-behavioural therapy is based on the premise that our emotions and behaviour are influenced by our perception of events, rather than simply by the events themselves. Within the context of CBT-based working, clients are encouraged to become more aware of patterns of thinking and feeling that promote maladaptive or abusive behaviour, and are assisted in the process of modifying those attitudes, beliefs and feelings that would tend towards further offending. They are also helped to practise new self-regulation and interpersonal skills through the use of role play and other experiential techniques. This is a three-stage process:

1. Identify problematic thinking, feeling and behaviour patterns in various contexts.

2. Change thinking, feeling and behaviour patterns in those contexts.

3. Provide opportunity to practise new thinking, feeling and behaviour patterns in those and other contexts (e.g. using skills practice, behavioural experiments and/or role play techniques).

Cognitive-behavioural methods tend to be educational, interactive and collaborative, with a strong emphasis on self-regulation and adopting healthier lifestyles. Socratic questioning (see Chapter 2) is widely used as a tool to emphasise the collaborative nature of the therapeutic process.

All of the exercises in this book are to one extent or another influenced by the CBT approach.

Attachment theory

Attachment theory (Bowlby 1969; Crittenden and Landini 2011) is also a crucial theory underpinning the exercises in this book. Attachment theory proposes that attachment relationships form during the earliest months of life. Depending on the attunement and predictability of the caregiver's response to the baby's cries or signals of distress, the baby – and later the child – will develop deeply embedded expectations about how relationships operate. These expectations will then influence their future behaviour and response patterns within relationships. Attuned and predictable care, for example, will tend to influence the development of secure attachment strategies as the person learns that closeness can be predictable, safe, protective and comforting.

Bowlby also introduced the notion of a 'secure base', namely a connection with a caregiver that will provide the safety and comfort that will enable an individual to feel sufficiently secure to explore and interact with the outside world, in the knowledge that the secure base will be there to return to. A secure base is promoted by appropriately responsive, attuned and consistent caregiving.

Bowlby's work has been further developed by theorists such as Mary Ainsworth, who introduced the idea of categories of attachment style, known as secure, anxious-avoidant and anxious-ambivalent (Ainsworth *et al.* 1978). Disrupted childhood experiences and unattuned or unpredictable care may contribute to the development of insecure attachment styles. If these insecure attachment patterns continue into adulthood, they may lead to difficulties in emotional self-regulation

and sustaining intimate relationships (Marshall *et al.* 2000).

This book is also informed by Crittenden's Dynamic-Maturational Model (DMM) of Attachment and Adaptation (Crittenden 2008). Crittenden proposes that all attachment responses are strategic, and that individuals have the potential to reorganise their attachment strategies throughout their life span in response to increasing maturity and life experiences – and sometimes therapy or other forms of reflection and self-development. The DMM focuses on the self-protective function of behaviour when people experience stress, threat or danger. The model also helps us to understand how and why some behaviour that is harmful to the self or other people may represent the individual's best attempts to resolve the need for safety, comfort, proximity and predictability when under stress or perceiving danger. Understanding how a person's behaviour has meaning for them is essential in identifying the drivers, pay-offs and risks of their behaviour.

Attachment theory also helps to explain patterns of behaviour, for example, why a person may commit crime or repeatedly sabotage their close relationships and what might be at stake if the person changes their behaviour. By focusing on the underlying patterns and function of behaviour (i.e. the reasons for the behaviour) we are much more likely to be effective in helping the person to change their behaviour than if we focus on the behaviour alone (Crittenden 2008; Senge 1990). We are also more likely to work with compassion for our clients, because we will have a better understanding of the underlying reasons for their behaviour. Alternatively, if the focus is only on changing the presenting behaviour (i.e. the symptoms/offences) we may miss the underlying pattern and function, with the result that the problem returns (see Figure 1.1 on the following page).

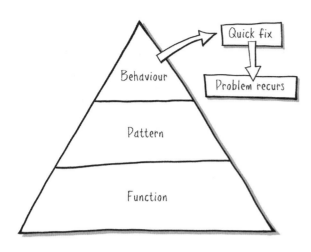

Figure 1.1: The behaviour, pattern, function triangle

Several exercises in this book, particularly *My Life Experiences* (Chapter 4) and *My Relationship History* (Chapter 5), draw on attachment theory and encourage the client to reflect on their history of close relationships and their coping strategies when under stress. More broadly, all of the exercises are meant to be delivered with a focus that looks beneath the surface appearance of behaviour and tries to understand the underlying meaning and function of the behaviour.

Social learning theory

Social learning theory (Bandura 1977) describes how most human learning occurs in a social context. For example, children learn an enormous amount through social processes that occur at a number of levels including the family, peer group, school and wider societal levels. For some children, the family environment may encourage – through modelling and reinforcement – attitudes and behaviour which are consistent with offending. Peer groups and wider society may also reinforce attitudes which are supportive of offending.

As well as forming the basis for our views of self and others, socialisation provides the opportunity to learn the host of skills that will be needed in adulthood, for example, interpersonal skills, self-management skills and problem-solving skills. However, poor socialisation may limit the range of skills which are learned and model inappropriate modes of thinking and behaving. For example, children who are beaten by a parent who is angry and drunk may learn that violence is an acceptable response to anger and may fail to learn other more appropriate methods of managing anger.

Social learning theory also helps us to structure interactive learning processes following a standard sequence that is based on the way that human beings naturally and instinctively pass on knowledge and skills (this process is used in the skills practice exercises in this book – see Chapters 4 and 5):

- *Assessment/self-assessment* of skills and roles that need practice.

- *Instruction* in the recommended steps of the skill.

- *Modelling* of the skill (e.g. by a more able participant or by a worker). Modelling works best when the person doing the modelling is like the person learning the skill, but perhaps just a little older/more mature (i.e. a positive role model).

- *Labelling*. During modelling, each micro-step of the skill is labelled (i.e. named) to make it clearly identifiable and to break the skill into digestible and learnable 'chunks'.

- *Multiple practice* of the new skill, with feedback. The skill should be practised in a step-by-step fashion in order to encourage incremental reinforcement of the skill. If the skill is practised element by element, gradually these can be joined together into a smoothly functioning sequence of micro-skills. As the person becomes more confident, the level of difficulty is raised in order to 'harden' the skill and make it more flexible and applicable to real-world scenarios.

- *Testing* of the new skill, to ensure it has been assimilated.

- *Real-world practice* including opportunities for positive real-world experience of the new skill within a relatively short time.

Motivational interviewing

Motivational interviewing (Miller and Rollnick 2002) originally developed from Miller's work with recovering alcoholics. It has been broadened over the years into an approach which can be applied to virtually any helping conversation where a person may lack motivation or have ambivalence about change.

The essence of the approach is that in order to help someone become motivated to make changes in their life, we must engage with them in a collaborative conversation that helps them to identify their motivations for making changes and the resources they can use to achieve their goals. As Miller and Rollnick emphasise in their description of the model, motivational interviewing is not just a set of techniques and methods. It is, just as importantly, a stance and a 'way of being' with clients that places them in the position of being the expert on their own life. It is also a stance that emphasises the client's autonomy and self-determination.

The motivational interviewing approach places a strong emphasis on collaborative discussion and 'drawing out' ideas rather than imposing them. The overall goal is to increase the client's intrinsic motivation to change by encouraging them to present the arguments in favour of change, as opposed to the therapist telling the person why they ought to change. There are five general principles that underlie the motivational interviewing approach:

1. express empathy for the person

2. develop discrepancies between the person's stated values and goals in life and their actions

3. avoid arguing or taking opposing views

4. roll with resistance and find a way to re-frame statements that avoids head-to-head confrontation

5. support the client's sense of self-efficacy and self-determination.

The exercises in this book are all meant to be delivered using the motivational interviewing stance.

Motivational cycle of change

Prochaska and DiClemente (1982) describe different stages through which individuals pass when they are making significant changes. While interventions need to be responsive to the individual's stage in the change process, it is important to note that motivation to maintain change is dynamic, and it is likely to be necessary at various times to undertake work to sustain or promote it. The stages identified by Prochaska and DiClemente are:

- *Pre-contemplation:* At this stage individuals demonstrate little awareness that their behaviour is problematic, either for themselves or others. They may justify their actions by use of minimisations and distorted thinking patterns or attitudes. The task for the worker at this stage is to help the individual to become more conscious of the negative impacts of their problematic behaviour, by promoting dissonance (i.e. a gap between the individual's stated aims and goals, and the current consequences of their behaviour).

- *Contemplation:* At this stage individuals are likely to be considering the consequences of their actions. They may experience ambivalence, due to the conflict between the pleasure and rewards they may have derived from their behaviour, versus an increasing awareness of the negative consequences of this behaviour for themselves and others. The task for workers at this stage is to maximise the individual's desire to work towards addressing their behaviour by enhancing the positive aspects of change and identifying achievable goals.

- *Determination:* At this stage individuals have taken an informed decision to change their problematic behaviour, but have not yet begun to do so. The task for the worker is to reinforce the decision to change, and to help the individual to construct a realistic action plan.

- *Action:* During this stage individuals will have resolved to address their problematic behaviour and to behave differently. The change is started and the new behaviour is put into action.

- *Maintenance:* It is during this stage that individuals learn to maintain new behaviours and healthier lifestyle choices. This may involve the identification and management of risk factors that may cause them to revert to previous patterns of behaviour.

One advantage of this model is that it helps workers identify the work that needs to be undertaken at each stage of the process. The exercises in Chapter 3, for example, are primarily focused on encouraging motivation to change.

Please see the exercise entitled *The Motivational Cycle of Change* in Chapter 3 (p.84), which draws very directly from Prochaska and Di Clemente's model and modifies it slightly, based on an adaptation by O'Reilly *et al.* (2001).

Risk-Needs-Responsivity Model

The Risk-Needs-Responsivity (RNR) Model (Andrews and Dowden 2007; Andrews *et al.* 2006) is a model of assessment and rehabilitation based upon three principles. The first is the *risk principle*, which states that in order to increase treatment effectiveness, the level of intervention must be matched to the risk level of the client (i.e. low risk offenders receive minimal intervention and high-risk offenders receive more intensive intervention). This is based upon an assumption that risk of re-offending is an approximate indicator of clinical need.

The second principle, the *needs principle*, says that treatment should target needs that are actually related to offending (i.e. criminogenic needs).

Finally, the *responsivity principle* calls for the use of methods of intervention and therapist styles that engage the client and cater to their learning styles and other relevant characteristics, such as cognitive ability, social/cultural factors and level of motivation.

This book is designed to be concordant with the RNR model. *Risk* should be assessed using the standard risk assessment processes common within your agency; in the next chapter, we offer guidance about assessing risk. Criminogenic *needs* and protective factors are initially identified during the pre-programme assessment phase and then modified as the sessions proceed. The number of sessions undertaken can be altered to directly reflect the risk level and the criminogenic needs presented by the client. Finally, the book is designed to cater for a very diverse range of *responsivity* needs. For example, the exercises can be delivered either in a groupwork or one-to-one setting, and each exercise can be delivered using a variety of methods according to the learning style and other characteristics of the individual client.

Systems theory

Systems theory is a vast field of theory, practice and research, encompassing biological and physical systems, political and organisational systems, large and small group systems, family and two-person systems, and other areas. Bateson (1972, 1979), among others, focused on systems theory in relation to psychology. Looking through the lens of systems thinking, we can understand that many psychological disturbances, including offending behaviour and many forms of mental illness, are partly a result of systemic contradictions and dilemmas faced by the individual. To offer just one fairly common example, an individual may commit offences within the context of a family system where offending is the norm, and where there may be negative consequences for the individual of not conforming to the family norm. Gang-related crime may be similarly understood. More broadly, in societies where there is a high degree of corruption or gross inequality of opportunity, the societal norms may themselves be seen as criminogenic. If everyone else is seen to be 'on the take' or at an unfair advantage, we may feel it is entirely justified to be 'on the take' ourselves. This is not to condone offending, but merely to understand the rationale offenders may use at the time to justify committing a crime.

Systems theory also offers a structured way of not just understanding the systems influencing the client but also forming constructive systems to help the client. Pincus and Minahan (1973), for example, offer clear guidance about how to formulate a systemic view of a client's life circumstances. They offer the following breakdown of the systems around the client:

1. *The client system:* Who is the client? Is it a person, a family? A group? A community? What is the contract that you have with the client? What is your role and the client's role in relation to the contract and the aims of the work you will do together?

2. *The change system:* Who can be a part of the positive change process for the client? You, another worker, a family, a community, a voluntary group, a support group, a statutory agency and/or another organisation?

3. *The target system:* What and who needs to change? Sometimes, it is not so much the client themselves but the system around the client that needs to change. For example, if a client has committed crimes under the strong negative influence of a peer group or a family member, this is a clear indicator that the focus of change needs to be not only on the client but on the system around the client, or the client's relationship to the system. In such a situation you can do the most powerful and productive work with the client but, if the focus is only on them and not on the system around them (or their relation to that system), the effort may be futile.

The invitational approach

The invitational approach is based on the work of Alan Jenkins (1997) and focuses on the individual's sense of responsibility for their actions. In the invitational approach, questions are addressed to the 'responsible self' of the person (as opposed to the 'irresponsible/offending self'). These questions invite the person to take on incrementally greater responsibility, often by promoting an internal dissonance between their emerging beliefs and their past behaviour. Invitational questions also encourage the person to reflect on their thoughts and feelings and what it means to become a responsible individual. To illustrate the invitational approach to people who are new to the concept, we use the analogy of two chairs: one chair for the irresponsible part of the self, and one for the responsible part. The two aspects of self can be seen as 'in dialogue' with each other. The task then becomes to strengthen and enhance the 'responsible self' while allowing the 'irresponsible self' to become, by comparison, weaker and less dominant. Taking the analogy a step further, the role of the worker is to encourage the client to develop their responsible self, whilst resisting the temptation to occupy that position themselves. It can be tempting for us, as workers, to sit in the chair representing the client's 'responsible self' from time to time, and engage in behaviours such as offering unsolicited advice, or telling the client what they 'ought to' or 'should' do or change. However, if we occupy the client's 'responsible chair', then we run the risk of rendering it unavailable to the client, and increasing the likelihood that they will continue to sit in the 'irresponsible chair'.

Using the lens of the invitational approach, an underlying aim of all of the exercises in this book is to encourage the person to develop the responsible part of themselves and to become more internally resilient. On this journey, one of the first challenges for many clients is to encourage them to identify that there is any part of them that is responsible, valued and competent.

Role theory

Role theory (Moreno 1946) offers a common sense framework for understanding and developing our roles, strategies and behaviour toward others. Much of human interaction can be understood by considering the roles, routines and 'scripts' we perform as we go about our daily lives. An individual may carry out hundreds of roles through the course of their life: son, daughter, mother, father, brother, sister, husband, wife, lover, friend, worker, boss, neighbour, patient, student, customer, commuter and countless more. Each role designates a cluster of behaviours generally associated with that role in a given cultural context. When we know how to perform a role, it is in our 'role repertoire'. The more roles that we are able to successfully embody, the more strategies we have to choose from and the more adept we will be at successfully navigating life's challenges.

If an individual does not have the opportunity to take on a particular role for themselves, and does not have the role modelled for them, then they may have a limited repertoire of roles available to them. For example, if a person grew up in a household where none of the adults was in paid employment, and they have never had a job themselves, then they may not be familiar with some of the basic behaviours expected of a person in the workplace, and may struggle to get or to keep a job.

Role theory thus offers a powerful rationale for why rehabilitative programmes should focus on the development of positive skills and roles. In Chapters 4 and 5, the skills practice role plays are prime opportunities to learn and practice new skills and roles. Skills practice can also be used at any point in any other session.

Person-centred therapy

Researcher and psychotherapist Carl Rogers (1967) developed the idea of the person-centred approach to counselling and psychotherapy. This includes within it the idea that when we interact with our clients we should always start from the stance of basic respect towards the person that recognises our common humanity, even when there may appear to be major differences between us. Rogers's concept is particularly important

in offending behaviour work, because the concept means that even when there are vast differences between us in terms of our life experiences, our values and our goals, we can, using a person-centred approach, maintain a fundamental respect for other people as human beings – flaws, strengths and all.

The person-centred approach is also based on another important idea: that when people experience warmth, respect and being valued, they will often make positive changes based on their own initiative as they develop their sense of confidence and self-worth. Rogers proposed the idea of 'self-actualisation'. Self-actualising people strive to make the most of their potential, and they can be thwarted or enabled by a variety of conditions. Therefore one of the aims of working with offenders should be to help them become – in Rogers's terms – more self-actualising. This is fundamental to the approach taken in this book.

Positive psychology and the strengths-based approach

Positive psychology (Seligman *et al.* 2005) demonstrates that an effective way of helping people to make positive changes in their life is to focus on their strengths and build on those strengths. Positive psychology research has found solid evidence that certain kinds of strengths can buffer us from mental illness and self-defeating behaviour. These are strengths such as courage, optimism, the ability to think about the future, diligence, perseverance and self-reflection.

While the term 'positive psychology' is relatively new, the concept is not. The idea first grew popular in the 1950s and 1960s, with authors such as Abraham Maslow (1943, 1954) and Carl Rogers (1967) advocating a strengths-based, humanistic approach to well-being and recovery. Earlier still, the ancient Greek philosophers made the study of the 'good life' the subject of deep enquiry.

Many of the exercises in this book might be thought of as strengths-based and drawing from the tradition of positive psychology.

Narrative therapy

Narrative therapy is based upon the social constructionist view that our ideas about the world shape our experience of reality. This approach was advanced by Michael White and David Epston, who developed an interest in how dominant stories accepted by individuals affect the way they view themselves, and thus influence their behaviour (White 2007; White and Epston 1990). A very large part of our identity consists of the stories and the narrative meaning we give to the events of our lives and our relationships. For example, if an individual holds the dominant story that 'I am a failure,' he will tend to focus more on experiences where he perceives himself to have failed, and will proportionately disregard experiences of success. Paying more attention to episodes which reinforce the dominant story will further entrench the perceived problem, rather than promoting a solution.

Narrative theory also observes that a key indicator of our psychological health is the coherence and integration of our own life story, for this is the basis of our sense of self. One way of thinking about an individual's life history is as an autobiographical story, including important people, places, events, interactions, relationships, emotions and conflicts they have faced (Dallos 2006). These stories shape who we are and what we do. Narrative therapy helps us to formulate one of the clear goals of intervention: to help clients to arrive at a more adequate understanding of their life story and to give meaning to the problems they face. These stories can be elicited by exploring questions such as:

1. How did I get here?

2. What are the stories I and other people have about me?

3. How do these stories help or hinder me?

4. How would I like things to be?

5. How do I get there? Who can help me?

Narrative therapy proceeds by encouraging individuals to view the problem as an external entity, separate from their own identity. Thus the individual would be encouraged to see themselves as a person with skills and resources, distinct from the experiences of failure. Then the client and the therapist would collaboratively explore times when they had succeeded, thus 're-authoring' their experiences and interpretations. Narrative therapy offers an individual an opportunity to rewrite the way in which they describe their life, to develop new, more positive stories about the way they have responded to and coped with the difficulties they have faced. Narrative therapy often involves the writing of letters or certificates as a way of formalising the process of rewriting alternative, richer stories.

Narrative therapy is also concerned with equalising the traditional power imbalance between client and therapist. This is achieved by an emphasis on collaborative working, genuine enquiry and jointly written case notes (White and Epston 1990).

This book contains a number of exercises aimed at helping the client to develop a more coherent and adequate understanding of their life story. The autobiographical exercises present opportunities for the client to consider the dominant stories which they have been told about their developmental history, and the dominant stories which they have accepted about themselves. Re-exploring these stories encourages the development of alternative narratives to support the construction of a pro-social self-identity.

The ecological-transactional model

Another very useful and rather comprehensive developmental model is the ecological-transactional model (Cicchetti and Valentino 2006). This model describes how healthy development requires us to negotiate challenges and transitions throughout our lives. We face these challenges in the context of our local environment and the supports and stresses that surround us. As the authors write:

> An ecological-transactional perspective views child development as a progressive sequence of age- and stage-appropriate tasks in which successful resolution of

tasks at each developmental level must be coordinated and integrated with the environment, as well as with subsequently emerging issues across the life span. These tasks include the development of emotion regulation, the formation of attachment relationships, the development of an autonomous self, symbolic development, moral development, the formation of peer relationships, adaptation to school, and personality organisation… Poor resolution of stage-salient issues may contribute to maladjustment over time, as prior history influences the selection, engagement and interpretation of subsequent experience.

(Cicchetti and Valentino 2006, p.143)

The ecological-transactional model helps us to see that the underlying reason why a person behaves as they do may be found in the cumulative history of their interaction across their lifespan, taking into account the stresses and supports affecting them and also their experiences of success and failure in many contexts. For example, a child growing up in a family where there is domestic violence, neglect, substance misuse or various forms of verbal, emotional or physical abuse, is facing significant stressors and risks to their development. Understanding and working with the nature, impact and meaning of the client's history are thus key tasks in enhancing their capacity to see themselves and their life history accurately and therefore to more adequately assess their perceptions of themselves and other people (Brandon *et al.* 2008). The ecological-transactional model suggests that the development of a coherent life story is a key task when working with troubled and troubling clients. Many of the exercises in this book take just such an approach, helping the client to understand their life history and the strategies they have used to meet their needs, and to prepare and practise for a hoped-for future.

Mentalisation

Mentalisation (Fonagy *et al.* 2004) is the ability to understand oneself and other people

by attuning to and reflecting on the mental states that underpin behaviour. Mentalisation is strongly connected to concepts such as empathy, perspective-taking, emotional and social intelligence, cooperation and – in attachment theory terminology – the idea of the goal-directed partnership. Mentalisation involves recognising and thinking about your own and other peoples' thoughts, feelings, actions and intentions. This can lead to a more accurate concept of the self and an enhanced understanding of the internal worlds of other people. Without a sufficiently developed capacity to mentalise, an individual may struggle to self-regulate and to form and maintain healthy relationships.

The capacity to mentalise develops during childhood within the context of a secure attachment relationship with a caregiver, through processes such as affect-mirroring. This is the capacity of the caregiver to mirror, through their face and voice, the mental states which they perceive the child is experiencing, in a manner which calms the child. The child learns to interpret and organise their own subjective mental experiences through the example of the caregiver. However, sometimes this process goes wrong:

> Suboptimal early experiences of care affect later development by undermining the individual's capacity to process or interpret information concerning mental states that is essential for effective functioning in a stressful social world. Insecurity in attachment relationships is a signal of limitation in mentalising skills.

(Fonagy et al. 2004, p.7)

Many of the exercises in this book encourage mentalising processes. Some are explicitly directed at aims that include perspective-taking and self-awareness. More broadly, all of the exercises have the potential to enhance the client's capacity to mentalise when used in the context of an attuned relationship with the worker. For example, as the facilitator, if you are attuned to, respectful of and listening to the client, you will very likely be modelling the skills and qualities of mentalisation. This will offer powerful role modelling for your client, and you can use this as a bridge, encouraging them to follow your lead.

Experiential approaches to trauma and loss

Many people who commit offences will have experienced trauma and loss which continues to impact negatively upon them. Research into the neurobiology of trauma suggests that traumatic memories are laid down in ways which render them more resistant to traditional forms of talk-based therapy (van der Kolk 1994; Perry 2009).

The Therapeutic Spiral Model (TSM) was developed by Hudgins (Hudgins 2002) as an expansion of classical psychodrama in order to provide additional safety and structure when working with people who have experienced trauma. It follows the goal of working experientially with experiences of trauma, while providing safety and containment at every step for the client as well as the professional. The model contains specific mechanisms designed to promote safety, which include warming up by identifying strengths, an incremental approach to the themes which are examined, and clear boundaries and contracts.

Whilst the TSM is a specialised form of psychodrama therapy, its principles can be used to inform the work of facilitators who use the exercises in this book. To offer one example of how TSM concepts are incorporated in this book, you will see that an early exercise in Chapter 3 is *Starting from Strength*. This is drawn directly from the TSM concept that, when working with difficult and painful life experiences (which includes offending behaviour), one always starts from strength.

Psychodynamic theory

Psychodynamic theory is deeply embedded in mainstream therapy and counselling approaches. It developed from psychoanalytic thinking in the early to mid twentieth century, based on the work of Freud and later such theorists and clinicians as Melanie Klein,

Wilfred Bion, Carl Jung, Alfred Adler and Otto Rank. Psychodynamic therapy contrasts with Freudian psychoanalysis in that it focuses more on here-and-now problems and practical issues in daily living and relationships. The psychodynamic approach seeks to increase a client's understanding and awareness of how the past has influenced present thoughts and behaviours, and how past patterns of response can be 'triggered' in the present – particularly when we are feeling under stress or threatened in some way. It also tends to be shorter term than traditional psychoanalysis. Some of the key principles underlying the psychodynamic approach are:

- Our perception of people and situations, and most prominently our perceptions of situations of danger, comfort and sexuality, will be strongly influenced by early experiences and patterns of response from early in our lives, often in infancy.

- The past plays out in the present: because so many of our patterns of response begin in infancy, later in life we may react in ways that are largely unconscious, because the patterns were created at a time in our lives that is inaccessible to our conscious memory (typically, this is before age four or five). It is because of this that many people with emotional and psychological difficulties react and behave in ways that seem to them to be mysterious, troubling, confusing and out of conscious control.

- Insight is an important step in the process of change. In other words, it is an important principle of the psychodynamic approach that people are helped to understand how and why they may be reacting as they do to current life situations, and how their past experiences have influenced their current patterns of response. This is seen as a crucial step before the client then can make full, conscious decisions to respond in new, more adequate ways to current and future situations.

- Very often, the client's patterns of response and the dynamics of the previous significant relationships will play out in their interactions with the worker. For example, if the client has to be a 'good boy' or a 'good girl' with their parents, they may behave the same way with the worker. As another example, the client may have played the role of 'defiant child' or 'helpless victim' in order to survive and get their needs met as children. Again, this dynamic may be played out in their sessions with you.

- Psychological defences are very common and can take many forms. Indeed, almost any form of behaviour can serve as a defence, depending on the person and the context. This will be highly individual. A psychological defence is any activity of the mind (which may also manifest itself behaviourally) that serves the purposes of defending the mind against difficult or painful emotions and insights. A common example of a defence would be drinking alcohol to numb or avoid emotional pain, or hitting someone in order to avoid the difficult and painful experience of containing (and facing) one's own rage and fear.

Psychodynamic theory underpins a number of the exercises in this book, particularly those exercises that encourage the client to think about the impact of their past relationships and experiences.

A good resource for learning more about the psychodynamic approach is Bateman *et al.* (2010).

Theory of spontaneity-creativity

The theory of spontaneity-creativity is a way of looking at human development from a cross-cultural, species-wide perspective that emphasises the innate creative impulses and potential of all human beings. The theory derives from Moreno's observation of children at play, and the natural and instinctive processes they followed when allowed to express themselves freely (Blatner 2000; Moreno 1946). He noted, for example, that the more

socially able children spontaneously took on a variety of roles in the games, dramas and stories the children created. He also noticed that the less socially able children tended to repeatedly take on the same roles; they seemed much more confined and fearful in their play and expression. Based on this observation, he encouraged all of the children to explore new roles and to widen their repertoire of roles and social interactions, as a way of enjoying their creative expression and also improving their social confidence and abilities. This later formed the basis of Moreno's creation of the theatre of spontaneity, psychodrama, sociodrama and sociometry, all of which contain processes and techniques for enhancing the spontaneity, creativity and psychological integration of individuals and groups. Out of these methods grew some very widely used techniques such as role play, the 'empty chair' technique, group therapy and groupwork. Moreno was also one of the first clinicians to organise self-help groups for people facing common difficulties, and was among the first authors to use the term 'self-help' in relation to psychological change (Moreno 1947).

The theory of spontaneity-creativity underpins many of the exercises in this book, particularly in the book's approach to the concept of responsivity and role development. The exercises are meant to be facilitated in such a way that at all times we encourage the client to use their own creativity and imagination to find solutions, to practice self-help skills and to work their own way through difficulties, with us offering support and guidance only where needed. At the same time, the exercises in this book should be facilitated in such a way as to encourage the development of more resilient, emotionally flexible and socially adept roles.

Moreno (1946) also highlights the importance of the warming-up process. If we wish to help our clients to use their maximum potential, we must use methods to encourage them to become fully engaged, alert and ready to think, feel and act in new ways. This involves creating a safe place for working, and using a wide variety of techniques to encourage trust, debate, energy, physical alertness, focus on the moment and the task in hand, creative solutions, 'thinking outside the box', and a willingness to try out different roles/points of view. Facilitators of the exercises in this book should therefore be mindful of how the client(s) are helped to prepare and warm up for all of the exercises, and how they are encouraged to use their own creativity in working through the exercises and the challenges they pose. Chapter 2 offers a range of suggestions for how we can adapt exercises to suit the learning styles and preferences of different clients. These adaptations can also be used in a strategic way to encourage the maximum involvement, creativity and spontaneity of your client(s).

Labelling theory

Labelling theory (Becker 1963; Goffman 1959; Mead 1934; Tannenbaum 1938) is the theory of how the self-identity and behaviour of individuals and groups can be influenced by the labels used to identify them. Many studies have shown the powerful effects of stigmatising language (such as 'deviant', 'criminal', 'offender' or 'delinquent') on the self-concept, social identity and life chances of individuals and groups living under the stigmatising label. In many ways, labels can become self-fulfilling prophesies, as any attempt to move beyond the label might be seen as reinforcing the justification for using the label in the first place. As Matza (1969) writes:

> To be cast as a thief, as a prostitute, or more generally, a deviant, is to further compound and hasten the process of becoming that very thing... In shocked discovery, the subject now concretely understands that there are serious people who really go around building their lives around his activities – stopping him, correcting him, devoted to him. They keep records on the course of his life, even develop theories on how he got that way... Pressed by such a display, the subject may begin to add meaning and gravity to his deviant

activities. But he may do so in a way not especially intended by agents of the state.

(Matza 1969, pp.157–164)

Understanding the powerful effects of stigmatising language, we must work at all times using a stance of respect for the individual and their sense of dignity, autonomy, responsibility and self-determination. All of the exercises in this book are meant to be facilitated from this respectful, non-judgmental and non-labelling approach.

Essential preparation and principles of practice for workers

Before beginning an assessment or intervention with a client, it is important for the worker to be well prepared and clear in their mind about their role and the principles of practice they will follow when working with the client. Here are some questions and points to consider (adapted from Baim and Morrison 2011):

Context

- What is the context in which I am working with this client?

- Why am I undertaking this intervention with the client?

- What do they understand to be the purpose and aims of our sessions?

- How does this compare with my understanding?

- What motivates the client to attend and engage in these sessions?

- What is the power relationship between me and the client? Am I in a position of power or authority over the client? How will this affect their willingness and ability to engage?

Rapport and empathy

- What sort of working rapport do I have with this client?

- How safe do they feel with me?

- Do they feel safe enough to allow themselves to be vulnerable in my presence?

- Can I put myself in their shoes and consider how I would react if asked to undertake these activities?

Self-awareness

- How aware am I of my own coping strategies under stress, my own emotional 'hooks', 'hot buttons' and 'no-go' areas?

- How aware am I of my own level of expertise, and where there are still gaps in my knowledge, skills or training?

- How open am I to feedback and critique from clients, colleagues and supervisors?

- Have I done these exercises and activities for myself in order to become better integrated and to know what I am asking my client to do?

Note: The exercises in this book will require an understanding of the potential impact and outcomes. Workers should be aware of the possible benefits and also the drawbacks for clients. (Example: some clients can be at greater risk of harm if they return to a home environment where they have made changes but their family members have not.) We strongly recommend that you do these exercises for yourself before you use them with your client. This will help you to understand and explain the exercises to the client, and it will also make you more sensitive to the nature of the exercises and the issues they raise.

Support, supervision and co-working

- What organisational or agency requirements may affect my ability to do this work with my client?

- Will my agency support this work, for example, by giving me adequate time to undertake this work, and by providing adequate supervision?

Note: Undertaking this sort of work with clients will require good supervision. It is also important to be realistic about your level of skill, training and experience when using exercises such as these. Opportunities for co-working and mentoring will also enhance and support good working practice. This may include accessing colleagues with particular experience of working in particular settings.

Reports

- What reports will I be writing at the end of my sessions with the client?

- How might this impact on issues of confidentiality?

- How will I negotiate these factors with the client so that they feel safe at whatever level of personal disclosure is appropriate for them in the context in which we are working?

- How do organisational expectations and context (e.g. criminal justice, social work, mental health contexts) impact on issues of informed consent with my client?

- Is there an imminent court appearance? Is there an active social work enquiry being undertaken?

Assessment, case formulation and treatment planning

- How well do I understand my client?

- How much time have I given to assessment, and in particular an assessment of my client's life history that takes into account their experiences of danger and attachment relationships, and any potentially unresolved loss or trauma?

- How well do I understand my client's strengths, vulnerabilities and external stresses and supports?

- How has my assessment taken into account the possibility that my client may not have a clear concept of what their problem is, because on a pre-conscious level their mind avoids the most painful and difficult topics?

- How will I therefore avoid missing the very thing that my client most needs?

- Have I developed a reliable formulation of my client's difficulties and how they have developed over time?

- Does this formulation take into account the function/meaning of the client's offending?

- How will I take into account this understanding when I undertake these activities with my client?

Collaboration and transparency – no hidden agendas

- How will I involve my client in an active collaboration, where they are helped to 'co-pilot' the process, as opposed to being led by me?

- For example, how can the client be involved in selecting the exercises and techniques that we will work on together, and the sequence in which we will use these? (This speaks to the principle of transparency, i.e. that we are as transparent as possible with the client about the process and the techniques on offer. The exercises in this book are meant to be delivered following the principles of 'purposeful eclecticism' – that is to say, a process where techniques and exercises are selected based on a consideration of what works for the individual client and what their needs are. Once selected and used, techniques and approaches should be subject to continual feedback from the client, so that the process is dynamic and collaborative – as opposed to something that is imposed and passively received.)

- How will I make decisions when the client clearly needs extra help and cannot 'co-pilot'?

Socratic approach

- How clear am I on the importance of using a Socratic approach with my client? (Socratic questions are described in Chapter 2.)

- How consistently do I ask questions that are collaborative, open-ended and non-leading?

- How will I check to ensure that I am asking open-ended, non-leading questions? Who can give me feedback?

Depth of engagement

- How willing am I to engage with this client in areas and on topics that may evoke difficult or painful feelings in them and also, potentially, such feelings in me?

- How will I be consistent and attuned with my client?

- If the client allows themselves to become vulnerable during these sessions, the implication is that I will be there to support them and to hear their story. Am I willing, prepared and supported to do this?

Conclusion

We hope that, in offering this overview of the theories and principles of practice that we integrate into the exercises this book, you can see how the various theories overlap and complement one another and how the principles of practice fit with the theoretical models. We hope that you can also see the advantage in using more than one theory, as each has a valuable insight or method to offer. Again, as a reminder, if you are trained in a method or theory not mentioned here, please bring that knowledge and expertise into play as you facilitate the exercises in this book.

CHAPTER 2

Essential Skills and Frameworks for Practitioners

In this chapter, you will learn about:

- assessment, planning and evaluation
- working with clients who deny offending
- the skills and qualities of the facilitator
- skilful questions – the fine art of promoting reflection, discovery and positive change
- variations and adaptations that can be used with any of the exercises
- several handy techniques with many applications.

Assessment, planning and evaluation

The broader context of risk management and community support

This book should be used within the context of the broader structures of risk management, public protection, social care, health care and criminal justice provision local to you. The exercises address those factors which are most likely to be criminogenic in the vast majority of offenders. There are also well-known additional factors which may prove criminogenic in some offenders, and these include substance misuse, gambling, prolific criminal background, having criminal associates, mental health conditions, lack of adequate family support, social isolation or exclusion, experiences of discrimination, community/cultural influences, lack of secure/ appropriately supervised accommodation, debt, poor money management skills,

unemployment, educational underachievement and poor use of leisure time. Where such factors are significant for an individual, a detailed risk management plan addressing these factors will need to accompany any risk management plan arising from delivery of the exercises in this book.

Similarly, it is understood that any self-change process will have far more long-term positive effects if the work accomplished during the sessions is supported with long-term follow-up. Some people undertaking these sessions will need ongoing support in maintaining the changes, new ideas and lifestyle practices that are begun during the sessions. For example, some clients will need ongoing access to informed individuals who can support them if they lapse and need help. This support might take the form of outreach/follow-up/after-care and may involve staff from probation, prison, police, social services, housing, health or ancillary agencies who have responsibility for or a duty of care for the individual. Follow-on support may also include informed volunteers or mentors. One of the most effective support systems could be the family and friends of the client, and any work you can do to engage with this system is likely to be very worthwhile. Where such supports are missing or inadequate, this has the potential to undermine the long-term efficacy of the work you do with the client.

Assessment and evaluation

The exercises will be best utilised if they are informed by a thorough assessment of each person that takes into account their strengths in balance with their needs, vulnerabilities and risks. Such an assessment will include all or some of the following:

- previous convictions, victim and witness statements, detailed information about offences

- education, care history, employment, relationships

- psychometric questionnaires, if used. See Browne, Beech and Craig (2013) for further information about this aspect of assessment

- reports/assessments from programmes attended during previous periods of supervision, imprisonment or institution-alisation

- psychiatric reports and relevant medical reports

- prison/hospital reports and/or security files

- information about other agencies involved, other professionals, other people in their support network, police intelligence, social work, risk management committees

- other assessments as relevant to the individual and their offence(s).

Other important areas to include in the assessment are:

- *All exercises in Chapter 3 – the preparation stage:* These focus on strengths, supports, values, motivation to change and life goals.

- *The client's experience of danger in the past:* The assessment should include understanding the client's experiences and memories of danger and comfort (or lack of comfort) across their lifespan. This should include consideration of unresolved trauma and loss.

- *The client's experience and perception of danger in their current life and in the present moment:* It is important to be aware of when and where the client may feel there is danger intruding on their life currently, and also in the present moment of the session. This may be implicit or explicit danger. One form of danger, for example, would be when the client is aware that making certain kinds of disclosures to you will result in sanctions or what they perceive as punishment. Or they may be concerned about current peer influences or threats which are currently active – for example, a threat from peers that 'you better not go soft'. This will keep them on alert, and we should be realistic about our expectations of clients in these circumstances. Another type of danger the client may perceive is the pain and fear associated with recalling life events, relationships, traumas and losses that are unresolved. Such topics will demand sensitivity, attunement and clear boundaries and contracting about what the purpose is of discussing these topics.

- *Relationships and sexuality:* Assessment and intervention should address how the client functions in relationships, particularly close relationships (including, where relevant, sexual relationships). This aspect of the assessment should also include how the client functions interpersonally with you. Are they engaged and cooperative? Are they confrontational or defiant? Are they people-pleasing or passive? Are they deceptive or elusive? To what extent is this affected by your approach and manner with them?

- *Information processing:* Assessment should also take into account how the client processes information – that is to say, how the client balances and integrates their perceptions, thoughts and feelings (Crittenden 2008). Does the client *omit* crucial information from their awareness, such as their own or other people's roles in an event? Or do they omit feelings and focus only on facts – or vice versa? Does the client make significant *errors*, such as misattributing cause and effect, or blaming the wrong person for an event? Do they *distort* information, for example by minimising or exaggerating feelings or responsibility? Does the client *deny* information that they are fully or partially aware of? Do they deny factual information, or deny their own feelings and perspective? Does the client *falsify* information about events, emotions or their actions or intentions, and treat this information as true? Are they deceiving themselves and/or you? Do they attempt to get you to collude with or believe the falsified version of events? How aware is the client of their self-deception or their deception of you?

- *Themes of identity, connection, significance and belonging:* How has the client tried to achieve a sense of being significant or powerful? Have they done this in any positive ways, or in negative ways? What interpersonal connections does the client have? What is the quality of these connections? How do they achieve a sense of belonging? What is their sense of who they are and where they fit into society (i.e. their sense of identity)?

- *Opportunities for personal growth and contributing/giving back:* What are the client's hopes and aspirations? Where might there be possibilities for positive growth, internally and interpersonally, in any aspect of life? Where might there be opportunities for the client to make a contribution to society, for example by volunteering, making reparations or assisting in support groups for ex-offenders?

- *The systems around the client:* We described systems theory in Chapter 1. Here is a brief reminder of some of the important questions for assessment arising from systemic theory:

  ○ *The client system:* Who is the client? Is it a person? A family? A group? A community?

  ○ *The change system:* Who can be a part of the positive change process for the client? An individual, a family, a community, a voluntary group, a support group, a statutory agency, another organisation?

  ○ *The target system:* What and who needs to change? Sometimes, it is not so much the client themselves but the system around the client that needs to change, or the client's relationship to that system. For example, if a client has committed crimes under the strong negative influence of a peer group or a family member, this is a clear indicator that the focus of change needs to be not only on the client but on the system around the client, too.

Based on the above process of assessment, a treatment plan should build on strengths and address needs, while also being aware of risks. It should specify the number of sessions the person should do, which exercises should be chosen, which adaptations/variations are likely to prove most fruitful, and what the aims are. The treatment plan should always allow for the possibility of modifying the plan as work proceeds. Thorough assessment should result in a comprehensive functional formulation of the client's psychological difficulties that looks beyond symptoms and into their underlying function in the client's bio-psycho-social history. What purpose did this strategy serve when it was first used? What purpose does it serve now?

At the end of your sessions with the client, a final report should be written which is informed by all or some of the following:

- session records
- out-of-session work
- post-treatment psychometrics, if these are included
- assessments and other information from professionals and volunteers who are familiar with the client and have a significant role in relation to the client
- information from family, friends and associates
- other assessment tools as used.

Appendix 2 offers a session recording and report template for you to use and adapt.

Working with clients who deny offending

Criminal justice workers will frequently find themselves in conversation with clients who deny all, or significant aspects, of offences for which they have been convicted. Engaging with clients who are 'in denial' commonly evokes strong feelings of frustration and even anger among workers. Many workers, either consciously or unconsciously, believe that it is an indicator of successful intervention to get the client to 'confess' and 'admit responsibility' for previously denied aspects of their offending behaviour. It can feel like a professional snub, or as though we aren't good enough at our jobs, when the client 'refuses' to confess (Blagden et al. 2011).

This process occurs in the context of a prevailing cultural view that it is important for those who have broken the law to admit their guilt and take responsibility for their behaviour, and that this step is a prerequisite for genuine remorse and the rebuilding of a positive life. Indeed, many treatment programmes will not accept people who publicly deny their offences, and the denial of guilt is often presumed to be indicative of a raised propensity to re-offend. Furthermore, the criminal justice system offers rewards for the admission of guilt, such as likely earlier release by the parole board and other sentence review panels, and discounted sentences at court for guilty pleas.

It is important to acknowledge that a client's denial stance can complicate the risk assessment process, as there may be information about the offence process which it is difficult to access. Furthermore, if a client's family support the client's position of denial, it can be difficult to monitor risk situations which may occur in the family. This is particularly relevant in the context of intra-familial sexual abuse (Nunes et al. 2007) or domestic abuse. In such circumstances, external measures to monitor risk will be a vital component of risk management, in addition to work with the client and the family, where possible.

It is commonly assumed by the general public, and reinforced by some aspects of the way that the criminal justice system functions, that motivation to lead a law-abiding life is closely related to the willingness to publicly admit guilt for previous bad behaviour. The result of this can be that people who are not prepared to, or are not able to, publicly admit their guilt, are sometimes denied access to the sorts of interventions which may be the most effective tools to reduce their risk of re-offending.

However, the messages from research suggest that the situation is more complex. Much of the research in this field has been conducted with men convicted of sexual offences, and so it is from this literature that we will draw most heavily. Most research finds no overall clear link between recidivism and denial (see Hanson and Bussiere 1998; Hanson and Morton-Bourgon 2005). There is no evidence that an increase in 'accepting responsibility' leads to a reduction in re-offending (Marshall et al. 2001, Ware and Mann 2012). One possible exception appears to be among men who are convicted of sexual assault within their family, if the family are supportive of the man's innocence (Nunes et al. 2007). The authors speculate that the mechanism at work here may be that the family members, in maintaining the position that the man is innocent, may not take any steps to monitor his behaviour or restrict his access to children, which may increase the level of risky activity in which he engages.

Additionally, the desistance theorists have offered an interesting perspective on this debate. It has been proposed that, rather than being an indicator of deliberate deception and raised risk, denial may be understood as a rational and self-protective strategy. If this is the case, then it follows that adopting the stance that it is our role to unpick denial and promote the acceptance of responsibility may be counter-productive in some cases (Maruna and Mann 2006). Looked at in this way, denial may be, in some cases, a positive sign, as it might indicate a degree of shame, guilt or remorse on the part of the client. Some research into private psychotherapy (voluntarily entered into and paid for by the client) indicates that the majority of clients lie or deliberately omit information which they fear would reflect badly upon them and potentially cause their psychotherapist to reject them or view them in a negative light (Kottler 2010). If this is the case in private psychotherapy, it is likely to be even more so in the context of the criminal justice system, where the behaviour in question is against the law and where the client may have less choice about engaging in the process.

Implications for practice

In the light of this, what should the worker actually do? First, there is a distinction to be made between denial, resistance and non-cooperation. Both denial and resistance may be seen as normal and expected parts of the change process, and they typically (but not always) reflect the earlier stages of the motivational cycle of change. Clients may begin the exercises with you and still have varying forms of denial and resistance. Very often these factors will lessen as the sessions proceed and the therapeutic alliance is built. However, if a person is non-cooperative and refuses to even begin the process of engagement, they must not be pressured into a therapeutic process. It

may be possible to return to this individual at a later date in order to offer help, or to engage with them on the basis that they will not have to speak about any of their offences.

If a person is willing to engage with you, a good place to start is to ask yourself the question, 'What is the function of their denial?' In other words, why, from their point of view, does it make sense for them to outwardly deny their offence? (By the way, it is useful to remember that, in a small number of cases, the client may have been wrongly convicted – miscarriages of justice are rare, but do occur.) Another crucial question to consider is whether the client *publicly* denies the offence or their responsibility for the offence; they may to one degree or another *privately* admit to themselves their culpability (Roberts and Baim 1999). If you sense that the client privately admits to themselves their role and responsibility for the offence, but for various reasons they feel unable to 'own up' publicly, this will have significant implications for how you engage with them. As you get to know your client during the course of your work together, you will get a strong sense of whether there might be a gap between what they publicly admit to you and what they privately admit to themselves.

Once we start to conceptualise denial in this functional way, we can be more open to the idea that it is not an immutable, or stuck, position. Your relationship with the client, and the depth of your rapport, will have an influence on the extent to which the client feels the need to use self-protective strategies (Mann 2000). Also, the way in which the client understands the nature of your working contract will have an impact. If the client feels that your goal is to extract a confession (rather like a dentist extracting a tooth!), they are more likely to adopt a defensive stance and cling on to denial.

Working with resistant or reluctant clients

It is crucial to acknowledge that the client's agenda may be quite different from our own. For example, if you are working in the context of court-mandated supervision, the client may initially have little or no motivation to engage with you (Calder 2008). They may attend because the court has mandated their attendance, and this will almost inevitably mean the client is ambivalent and that you are in a position of power over them. The person might feel vulnerable – although many will refuse to show this. They may fear being judged or humiliated in their sessions with you, or they may fear being made to sacrifice part of their identity. Or perhaps they have previously had a bad experience of counselling or other forms of change-oriented work, and fear repeating the experience.

These are genuine fears and must be heard and validated. We can start by acknowledging their fear and helping them to re-frame it as ambivalence. Then we can help them focus on the reasons they want to participate on the sessions (e.g. 'I'm here because I want to stay out of prison,' or, 'I'm here because I want to make something of my life,' or, 'I don't want to lose my girlfriend/boyfriend') as opposed to focusing on the reasons they don't want to engage.

Of course there will also be occasions when all our best efforts will not engage an individual because the context is inappropriate; it is simply the wrong place and time for them.

Practical strategies

There are a range of motivational strategies which you can use to engage confidently with reluctant and resistant clients. It is possible to adapt all the exercises in this book to respond to clients who deny significant aspects of their offending and even to those who completely deny their offence (i.e. 'I didn't do it'). For those people who categorically deny their offence, a range of options and approaches can be used. A common variation is to use hypothetical examples and examples from stories in the news, asking the person to engage with the themes of the programme at *one step removed* (see the description of the *one step removed* technique later in this chapter).

Perhaps the most useful and wide-ranging adaptation is to help the person develop a relapse prevention plan aimed not at preventing a further offence (as they say they committed no crime), but aimed instead at ensuring that they are *never again accused or suspected of committing an offence*. Instead of discussing the disputed offence, pose the question, 'What was it about your lifestyle, or your patterns of thinking or behaving, which meant that you were arrested for, and subsequently convicted of, this offence? What changes do you need to make to ensure that you are never at risk of being suspected or accused of an offence again?' A *New Way of Living Plan* (see p.177) designed on this basis can be just as detailed as a plan developed by an 'admitter', and the end result is as likely to be safe behaviour as it would be if the individual was an 'admitter'. Moreover, experience has shown that, with some imagination and adaptation on the part of the facilitators, all of the exercises used with 'admitters' can be adapted for work with 'deniers' (Roberts and Baim 1999).

The skills and qualities of the facilitator

The skills and treatment style used by the worker are crucial to successful outcomes (Cooper 2008; Marshall *et al.* 2003). The exercises in this book are likely to be most effective when delivered by facilitators who work consistently at a mindful level which demonstrates the following skills and abilities:

- the ability to establish rapport with the client

- the ability to offer both high challenge and high support

- the skilful use of Socratic questioning and dialogue, combined with collaborative enquiry and motivational interviewing

- working with the whole person and not just with the 'offender' or 'client' role

- attuned communication and emotional intelligence

- working in a way that increases the person's sense of self-worth and self-efficacy

- pro-social modelling of mature communication around troubling topics, and acting as role models for responsible approaches to life's challenges

- maintaining boundaries while also being willing to be present with the client as a fellow human being (as opposed to a 'blank screen' or 'scientist performing an experiment on a guinea pig', as some clients have referred to it)

- using the quality of the collaborative relationship as a key to effective working

- instilling hope in the client, e.g. the hope that change is possible and that long-term positive life goals are worthwhile

- an understanding of the limits of what we can influence, balanced with the responsibility of the client for their part in the process

- the ability to use theoretical knowledge and models to facilitate effectively

- the ability to reflect on one's own thoughts, feelings, behaviour and experiences in order to develop as an effective facilitator

- the ability to positively seek feedback about one's strengths and areas for development and then make changes

- the ability to use different techniques to help people challenge their ways of thinking or behaving and practise new skills.

Many of these skills and abilities are encompassed in the handy acronym WERD (Marshall *et al.* 2003):

- **W**armth, e.g. as conveyed through voice tone and non-verbal communication.

- **E**mpathy, e.g. as conveyed through acceptance and attuned communication.

- **R**einforcement, e.g. through the use of specific and motivational praise.

- **D**irectiveness, e.g. assisting the person to work through problems by using strategic, open-ended questions.

By contrast, a confrontational approach is likely to be destructive. Challenge can be useful, but this is only effective if a true working rapport has been developed between the facilitator and the client. Otherwise, an approach of high challenge is likely to lead to mistrust, shutting down and possibly entrenchment of pro-offending attitudes and increased resistance to treatment.

Skilful questions: The fine art of promoting reflection, discovery and positive change

In this section, we focus on the types of question that facilitators can ask clients in order to promote reflection, personal discovery and positive change. There are many different types of question, and we will focus on several of the most crucial and important types: Socratic questions, solution-focused questions, active listening, reflective questions and questions that encourage change talk. We also focus on the related concepts of asking genuine questions and allowing thinking time.

Socratic questions

Socratic questions and the Socratic approach to dialogue are the bedrock of the motivational approach we take in this book. Socratic questions are intended to lead the individual to make their own discoveries and insights based upon the worker's strategic, incrementally adjusted questions and answers. Socratic questions are used to stimulate critical thinking, explore alternatives, clarify meaning and encourage insight.

One way of describing Socratic questions is that they are questions that 'lead from one step behind'. This is also known as the stance of the naïve enquirer – sometimes also called the 'Columbo' approach, after the television detective played by Peter Falk. Socratic questions have the great advantage in that they encourage the client to do most of the work, because they must actively think through problems and arrive at solutions that have personal meaning for them. The approach is based on the principle that people are more likely to integrate knowledge they come to through their own thought process rather than that which is delivered or imposed upon them. Socrates' novel insight as a philosopher and teacher was to, in effect, reverse roles with his pupils and turn them into the 'experts'. Through his deliberately naïve questioning, he allowed his students to find their own way towards discovery, insight, knowledge and truth, and to apply this learning to their own circumstances.

A good way to craft Socratic questions is to bear in mind that there are different levels of questioning that relate to different levels of cognitive processing. The following breakdown derives from the work of Bloom (1956), and starts from the simpler levels of cognitive processing to the most complex and demanding:

LEVEL 1: GATHERING AND RECALLING INFORMATION

The purpose of level 1 questions is to cause the client to gather information by recalling it from short and long-term memory. Behaviours elicited by level 1 questions include *completing, counting, defining, describing, identifying, listing, naming, observing, recalling, reciting, scanning* and *selecting*.

Examples

- Completing: *'How would you complete this story / case study?'*

- Counting: *'How many possible sources of support and strength have you illustrated in this diagram?'*

- Defining: *'How would you define what success means for you in relation to the sessions we are doing together?'*

- Describing: *'What do you see in this picture?'*

- Identifying: *'Who are three important people in your life and why are they important to you?'*

- Listing: *'What are your strengths? (e.g. internal, interpersonal, spiritual and / or past accomplishments).'*

- Naming: *'What do you call it when you start to feel like that?'*

- Observing: *'What do you notice?'*

- Recalling: *'What is one thing you remember from the last session?'*

- Scanning: *'In this picture, where is there anything that might be dangerous? That might be safe?'*

- Selecting: *'From this list, which option would you like to try?'*

LEVEL 2: MAKING SENSE OF GATHERED INFORMATION

Level 2 questions aim to help the client to process the information gathered and recalled. Level 2 questions are often useful for following up new information in order to clarify and analyse the relevance of the information. Behaviours elicited by level 2 questions include *analysing, classifying / grouping, comparing, contrasting, distinguishing, inferring, planning, sequencing, synthesising, translating* and *clarifying thinking*.

Examples

- Analysing: *'Looking at this case study, what would you say Steve's risk factors are?'*

- Classifying / grouping: *'How would you draw that as a diagram? What would you include / not include in the diagram?'*

- Comparing / contrasting: *'Looking back now, what do you think of your behaviour on that day? What might you think or do differently, if you had the chance?'*

- Distinguishing: *'What are you responsible for and what are you not responsible for? (e.g. in the past, present, future).'*

- Inferring: *'What does that tell you about how that thought affected your feelings and actions?'* *'What does that tell you about what the person was thinking?'*

- Planning: *'What are three tasks that you want to accomplish today? How can we plan together to help you get them done?'*

- Sequencing: *'What was the order of events in that episode? What happened first?' 'What was the sequence of thoughts?'*

- Synthesising: *'What is your understanding of how the pressures in your life contributed to your offence?'*

- Translating: *'How would that idea look in practice? Can you think of an example?'*

- Clarifying thinking: *'What do you mean by that?' 'Please expand on that thought/explain further.'*

LEVEL 3: APPLYING AND EVALUATING INFORMATION

Level 3 questions help the client to make and defend a judgement, to discuss a value system or to use and apply information in novel or hypothetical situations. A well-crafted level 3 question is often an efficient path to rich and significant discussion. Behaviours elicited by level 3 questions include *applying a principle, evaluating, prioritising, generalising, hypothesising, imagining alternatives, perspective-taking, judging, utilising resources, reflecting, evidencing, expanding, predicting, looking at implications/consequences, meta-questioning, challenging assumptions/bias* and *clarifying values.*

Examples

- Applying a principle: *'Based on the idea/value you have just stated, what do you think is the best way for you to handle the situation?'*

- Evaluating: *'What is important to you? (e.g.: family, community, work, spirituality, education, friends, etc.).'*

- Prioritising: *'Which way do you think is the best way?' 'Which part is most important to address first?'*

- Generalising: *'What learning can you take from that? Where else can you apply it?'*

- Hypothesising: *'What explanation might there be for A's behaviour?'*

- Imagining alternatives: *'What might be a different way to see that?' 'What is the counter-argument?' 'Did anyone see this another way?'*

- Perspective-taking: *'How might other adults view that problem?' 'How might the victim view that?'*

- Judging: *'In this role play, was Bobby justified in saying that he was "just testing" himself?' 'Do you think his actions were right or wrong?'*

- Utilising resources: *'What will help you find the courage to face it?' 'The next time you are angry, what would be an effective coping strategy for you to take?'*

- Reflecting: *'How are you managing to cope with your anxiety and still do this important work?' Or: 'What might you have to give up in order to move on?' Or: 'What's holding you back from making that decision?'*

- Evidencing: *'What is the evidence that that way of thinking is safe/risky for you?' 'Why do you say that?' 'Is there reason to doubt this evidence?'*

- Expanding: *'What are some different options that you could think about?' 'What other thoughts do you have about that?'*

- Predicting: *'What might get in the way of your positive changes?' 'What would be a high-risk situation?'*

- Implications and consequences: *'If X happened, what would the result be in the short and long term?' 'How does X affect Y?'*

- Meta-questions (questions about questions): *'Why do you think that might be an important question to ask?' 'Why do you think I asked that question?' 'What is the most important question to ask right now?' 'What would be a useful question to ask yourself about that problem?' 'Which question was the most useful?'*

- Challenging assumptions/bias: *'What assumptions are you making there?' 'Is that assumption warranted?' 'Is this always the case?' 'Why do you think that this assumption holds here?' 'Where might there be a bias?' 'What might be the missing information?' 'Where could* the missing information be obtained?' 'Does it exist?' 'What is a matter of fact and what is a matter of opinion or judgment?' 'Do "known facts" and "well-established truths" ever change over time?'

- Clarifying values: 'Why is that important?' 'What is the value system underlying that statement?' 'Why should we care about that as a human society?'

Solution-focused questions

The solution-focused approach to asking questions is aimed at helping clients to identify their strengths, abilities, skills, resources, support systems and interpersonal resources. This is meant to help the client construct a narrative about themselves where they are internally competent and externally supported. The discussion prompted by solution-focused questions is also intended to find new ways to bring existing resources to help with current problems. In this approach, the facilitator helps the client to identify resources using techniques such as focusing on *coping skills*, encouraging *problem-free talk*, *finding exceptions*, using the *'miracle question,'* *focusing on strengths* and using *scaling questions* (Greenberg, Ganshorn and Danilkewic 2001).

Examples of solution-focused questions

Comment: 'It's all too much. I'm overwhelmed by problems.'

Solution-focused response, focusing on the client's *coping skills*: 'Let's think of a time together when you have managed to cope with a situation. Let's think of a time, no matter how small or insignificant it seems. What was happening when you coped well and had a successful outcome? What thoughts and feelings did you have? What did you do to affect the situation? What evidence does this give you that you can cope now and in future?'

Comment: 'I don't think I can change.'

Solution-focused response, using *problem-free talk*: 'What would one positive change look like? What would I see you doing if you made one small change? What would that look

like? What would you think and feel about yourself if you made this change?'

Comment: 'I don't see the point of trying; I've always been like this, and a leopard can't change its spots.'

Solution-focused response, finding an *exception to the rule*: 'Tell me about a time when the problem did not exist. How old were you? Where were you? Who was around? Looking forward, picture a different future. What would the imagined 'new you' look like and be like? What needs to change in order to help you get there?'

Comment: 'I don't know what needs to change, and I don't know what I want.'

Solution-focused response, using the *miracle question*: 'Imagine you have come to the last session of our work together. How are you different now as compared with the start of the sessions? Looking back over your time in the sessions, what was the key session for you? What happened in it? What insight did you have that made all the difference? How did this help you to change/to move in the direction you want in your life?'

Comment: 'I know I need to turn my life around, but I'm a million miles from there. It's hard. It's really hard.'

Solution-focused response, *focusing on strengths*: 'What are some of the strengths you can draw on as you make some changes in your life? What are the strengths you have inside you? Who are the people in your life who give you strength? What other strengths do you have, for instance a place that makes you feel good and confident, or a belief/faith, or a form of creativity, work or expression? What have you accomplished in the past that can give you strength, even if it is the strength to survive in difficult circumstances?'

Comment: 'It all feels pointless and hopeless.'

Solution-focused response, using *scaling questions*: 'What is the worst this feeling of hopelessness has been? (This is marked zero on the scale.) What is the best this feeling could possibly be? (This is marked 10.) Where would you mark it now? If you are having a better day, how will you know? What tells you it is a better day? When you are having a better day, mark it precisely on this scale. What point on the scale would be good enough for you? What would it feel like on a day like that? What would you be doing differently? How did you manage to make such a day a reality for you? What resources do you have to support you as you develop a way to cope and move forward with your life?'

Active listening

Active listening encompasses a number of different techniques and is based on the principle that deep listening is an active process and not a passive one. In addition, the techniques of active listening allow the facilitator to engage with the client more effectively, to maintain focused discussion and to use time most efficiently. Some of the key techniques within active listening are:

- **Summarising:** You pause the conversation to summarise what the person has said.

- **Repeating:** You repeat a word or phrase the person has said using the exact wording.

- **Paraphrasing:** You repeat back what you have heard in your own words.

- **Clarifying:** You pause in order to check your understanding of something the person has said or to make sure they intended to say that. This can be a very efficient and empathic way of maintaining control of the conversation. It is a particularly important and valuable technique to manage participants who speak very quickly, who lose focus, who bring in too many topics or who change the topic.

- **Verbal underscoring:** You note the importance of something the person has said and why you think it's important.

- **Expanding:** You ask the person to say more about something they have said.

- **Giving time:** You reassure the person that it is fine for them to take their time in thinking or expressing a feeling.

- **Connecting:** You note a connection between things the person has said.

- **Observing:** You note with the person something that is happening to them during the conversation, for example, that they are smiling, or becoming agitated.

- **Body language:** You use your body language in a non-distracting way to foster good communication and rapport. You observe the person's body language and use this information to inform your approach with them.

- **Non-verbal prompts:** These include prompts such as nodding, smiling, leaning forward, tilting head, gesturing with hands, and simple prompts such as, 'Yes…', 'Hmmm hmmm…'

- **Listening with high hopes and expectations:** As you listen, you work with a hopeful stance that conveys a message to the person that you can see the best in them. You treat them as if they are the best person they can be, and your manner with them conveys that you believe they can fully inhabit such a role (i.e. that they are such a person).

- **Validation:** To validate means to acknowledge and try to understand the unique perspective of a person. When you validate someone, you allow them to safely express their feelings and thoughts. By doing so, you allow the person a chance to feel heard, understood, acknowledged and accepted. You send a message that you truly care enough about the person to try to see the issue from their perspective. In turn, the person feels heard and validated. It may be at this point that they display a willingness to engage. Until a person feels validated by you, the focus is likely to be on defending a particular position. And this destroys the forward movement of the discussion.

  Validation allows the person to release their feelings in a healthy, safe and supportive manner. It's also an effective tool to help you get to know the person better, thus building bonds of support, acceptance, understanding and trust. By practising validation, you'll display genuine concern for the feelings of the participants, which is a key aspect of effective facilitator style.

Reflective questions

Reflective questions are, as the name suggests, questions that encourage the person to reflect on their thoughts, feelings, actions and relationships. They are also questions that include some of the reflective thinking of the worker. In general, reflective questions are questions that make use of statements by the client, and use those statements in order to move to the next level of integration, insight or discovery. Here are some of the types of reflective question:

SIMPLE REFLECTION

You reflect back what you have heard the person saying or expressing, in a way that validates the person's feelings or point of view and gives words to their perspective or names their feeling. Example: 'It sounds like you're feeling really sad about what's happened.' This could also include reflecting back your observations of a person's non-verbal communication. For example: 'I notice that when you talk about your ex-partner, you raise your voice slightly, and clench and unclench your fists.'

SUMMARISING REFLECTION

You offer a reflective summary. Example: 'I notice that you talk a lot about how you were feeling angry when that happened to you.'

DEEPENING REFLECTION

You ask a question that is intended to allow the speaker space and time to reflect and to challenge him/herself. Example: 'I notice that you spoke about feeling very angry with your partner at the time. How did you feel *within yourself* during those times? What was happening and not happening in your life that fueled your anger and frustration? Take a moment or two to think about that before you reply.'

'NEXT STEP' OR SCAFFOLDING REFLECTION

You reflect on something the person has said and you help them to focus on the implications of that statement for the next step they take. The *Motivational Cycle of Change* in Chapter 3 (p.83) is a very useful reference point when using scaffolding questions. Example: 'I can see that you are frustrated about the problem and the way that it keeps ending up with you getting arrested. What role do you think you have in the problem?' Then: 'What role do you think you have in the possible solution?' Then: 'What might be the first step towards change?' Then: 'What resources do you need to help you make that first step?' Then: 'When do you think you can begin to make that change?' Then: 'How many days has it been since you last (X)?' Then: 'What steps can you put in place to maintain this change?' etc. (This may continue for many months until the change is deeply embedded.)

DOUBLE-SIDED REFLECTION

This type of reflection emphasises the role of choice and highlights ambivalence. Example: 'What I hear you saying is that on the one hand you are trying to change your thinking and behaviour, and on the other hand you are still struggling to understand what you have done that was wrong. Have I got that right?' Then: 'Let's give some attention to both of these issues and see where you want to go from there.'

AMPLIFIED REFLECTION

This type of reflection exaggerates a statement to the point where the person is inclined to back away. Example: 'It sounds like you are saying that you had no choice at all, and that you *had* to commit (the offence).' Or: 'It sounds from what you are saying that in your opinion the victim was asking for you to commit the offence against them.' Or: 'It sounds as though you are giving 100 per cent of the responsibility for the offence to the other person/victim and that you had no responsibility for what you said or what you did.' (Note: If the client admits to as little as one per cent responsibility, you can build from there.)

PARADOXICAL QUESTIONS

These are questions that, by their phrasing, encourage the person to take an opposite view. They are paradoxical because, in their phrasing, they acknowledge the temptation to commit crime while also encouraging the person to argue against committing a crime. Examples: 'Why didn't you steal the money?' 'Why didn't you punch him in the nose?' 'Why didn't you take advantage of that person?' 'Why don't you commit a crime any time you feel like it?'

Questions such as these are very useful in highlighting the thought processes that lie behind the decision to commit or not commit a crime. This is a powerful and significant step towards taking full ownership of and responsibility for one's thinking.

AGREEMENT WITH A TWIST

These are questions that build on what the person has said and then use their stated values to highlight a crucial decision or thought process they used during their offending. This can then be used as a bridge to help the person challenge their 'permission-giving' thoughts. Example: 'I can see how, as you say, you were and are a good father, a good husband, a good provider and a respected colleague. How then were you able to give yourself permission to commit (the offence)?' Then: 'What is your opinion now about that permission-giving thought you had at the time?'

Questions that encourage and develop change talk

At any point in the sessions with the client, you may want to encourage them to develop their 'change talk' – that is to say, their statements about how they are moving on from their past offending and towards a more positive way of being in the world (Miller and Rollnick 2002). In asking questions that promote change talk, you can also encourage the person to contrast their old thinking with their new thinking. This usually has the powerful effect of freeing up the participants to disclose more fully their pro-offending thoughts, feelings and behaviour, because they do not feel trapped by your suspicion that they are 'still like that'; they feel they are being given some credit for already having changed (even if only slightly) from the time of their offending.

Examples of questions designed to elicit change talk:

- How have you moved on since the time of your offending?

- What are your beliefs now about what you did then?

- Looking back now, what is your opinion of your behaviour on the day you offended?

- What would the (present-day) 25-year-old you say to the 21-year-old you about having those thoughts/committing that offence?

- What would be an example of how your thinking has changed in relation to the offence you have been convicted of? Do you still think it was the right thing to do? Why or why not?

- What new decisions, actions or directions does this suggest to you? Which direction do you want your life to start heading?

- Are there any blocks to you making that first step?

- What is your evidence that you are already starting to make these changes?

- What strategies and support networks and other resources can you (or do you) draw upon to help you make these positive changes?

Asking genuine questions

A useful guideline to follow when asking questions is to ask genuine questions. A genuine question is simply one that you do not know the answer to. It is asked in a spirit of enquiry and with genuine interest in the perspective and thoughts of the client, even when it is covering basic or review material. The alternative, sometimes referred to as a 'dead' question, is one that you already know the answer to. Such a question forces the client to give only the one response you are looking for, which can be patronising, frustrating and boring.

Thinking time

Time is essential to any critical thinking activity. Therefore it is important to allow time for silence and for thinking, particularly when you have asked a genuine question and it requires real thought on the part of the client. It is not unusual to have to wait 30 seconds or longer to allow appropriate thinking time. If the client is taking a very long time to think, simplifying or rephrasing a question may help.

A tip: it can be useful to tell the person/ group in advance if you are going to give them extra time to think. This will decrease their anxiety about the silence. Example: 'Take a moment to think about that question before you reply.'

Variations and adaptations that can be used with any of the exercises

The exercises in this book are designed with flexibility and adaptability in mind. This is a cornerstone of effective intervention. Such adaptability will allow the exercises to be undertaken with virtually any client or service user, according to their needs and learning style. Adaptation of the material should take into account culture, ethnicity, literacy and numeracy, gender, age, social background, optimum learning style, sexual orientation, disabilities and life experiences of clients. This includes the responsivity needs of clients diagnosed with personality disorder, intellectual disability or mental illness/ disorder. The exercises can be delivered with the following variations, and you are encouraged to work collaboratively with your client to find methods that work for them.

Active methods

EXPERIENTIAL/PHYSICAL/GAME-BASED VARIATIONS

For example: doing a simple activity where trust is involved and then talking about the issues of trust in one's life.

AUDIO-VISUAL AND MULTI-SENSORY METHODS

There is enormous scope for creativity with audio-visual and multi-sensory ideas. For example, the client(s) might create colourful posters and notice boards. In one probation centre where we have worked, the staff and clients created a small theatre, with curtains and a small raised platform. This became the 'practice area' for role plays of various types. The clients enjoyed the heightened sense of importance conveyed by the theatre space, and the stage area also served as a useful dividing line between role play and discussion.

We have also incorporated mask making, crafts, sound recording, video creation and radio documentaries into various offending behaviour programmes we have facilitated. As you get to know your clients and what interests and motivates them, you will be better able to work with them to generate visual, auditory and kinaesthetic modes of working that make the learning more meaningful and involving for them.

PROJECTIVE METHODS

A projective method is one where the client is encouraged to 'project' meaning onto objects and to use these to facilitate discussion and exploration. The objects can be everyday objects such as a book, a pebble, or a pen, or they can be objects or toy figures specifically included in the session to encourage symbolic thinking (for example, an Aladdin's lamp, a puppet, a magnifying glass or an action figure).

Projective methods are extremely useful and can be used and adapted in many ways. They can prove very useful in helping the client to focus on their own perspective, because the client does not have to look at the worker as they do in normal conversation. Instead, they can focus entirely on the objects and the issue they are thinking about. The worker becomes a witness to the story and an interested observer, offering prompts for further exploration as needed.

PRACTISING

Skills can be practised at any point where it is appropriate in order to meet a learning need that emerges. Skills practice can sometimes be done very briefly if the skill is straightforward and clearly defined. More complex skills will take longer to practise, and require more repetitions, so they need advance planning if they are to be part of a session. See Chapters 4 and 5 for more on skills practice.

CONCRETISATION

In this technique, abstract concepts are made tangible or 'concrete'. Example: the client is torn between two competing impulses. Ask them to sit in one chair and speak from the point of view of one of the impulses, and then speak from a different chair from the point of view of the opposite impulse. Or: the client feels terribly disappointed about something. You ask the client to choose an object or draw an image to represent disappointment. You then ask them about the disappointment, and where appropriate you then ask them to choose another object or draw another image representing hope, or a way out, or a supportive person, etc.

ONE-STEP-REMOVED WORKING

This is when you use hypothetical examples, news stories or close-to-life examples. These examples are meant to be highly relevant to the client's experience, but they also allow some distance, which can help to free the client from feeling too pressured to reveal more than they feel comfortable with. An example of this is the client who put a good deal of work into creating a character he called 'Mr Healthy'. This character was often referred to, and the client found it useful to refer to 'what Mr Healthy would probably do in this situation'. Of course, the client was generating the ideas himself. Mr Healthy provided a necessary distance for the client to consider difficult and painful topics.

Typically, working at one step removed is a stepping stone to working at the directly personal level, but not always. With some clients, such as those who do not publicly admit to having committed any offence, working at the level of one step removed is the best way to address offending behaviour issues and achieve most of the learning aims, without having to talk directly about the client's offences.

SOCIODRAMA

Sociodrama is a process where people are helped to enact social issues and dilemmas that affect them, as a way of exploring the impact and testing out solutions (Weiner, Adderley and Kirk 2011). Sociodrama has a lot in common with the previous concept of working at one step removed. It is an active method of working that explores the social forces and systems that shape people individually and collectively. During the process, each participant has the opportunity to speak from a number of different character roles and points of view.

Here is an example: in group discussion, ask the group to think of some key details of a fictional crime that can serve as the basis of this exercise. Alternatively, you can use a news article. Set out three to five chairs, each representing a different person who has some relationship to the crime. For example, if the crime being considered is an armed robbery, the chairs may represent the offender, the victims, the police, the witness, and the partner, child or parent of the victim. There could also be chairs for members of the offender's family. The offence and its aftermath are re-told (not enacted) as a series of improvised monologues by each of the characters from their different points of view. Questions can come from anyone in the group and from the facilitators. Allow and encourage the participants to discover the validity and importance of each perspective. Each character will have their own version of 'the way I see it', and their own particular interest in the events. Swap round the participants, so that several people have an opportunity to play the key roles.

This process is meant to be delivered in the spirit of Socratic dialogue and debate, encouraging the participants to make their own discoveries and draw their own conclusions. The technique generates a language for discussing difference that moves beyond black and white, all-or-nothing, I-am-right-and-you-are-wrong thinking. In the discussion afterwards, people are encouraged to say how they connect with the issues raised in the sociodrama and what learning they want to take from the work.

Sociodrama can also be adapted for one-to-one working. In this situation, you can use chairs or objects to represent the various characters in the drama or the situation. You can then encourage the client to speak from each of these roles in succession. Where appropriate, you can speak from one or more of the roles, too.

INTERVIEWING IN ROLE

This is a technique drawn from the method of psychodrama. Using the interviewing in role technique, you interview the client in role as any aspect of themselves – for example, their thoughts, feelings, actions – at any point in time, past, present or future. You can also interview the client in role as another person, for instance, a family member, their victim, the police, the judge, a family member of the victim. Again, the 'interview' can be at any point in time. The client can enter and speak from virtually any role if it is relevant to their exploration of their life, alternatives to offending, their well-being and their future aspirations. The client is encouraged to speak in the first-person present tense 'as if' they are

that person, concept or aspect of being (Baim, Burmeister and Mariel 2007; Blatner 1997; Moreno 1946).

Reading, writing and talking methods

READING

Where appropriate and of interest to the client, they can be encouraged to read from relevant resources. This will be a viable option for some clients but not for others.

WRITING, INCLUDING CREATIVE WRITING

Some clients who particularly like to write can be encouraged to keep a reflections journal, do autobiographical writing, or write poetry, plays, songs, fiction or non-fiction which is related to their process of moving away from offending and towards a more positive life.

DRAWING/ARTISTIC EXPRESSION

Clients can be encouraged to express themselves with drawing. This can include even very basic stick figures to represent people and situations. Clients can also be encouraged to illustrate their thought process and inner world using Mind Maps (Buzan and Buzan 2010) or other forms of illustration.

IMAGES

As a related idea, you can use images of various themes and topics and create simple laminates. These can be used as prompts for discussion and skills practice. The client can even create their own, covering any topic that they see as relevant. This may include thoughts, feelings, actions, attitudes, places, people, ideas, etc.

TALKING AND SILENCE

While talking is normally the basis of working with clients, it can also become something that is used more consciously and strategically. For example, there may be times during a session where you deliberately agree with the client that neither of you will speak for a period of time while the client continues with a task. Additionally, you may suggest certain talk-based assignments for the client to undertake between sessions. This might include 'assignments' to have a conversation with a member of staff, a family member, a friend, a volunteer, or even the local shopkeeper.

Note: Baim, Brookes and Mountford (2002) contains more than 100 experiential exercises with multiple applications.

General guidance on responsivity

The wide range of variations listed here should make it possible to adapt the exercises to take into account the capacities of most clients. For example, where a high-intensity, personal level role play is called for, it may be necessary with some clients to begin with *projective methods*, then move into *one-step-removed* role play, and then potentially into directly personal level role play (i.e. simulations of real-life situations they face). However, in some cases, using projective methods and/or working at one step removed may be all that a client can tolerate. Facilitators and supervisors should consider what the individual capacity of clients is with regard to high impact exercises (particularly those addressing victim empathy and disclosure of offending behaviours and pro-offending thoughts). Clients must not be labelled as 'resistant' because they cannot or will not do an exercise at the same level of personal focus and intensity as another client. One client who works at one step removed using projective methods may be working just as hard and with as much integrity as another client who works on the personal level. The idea is to use and adapt appropriate techniques in order to focus each exercise at the right level of intensity for each client to gain optimal learning.

Out-of-session work

Some sessions will include an element of out-of-session work. Where literacy is an issue, clients can be helped to find creative solutions (e.g. using imagery, audio recording, or asking for assistance). Where appropriate and feasible, special 'homework sessions' (e.g. with a mentor) can be scheduled between sessions, in order to help clients with out-of-session work. This can greatly enhance the efficacy of the process, and may be particularly helpful for clients with intellectual disabilities.

Several handy techniques with many applications

In this section, we offer five very widely adaptable techniques. These can be used at any point in your work with the client in order to encourage reflection, focus on a particular theme or begin discussion on a given theme.

The pie chart

Pie charts can be used in many ways. One way, for example, is to have the person divide up the slices in to 'all of the factors that led to my offending'. Then, 'all of the factors that will lead me away from offending'. Or: 'Who is responsible for my decisions about what I do, where I go and who I talk or interact with?' Or: 'What percentage of my day is spent doing W, X, Y and Z?'

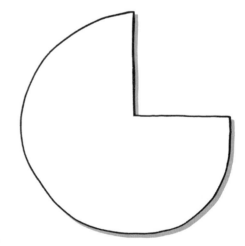

Figure 2.1: A pie chart

The decision matrix or cost/ benefit analysis

The decision matrix is a very simple tool to help the client weigh up the pros and cons of various themes affecting their life. Here are two examples:

WHAT ARE THE PROS AND CONS FOR ME OF DRINKING ALCOHOL?
(Can be done for short and long term)

	DRINKING	NOT DRINKING
Advantages		
Disadvantages		

WHAT ARE THE PROS AND CONS FOR ME AND OTHER PEOPLE IF I STOP COMMITTING OFFENCES?
(Can be done for short and long term)

	FOR ME	FOR OTHER PEOPLE
Advantages		
Disadvantages		

Continuums

Continuums are useful for addressing almost any topic or theme. They are very useful for revealing values, beliefs and opinions, and prompting discussion about these themes. In a group setting, you can ask the group members to arrange themselves along an imaginary line according to their replies to the continuum question. In one-to-one working, you can simply ask the client to point to a place on a line drawn on a sheet of paper. Here are some examples:

- How in control am I of my own behaviour? (0%–100%). Six months ago? Six months in future (goal setting)?

- How responsible am I for my offence? (0%–100%)

- How responsible is my victim for my offence against him/her/them? (0%–100%)

- How much control do I have over what I think about? (now/6 months ago/6 months from now)

- How much alcohol have I had this week? (0 units–70 units)

- How many times in the past week have I felt angry/been violent/lapsed/used an intervention?

- I am responsible for my own behaviour. (agree/disagree)

- I can make choices about how I behave in future. (agree/disagree)

- In the heat of the moment, I stop and think of the consequences before I act. (always/never)

The continuum is related to the technique of 'scaling', for example, 'On a scale of 1 to 10, how angry am I about that?' For more examples of scaling questions, see the section earlier in this chapter on solution-focused questions.

Future projection

In this technique, a future scene is examined and/or enacted. This may be for the purposes of relapse prevention, rehearsal, confronting fears, practising a hoped-for role or outcome, testing expectations, etc. The person in focus speaks in the present tense as if they are in a future moment in time. This technique can be combined with the idea of the 'miracle question', described earlier in this chapter in the section on solution-focused questions.

Warm-up questions

The purpose of a warm-up question is to open up discussion around a particular theme. Here are some examples (adapted from Baim *et al.* 2002):

MOTIVATION AND GOAL SETTING

- What is one thing you would like to get from these sessions? How able are you to do this now, in percentage terms?

- What is one reason you don't want to be here, and one reason you do?

- What do you want to achieve this week/ by the end of the course/this year/in your life?

- Who will benefit from you being here and making progress toward change?

- What is one thing you are good at and one thing you'd like to improve?

THE GROUP PROCESS: RESPONSIBILITY FOR OWN CHANGE PROCESS

- What do you think you have in common with the other people who have done this programme/these sessions?

- What are the most important questions you should ask yourself? Ask them, and try to answer.

POWER AND CONTROL

- Describe a situation where you had power and used it well/where you misused power?

- Describe an area of life where you have power/have no power?

ANGER MANAGEMENT AND VIOLENCE

- When was the first time you were violent?

- What is the smallest thing that makes you angry?

- When you are angry, what do you do to stop yourself being violent?

THINKING ABOUT THINKING: SELF-TALK, SELF-CONTROL AND RESPONSIBILITY

- Do you control your thoughts or do they control you?

- What actions are you responsible for and not responsible for?

- When are you likely to convince yourself that you are not responsible for your actions (e.g. when feeling bad/using alcohol)?

- How do you deal with the bad times?

CORE ATTITUDES AND BELIEFS ABOUT SELF AND OTHERS, SELF-ESTEEM, SELF-DISCLOSURE

- What messages have been given to you that have discouraged you from achieving what you wanted to?

- If you could teach everyone in the world one thing, what would it be?
- What is one rule you live by?
- What is one thing you don't like about yourself/one thing you do?
- What is the hardest thing you've ever done?
- Where does your name come from? Does it have a meaning? What do you think of it?
- Who was your first friend?
- What will be your epitaph?
- If you could be talented in something you are not, what would it be?
- What is something few people know about you that you are proud of?
- Name someone you admire/respect. Name someone you have considered to be a hero or heroine.
- Who has had the most impact on your life?

RELATIONSHIPS/GENDER TRAINING AND BELIEFS

- When did you become an adult? Or, more specifically, when did you become a man/woman?
- What did your father teach you about being a man/mother teach you about being a woman?

FAMILY AND EARLY LEARNING

- What did you get from your parents that you wish you hadn't/are glad you did?
- What is your favourite memory of playing as a child?
- Who was your favourite/least favourite teacher?
- What was the first rule you broke and what was the consequence? What was the lesson you take from that, looking back?

RELAXATION, TAKING A TIME OUT, FREE TIME

- Which room do you like to spend time in?
- How would you decorate a room of your own?
- What is your favourite place? Where would you most like to visit in the world?
- What is your favourite T.V. programme/film/music/book?
- What is your idea of a relaxing time?

RELAPSE PREVENTION AND HIGH-RISK SITUATIONS

- What was the last high-risk situation you handled well/didn't handle well?
- What would be your first indication that you are getting into an offending cycle? Who would you contact?

PART II
Exercises to Promote Positive Change

CHAPTER 3

Building on Strengths and Motivating Change

This chapter has ten exercises aimed at helping the client to think about their life, how they have arrived at this point, and what directions they want their life to go. The exercises help the person to locate their strengths, their values, their sense of self-worth and their understanding of the challenges they face. By addressing issues such as family and social networks, life experiences and values, the facilitator has an opportunity to engage constructively with the client, build a basis of trust and provide a realistic opportunity for successful engagement. The exercises will also help the person to understand their role in the process of change, and what is involved in the process of change. They will be helped to begin to set in place changes they can begin immediately.

In some cases, such as where the person is only capable of participating for short periods of time, or where the person has very low intellectual functioning, there may be more sessions and the process may involve creative strategies (e.g. projective methods using objects/toys to tell the personal life story).

There is a great deal of emphasis in this chapter on building a positive rapport and working relationship between the client and the facilitator. The work is designed to be taken at the pace which is right for the individual. Typically, a session will introduce an exercise and involve some exploratory thinking with the client. Where appropriate, the client may be asked to take the exercise away and work on it between sessions. When both the worker and the client are satisfied that sufficient work has taken place (this may take more than one session), the next exercise is introduced, and the process is repeated.

Establishing a contract for working together

Gaining informed consent, building a foundation for working together, motivating change

Time: 1 hour to 3 hours

Materials: a written contract that allows space for adding in items as needed

Aims

- To gain informed consent.

- To offer an orientation to the sessions and an overview of the process to come.

- To answer the client's questions about the sessions.

- To establish a working rapport.

Method

Discuss with the client their understanding of why you are beginning work together. Explain the mandate for working together. For example, is this part of a court order or a requirement of their statutory supervision? Is their participation entirely voluntary, or will there be possible ramifications if they do not undertake the sessions? Encourage the client to weigh up the pros and cons of participating in the sessions, so they can decide whether or not they wish to begin.

Note with the client that you intend to work with them on the selection of exercises that they feel are relevant for them, and that it is possible not all of the exercises in this book will be relevant for them. Explain how long the sessions are likely to take, how many sessions there are likely to be, and that this is subject to change, depending on their pace of progress and their emerging needs. Ask about any concerns. Identify any special needs/possible problems/difficulties.

You may wish to have a pre-printed contract (see sample below), with space for writing. Written contracts can help make sure that the client and the facilitators agree on the aims and the practical details. For clients, contracts can

be part of the motivational process, as it gives them a clear role and stake in the process. It is also a respectful and thorough way to gain informed consent.

Explore previous times the person has done personal growth work, or previous times they avoided it. What might be good/difficult about the process? Where can they go if they need follow-up/support between sessions?

If you are using pre-programme questionnaires, for example psychometric measures or lifestyle/mood questionnaires, check that the client has done these. Any that have not been completed may be completed on the same day as this session if alternative arrangements are not in place.

Explore any questions the client has about the process and what's to come.

The contract should be agreed, signed and dated by you both. Once the client signs, give them a folder for their contract and their other paperwork and worksheets and explain that you will also keep a folder for their completed work. If the client is living in the community and prefers to leave their folder and worksheets at your office, this option should be offered.

Variations

Where there are concerns about whether the client understands, explain the concept and then ask them to explain it back to you. Clarify and repeat as necessary. Where clients still struggle to understand, it may be that the contract needs to take another form, for example, a flipchart with images and words or audio recording.

Contract for Participation

I, (name) _____, enter into this contract

with (agency) _____ in order to begin a

programme of sessions with these aims:

a. **To help me live a fulfilling and offence-free life.**

b. **To help me to improve my interactions with and relationships with other people.**

c. **To help me to understand and take responsibility for my thoughts, feelings and behaviour.**

d. **To help me meet my needs in ways that work with other people, not against them.**

1. I understand that this programme of sessions is being offered to me to help me make a new start and develop a fulfilling and offence-free life. Respect will be shown to me at all times and I will show respect at all times to my facilitator(s)/key worker(s)/therapist(s), etc. This includes respect for personal boundaries and safety.

2. I will attend all sessions and I will be sober, ready to work and on time. I understand that the only acceptable excuse for absence or lateness is a medical or personal emergency, and I will give notice as soon as I know if I will be late or miss a session.

3. I will fully participate in the sessions. I understand that this consists of weekly or twice weekly sessions and may last between _____ and _____ months (example: between 12 and 24 months), depending on my needs and progress and also on whether or not the programme is delivered in a group setting. I agree to complete out-of-session work and to ask for help to complete this work if I need it.

4. I understand that the sessions will focus on four areas:

a. Building strengths and motivation to change

b. Understanding myself and my patterns of behaviour

c. Understanding myself in relation to other people

d. Setting future goals and preparing for the challenges ahead.

5. I understand that the sessions include some or all of the following: talking, writing, reading, films, explaining, role play, drawing, discussion and other possible techniques.

6. I understand that I may be asked to discuss my progress and assignments with various members of staff and other significant people in my life.

7. I understand that ongoing assessment of my progress may be a part of the work.

8. I understand that, during these sessions, I will be asked to speak about my life history and my offences in order to understand myself better and to make links that I may not have thought about before. I understand that I may find certain aspects of the sessions stressful. For example, discussing very personal issues may cause me to feel difficult or

painful emotions. I understand that there is support available should I need it.

9. I understand that I have the right and will have the opportunity to have each activity explained to me before proceeding. I understand that I have the right to refuse to participate in any activity and the right to ask for it to be done in a different way if at all possible. I also understand that if it becomes too difficult for me to participate in these sessions, the sessions can be stopped. This may mean that I withdraw from the programme or that I become ineligible. This will be fully discussed with me.

10. I understand that staff may provide periodic verbal and written reports to other individuals and agencies. I understand that the information in reports provided by staff may influence matters such as court decisions. I will always be informed when information about me is being shared, and wherever possible staff will tell me who the information is being shared with.

11. If participating in a group I will not disclose any information regarding another client to anyone outside this programme.

12. I understand that if I disclose any information related to activity which may be subject to criminal prosecution, the staff may pass this information to appropriate agencies or personnel, including those agencies with statutory responsibilities for public protection.

13. *If relevant:* I understand and give permission that some sessions may be audio or video recorded, which is solely for the purpose of ensuring the quality of delivery and will not be used for any further assessment of my performance. If sessions are recorded, the recordings will remain the property of _____. Such recordings may be used to train other professionals, and if they are used in this way my surname will be protected and confidential.

14. I acknowledge that no guarantees have been made to me about the results of the sessions. I also recognise that should I re-offend it will be entirely my own responsibility.

15. I agree to avoid situations and behaviours that will place me at risk of re-offending.

I have read, understand and acknowledge that I am required to follow all the conditions listed above. If I have any questions about this contract, I have discussed them to my satisfaction with the relevant person. By signing this contract, I give voluntary consent to participate in all the above.

Signed by client: _____ **Date:** _____

Name printed: _____

Signed by member of

staff/key worker: _____ **Date:** _____

Name printed: _____

Signed by supervisor/line manager: _____ **Date:** _____

Name printed: _____

Starting from strength

Strengths, self-worth, self-efficacy, identity, motivation to change

Time: 30 minutes to 1 hour, or more
Materials: worksheet

Aims

- To promote self-efficacy and self-reflection.

- To increase motivation to make positive changes.

- To identify as many strengths as possible within the client and in the systems around the client.

Method

This exercise is based on the principle that, when we are facing major challenges in our lives or struggling to find hope, a useful starting place is to focus on strengths. This helps us to begin to face the major challenges of life, and can also prepare us to remain strong if this becomes even more difficult during the process of change. These strengths are divided into five categories in order to help the client think about different types of strength. The types of strength include *internal strengths; people who give me strength; transpersonal strengths such as faith, art, nature; accomplishments and things I have achieved in my life that give me strength; strengths in the systems around me.*

To do the exercise, you can use the worksheet to help the client identify the different types of strength. The client can work in any order that they find useful. When they identify a strength, try to help them identify one or more examples of when that strength has helped them in the past, and/or how the strength can help them in the future. For example, under '*people who give me strength*', the client may identify their brother. In the right-hand column they can offer one or more examples of when and how their brother has helped them.

The worksheet can be done together or be completed as out-of-session work.

Variations

Identify strengths using toys, objects, props, drawings or any other means to 'concretise' the concepts. For example, a picture of an arrow could represent a sense of determination, or a book could represent learning or knowledge of a certain topic or subject. Empty chairs can also be used to represent the different strengths.

For clients who like to learn in a more physical or kinaesthetic way, you can ask them to find a physical stance that feels like a strong and firm stance (e.g. a martial arts stance) and then ask them to find ways to make it even stronger. You can them help the client to consider what strength means and the other strengths they have available to them.

A useful addition to the exercise is writing a 'letter to myself in the future, when I am living a better life and no longer committing offences'. This is a letter that can be saved until the last session, where it can be read and discussed. Or the client can address it to themselves in five years or even further into the future.

Credit

We have drawn from the work of Hudgins (2002) in creating this exercise.

Worksheet: Starting from Strength

Name: _____   **Date:** _____

This worksheet is about strengths that are important to you. You may need to remind yourself about these strengths if the work ever becomes tricky, painful or difficult for you. Try to identify strengths, even if they don't seem to be that important. Over time, you may find more or develop more.

As you go through the worksheet, say how the strengths operates, e.g. what a friend gives you, or what an internal quality helps you to do.

TYPE OF STRENGTH	HOW THIS HELPS ME (GIVE EXAMPLES WHERE POSSIBLE):
Internal strengths: (e.g. honesty, sense of hope, concern for others, my ability to stay alive, my sense of fairness for myself and others)	
People who give me strength: (e.g. family, friends, colleagues, people in the community, social workers/ probation officers, etc.)	
Transpersonal strengths: (e.g. belief system/religious faith/spirituality, places that give me strength, animals, pets)	

★

TYPE OF STRENGTH	HOW THIS HELPS ME (GIVE EXAMPLES WHERE POSSIBLE):
Things I am proud of: (e.g. work, education, social, hobbies, any accomplishments I can take pride in having accomplished. What am I good at? It doesn't matter how 'little' the accomplishment is – list it here anyway)	
Strengths I gain from the systems around me: (e.g. my housing association, the job centre, the charity that provided me with furniture/ food/other support, the education department here in the prison, the local library, my local government, the general public who fund this programme and provide me with a chance to change)	

Positive changes I can make today

Motivation to change, self-efficacy, building support network

Time: 30 minutes to 1 hour
Materials: worksheet

Aims

- To make positive changes, starting today.

- To think about times when the client has made positive changes, or coped with change that has been beyond their control.

- To help the client to think about themself and their life, and the things that they are capable of.

- To think about talking to people in the client's support network, and asking them for feedback and encouragement about the changes the client is making.

Method

Look together at the worksheet *Changes I Can Make Today*. This exercise is about small changes that can be started immediately, as opposed to more fundamental changes that will need to be made over time.

Ask the client to use the worksheet to write a list of positive changes that they may have already made, which promote a healthier, safer and (ultimately) offence-free lifestyle. This is an opportunity to acknowledge that many clients are already engaged in a change process, or at least contemplating change, prior to their work with you. Make sure to validate and reinforce these changes as a way of showing respect and enhancing motivation. It is possible that these changes may not appear to you to have a direct link to the nature of the offending behaviour itself. This is ok – it is the client's perception of which changes are relevant which matters

here. For some clients, just engaging with you in this work might represent a big change.

Some changes can appear to be daunting, and out of the client's control. If the client's perception is that there are too many obstacles to change, ask them to consider examples of times when they might have adapted well to changes which were beyond their control (e.g. changes in foster home, new school, new colleagues at work, moving house, etc.). This may help the client to build up evidence that they can be resilient in the face of change.

Work together to identify who can help the client to make and maintain these changes, and who can offer feedback about their progress. Ask the client to identify what changes in behaviour would be visible to members of their support network, and who would be most likely to notice the signs. This exercise can be revisited during your work together, as an opportunity to pause and reflect upon progress made. If it seems appropriate, you could encourage the client to set a goal, and make a contract to feed back to you at your next meeting. You may also be a valuable source of positive feedback for your client.

Variation

For an active version of this exercise, try using the game *Tin Soldiers* from Baim *et al.* (2002). This is a useful exercise for highlighting the idea that all of our actions stem from a decision, however small and fleeting it might seem.

Worksheet: Changes I Can Make Today

Name: _____ **Date:** _____

Making some small changes can help to boost your morale and build your energy for making the bigger changes. Here are some examples of small changes:

- Carry in your pocket, or put up in your room, pictures of significant people who would be supportive of you building a new life.

- Develop new thinking habits about situations that get you down (e.g. coming to terms with the ending of a relationship or the loss of a job).

- Begin to practice a new pattern of behaviour that leads towards a feeling of well-being (as opposed to isolation, conflict or anxiety).

- Become involved in a positive, legal activity that brings a sense of achievement or calm.

- Encourage feedback from friends or family: 'How am I doing?'

- Keep a thoughts diary or a behaviour diary related to anything that you are trying to manage/change.

What evidence do you have that you are capable of making changes in your life? (For example, when have you made changes to your behaviour, however large or small?)

When have you coped well with changes that were out of your control (e.g. loss of a job or relationship)?

Using the list, and adding any ideas of your own, make a note of any positive changes you want to make in the short term:

When you are trying to make changes to the way you think, feel and behave, it can be helpful to have people who can offer you support and feedback. Use this sheet to record what changes in the way you behave would be noticeable to your support network, if you were to be successful in making changes. If you want to, you could use this list to start a conversation with people in your support network about how they can help you.

DESCRIPTION OF THE CHANGE	WHAT WILL PEOPLE NOTICE?	WHO WILL NOTICE THE CHANGE?
E.g.: I am trying to cut down on my drinking. I will have two alcohol-free days per week, and alternate alcoholic and non-alcoholic drinks.	I will have more energy in the mornings, and will be more able to have conversations with my partner in the evenings.	My partner and my children.

Family tree

Identity and roles, understanding myself and my relationships, self-worth, motivation

Time: 1 hour to 3 hours, or more

Materials: worksheet and paper, and other materials as needed

Aims

- To help the client to notice and reflect upon themes or repeated patterns in their family history.

- To understand what may have been 'passed down' the generations to the client (both positive and negative things).

- To think about how the client's family has coped with difficulty, such as loss or trauma, and to identify hidden strengths, or the capacity for resilience.

Method

The family tree exercise (or 'genogram') is commonly used in therapy, coaching and personal development work. The exercise involves drawing a diagram to represent the people in the client's immediate and extended family, going back in time as far as the client is able to. This should include the significant people the client is related to, either through birth, marriage, cohabitation, adoption or fostering. If the client has owned pets who have been significant to them, then include them as well.

It can be of use to the client to add in very significant cultural and historical factors or events, such as moving between countries, losses, traumas, poverty, etc. This may enable the client to identify themes or repetitions, and previously unforeseen connections. There can be tremendous benefit for some clients in seeing how certain themes may have been played out over generations. This approach can also help clients to identify the coping strategies which have been adopted by family members, and strengths which have been drawn upon across the generations.

Using the worksheet, and the key to the symbols, help the client to draw a family tree. A fictional example is included, to help you get started. It is usual to start with the client and their immediate family, and then continue as far into the extended family, and previous generations, as the client is able to. There is more than one way to do this, so follow the client's lead. Some people prefer to take the piece of work away, and complete it on their own, and others would rather you helped them with drawing the family tree. Don't be overly concerned with getting the symbols and lines completely accurate – it just needs to make sense to the client.

Once the client has filled in as much of the family tree as they are able, you can then both look at it, reflect, and offer thoughts about recurrent themes or patterns. Use the questions below to deepen the significance of this piece of work:

Questions for reflection

- What lessons did you learn from growing up in this family about how to stay safe and get your physical and emotional needs met?

- How useful are these lessons to you now? Are some of them helpful? Are others unhelpful, and out of date?

- Does this family have secrets, or things which are off limits? What might happen if these forbidden things are talked about?

- What are the spoken and unspoken rules in this family? Who makes the rules? Can they be challenged?

- What are the important 'family stories' that are told within this family about our family history? What is their meaning and their purpose?

- What legacies might there be in this family, passed down like a hot potato from one generation to the next? What decisions can you make about this legacy and how it affects you?

Variations

If the client prefers to work in an active way, encourage them to set out pebbles or other small objects to represent family members. The brief family stories could be told by setting out empty chairs to represent the different people in the story. Or the client could draw pictures to represent different people, make a computer graphic, or make audio recordings for you to listen to together.

An advanced version of the family tree exercise would have the client taking on the role of one or more significant people in the family tree, and speaking from their perspective, using the technique of *interviewing in role*. A variation on this would be for the client to write themself a letter from the perspective of someone in their family tree. Example: 'A letter to me from my great grandfather/mother'.

Links

This exercise links closely with the following exercise, *My world diagram.*

Worksheet: My Family Tree

Name: _____ **Date:** _____

This exercise will help you to draw a diagram of your 'family tree'. This should include the significant people you are related to, and who you consider to be part of your family. Here are some examples of symbols to use, but feel free to adapt them:

Male Female Gender unknown (e.g. pregnancy) Death (Name / Name)

Family Tree Symbols

Enduring relationship (marriage or cohabitation)

Separation

Transitory relationship

Divorce

First child Second child Miscarriage or abortion Female twins

- Use circles to represent females.

- Use squares to represent men.

- Use crosses to represent people who are deceased (e.g. a cross through a square represents a deceased male).

- Put the age of the person in the circle or square, as well as their name and relationship to you.

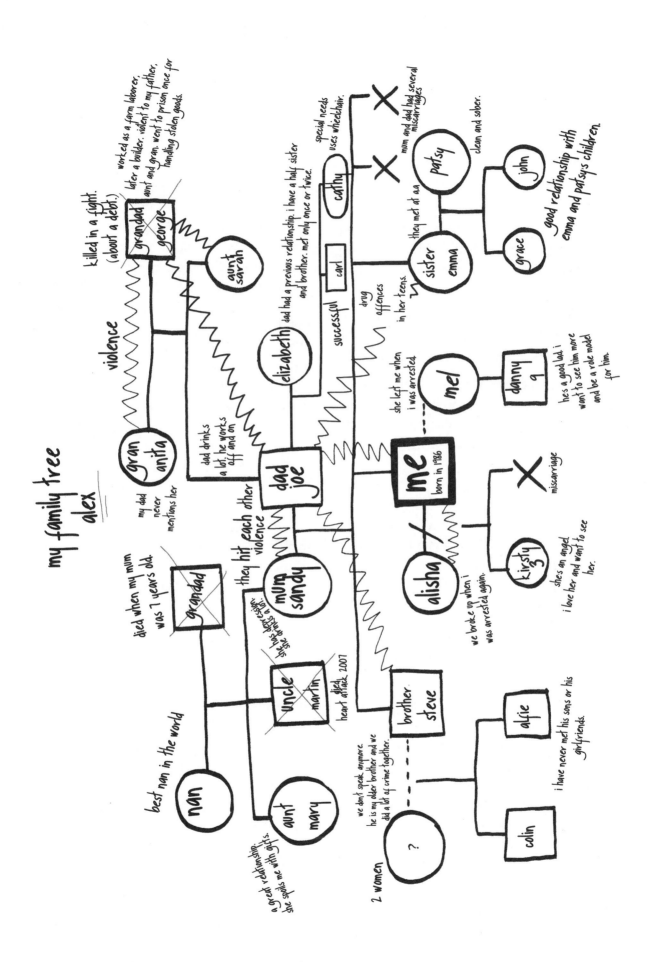

my family tree
alex

killed in a fight.
(about a debt.)

worked as a farm laborer. later a builder. violent to my father. aunt and gran went to prison once for handling stolen goods.

grandad george

aunt savah

violence

special needs uses wheelchair.

cathy

mum and dad had several miscarriages

patsy

clean and sober.

john

good relationship with emma and patsy's children.

grace

dad had a previous relationship. i have a half sister and brother. met only once or twice.

elizabeth

carl

successful

drug offences in her teens.

they met at a.a.

sister emma

gran anita

dad drinks a lot. he works off and on.

my dad never mentions her.

dad joe

she left me when i was arrested.

mel

danny 9

he's a good lad i want to see him more and be a role model for him.

me
born in 1986

miscarriage

died when my mum was 7 years old.

grandad

they hit each other
violence

mum sandy

she has aggression. she has a temper a lot.

alisha

we broke up when i was arrested again.

kirsty 3

she's an angel. i love her and want to see her.

best nan in the world

nan

uncle martin

died heart attack 2007

brother steve

a great relationship. she spoils me with gifts.

aunt mary

we don't speak anymore. he is my older brother and we did a lot of crime together.

alfie

colin

?

2 women

i have never met his sons or his girlfriends.

My world diagram

Self-awareness, identity, motivation

Time: 1 hour to 3 hours

Materials: worksheet, paper and other materials as needed

Aims

- To offer the client the opportunity to map out the important sources of connection and influence in their world, including things which are both positive and negative.

- To help the client to reflect on how the *My World Diagram* may have looked at different points across their life history.

- To help the client to think about how the different sources of influence might sometimes make conflicting demands which are difficult to reconcile.

Method

The *My World Diagram* (or 'eco-gram') has some similarities to the *Family Tree* exercise. The focus is different as it includes people who are outside the client's family, and it can also include cultural features, spiritual beliefs, and places and objects which are important to the client. It offers a rich opportunity for the client to reflect upon their important connections, and the different sources of influence upon them.

Begin with a large piece of paper, such as a page of flipchart paper. Ask the client to draw a symbol to represent themselves in the middle of the page. Then, ask the client to think about the main people, places, and things which they feel connected to, and which influence them in their life. This could include people, pets, places, sources of strength, spiritual beliefs, hobbies, clubs, groups, etc. The client then uses symbols, lines and words to draw a representation of the different influences, and the connections between them. The worksheet contains suggestions, and an example, to give you some ideas.

This exercise can be a valuable trigger for conversations about whether the client feels that, sometimes, different influences might conflict with each other. For example, the client's friends at work might not understand (or know about) the client's spiritual beliefs, or the client's parents might think that certain of the client's friends are a negative influence. The client may find it useful to evaluate the different types of influence which these different groups may have upon them and whether they are positive, neutral or negative. This may link well with the *Wheel of Life* exercise (p.78) which examines the client's goals, values and level of satisfaction with aspects of their life.

Variations

One possible variation is to use objects or small pebbles to represent the different people or sources of influence, which the client lays out on a flat surface. You could take a picture of this, using a digital camera, and both keep a copy.

An advanced version of this exercise could include the client speaking from the role of different people or sources of influence, using the technique of *interviewing in role*. This can be a positive and motivational experience if, for example, the client goes into role as a close friend or family member, and says that they don't approve of their offending, but that they still accept and love them. Or, if the client is facing a difficult decision, or a crisis, they could speak from the point of view of different people or sources of influence. You could then record, and later compare, the different perspectives gathered.

As a variation, the *My World Diagram* can be done to represent various 'snapshots' of time in the client's life. For example, this could include periods living away from home, with foster parents or in care, time in prison or hospital, or living in different countries. This can demonstrate how the client's social and cultural network has changed, or remained stable, over time. It can be very useful for clients who have experienced fragmented lives to consider who or what have been the main sources of influence upon them at different stages in their lives. It can also provide useful food for thought to consider what their world looked like very early in their lives, beyond conscious memory. This can often prompt reflection and reconsideration of received stories or unchallenged ideas about one's past.

Reflections and learning points

- We can be attached to, and influenced by, family members, friends, partners, colleagues and pets. Their influence may even continue, in some cases, after their death.

- Many people also have strong connections to places, or to buildings/houses, or activities like sport, or to cultural practices or spiritual beliefs.

- We can be influenced in positive or negative ways by the people and other elements in 'Our World'. Sometimes, different elements can influence us in conflicting ways, which can lead to us feeling confused or compromised, and unsure how to act.

- It can help you to make difficult decisions, or to cope in a crisis, if you have a greater understanding of the elements of 'Your World' and the ways they influence you, both positive and negative.

Worksheet: My World Diagram

Name: _____ **Date:**_____

The *My World Diagram* is a map of your social and cultural world. It can include family, friends, colleagues, strengths of any type, important objects, beliefs/ideas, values, pets, places, buildings, books, films, music – anything that you consider important to your values and your life as a whole.

As you draw the diagram, start with a symbol for yourself in the centre, and draw the other elements around you. Pay attention to distance and closeness, size, colour, etc. You may wish to draw different types of lines to represent the sorts of connection, e.g. solid line for solid connection, jagged line for a jagged relationship, line with an 'X' through it to represent negative relationship. Use your own creativity and imagination to draw a diagram that is right for you. Your diagram will be completely unique to you.

Here's an imagined example:

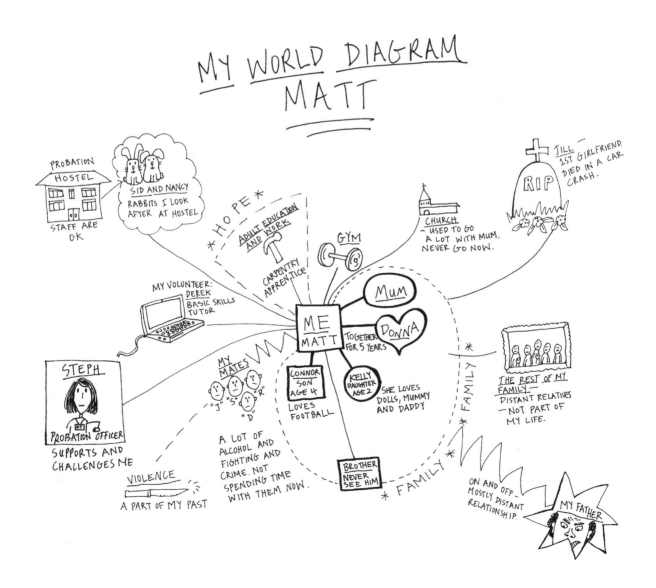

My local support systems

Asking for help, using the resources available to help me

Time: 1 hour to 3 hours

Materials: worksheet or other visual or IT materials

Aims

- To identify support systems around the client.

- To help the client develop connections and supports.

- To help the client understand that they can ask for help.

- To identify places, people or systems that are *not* helpful to them.

Method

This exercise has some cross-over with the *My World Diagram* exercise, but it focuses more specifically on helping the client to think more broadly about the supports that may be available to them. In addition, the exercise is intended to serve as a prompt to help the client forge new links and supports, and to feel more confident about asking for help when they need it.

To do the exercise, work with the client to draw a map of their local community, with areas beyond indicated with boxes or circles, to indicate they are beyond the edge of the map. On this map, work with the client to draw, write or illustrate where the supports are. For example, where is the probation office? Where is the local doctor and hospital? Where is the community centre, the health club/swimming pool, the job centre, the shops, the benefits office, the police station, the community college, the library, the adult education centre, the children's and families support centre, the drug advisory service, the charity shop selling inexpensive clothes, the food bank, the homeless shelter, the housing office, the local government office, the Citizen's Advice Bureau, the mental health centre, the

volunteer group looking for volunteers, the post office, the church, etc. Include support and help lines, for example, the Samaritans. What are the client's interests? What do they enjoy doing? Are there any groups of people they can join, and where are these located? Are there any particular skills they would like to gain, including literacy and numeracy skills, or any other basic skills? It may be that you can use the time with the client to go online and find local resources. This would also teach them how to do this for themselves.

Ensure that, as part of this discussion, the client is helped to understand the restrictions that may be placed on them due to their conviction. For example, someone convicted of sexual offences against children should not be attending a swimming baths at times when children are present. Similarly, the client should be helped to understand those situations where they would need to declare their criminal record to an employer or volunteer group/charity.

Where appropriate and needed, discuss with the client any parts of the map where there may be people it is not helpful to associate with or places where it is no longer helpful for them to go. Discuss how they feel about this, and what are the pros and cons of making decisions that take them in a positive direction. Do they think they deserve a better life, or the opportunity to make decisions of their own? Is anything getting in the way of them making clear decisions about how to live their life?

Variations

This exercise can be delivered in many different ways, depending on the skills and needs of the client. You can use simple pen and paper to draw the map, or you could use a printed street map. You can use objects to represent people/organisations/systems. You can use role play to help the client practise the skill of asking for help at a job centre or housing association, or asking for help with a learning task at the local adult education centre. You could use role play to help the client practise explaining to a friend, family member or partner the changes they are making, in order to gain the person's support.

Ask the client what help they will need to forge these new links and supports. Where needed, help the client to forge these links, or help the client find a volunteer or charity that specialises in helping people to make links in the community.

Worksheet: My Local Support Systems

Name: _____ **Date:** _____

A map of my local area, with my support systems shown:

Include these and other resources you can think of:

- probation office
- doctor
- hospital
- community centre
- health club
- job centre
- shops
- benefits office
- police station
- further education college
- library
- adult education centre

- children's and families support centre
- drug advisory service
- charity shop selling inexpensive clothes
- food bank
- homeless shelter
- housing office
- local government office
- Citizen's Advice Bureau
- mental health centre
- volunteer groups looking for volunteers

- post office
- parks/recreation facilities
- groups I can join, including support groups
- local transport, e.g. trains and buses
- church, etc.
- beyond the local: web-based resources, national resources
- support and helplines available to me 24/7.

The wheel of life

Motivation to change, values clarification, self-understanding

Time: 1 hour to 3 hours

Materials: worksheet or other visual materials

Aims

- To think about many different aspects of the client's life.

- To clarify what is important to the client in life, that is, what their values are.

- To think about how the client is living their life.

- To think about the person they want to be and how they want to live their life.

- To develop the client's confidence that they can make decisions about how they want to live their life.

Method

The idea of the wheel of life is an ancient one, found in indigenous cultures and in Buddhist ideas. In recent years, the idea of the wheel of life has been increasingly used in counseling and rehabilitation contexts and is perhaps best captured in the Good Lives Model of offender rehabilitation (Ward and Gannon 2006). It is a simple and accessible way to look at values and to think about what is most important to each of us. It is an exercise that focuses on what might be thought of as the ingredients of desistance of crime, that is, living a good and offence-free life.

Use the worksheet or draw a circle on a sheet of paper. Divide the circle into 11 equal 'slices', each representing a facet of life: family, social life/friends, healthy living, finance/wealth, work/studies, self-image, spirituality/meaning and purpose in life, personal growth/creativity, making a contribution to society/'giving back', pleasure/enjoyment/recreational pursuits; love/intimacy. You can add and subtract 'slices' of the pie, and rename them if other categories make more sense to the client.

Discuss with the client each aspect of life represented by the section of the circle. Help the client to identify how important each aspect of life is to them, and encourage them to rate its importance on a one to ten scale by drawing a line across the 'slice' of the pie at that level. The 1 to 10 scale starts at the centre of the circle and moves to the edge. For example, if 'family' is very important and rated '9', the client would draw a line across the 'family' section very near the perimeter of the circle.

Next, ask the client to think about each section of the circle and give a rating to how they are actually living their life. Again, they should draw a line across the section at that level. Very often, there will be a gap between the 'desired' and the 'actual' level. This can be used as an opportunity to think about what is important in life, and how one wishes to live.

Help the client to identify any areas of life they would like to develop. Rather than focusing on goals, which can either be achieved or not achieved, the emphasis in this discussion should be about the way the client wants to live their life, and the advantages of doing so. For example, in the section on 'finance/wealth', encourage the client to discuss what sort of lifestyle they see for themselves, and how they will feel when they are living this life. Encourage the client to think in the medium to long term, and to think about the steps needed to achieve the sort of lifestyle they want. Encourage the client to think in terms of what can be achieved in the near term and in one step at a time, rather than achieving some distant goal in one giant leap, which can set them up to experience failure. The wheel of life is not something that should be thought of as a single exercise to be 'completed', but instead should be seen as a reference point for lifelong growth and development.

Variations

Encourage the client to use visual materials to illustrate the different sections of the circle. The circle can be made highly autobiographical and personal through the inclusion of family photos, pictures of friends, specific places of work or other imagery that has personal meaning to the client.

Where appropriate, interview the client 'as if' they are at a given time in the future. For example, they can speak as if they are living their life in such a way that they are feeling good, living a successful life (by their own definition of success) and they have left offending behaviour far behind.

Encourage the client to think of examples of people they know, or who they have heard of, who could serve as role models in the different areas of life.

Worksheet: The Wheel of Life

Name: _____ **Date:** _____

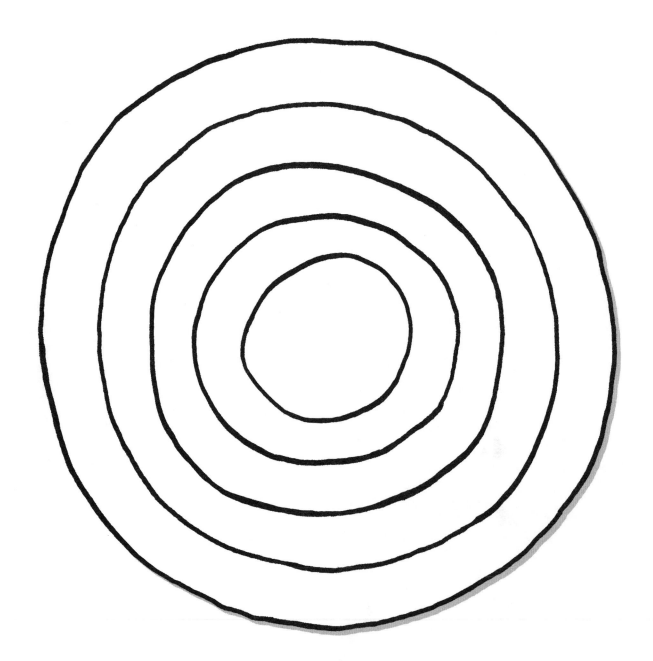

Do I want to change?

Motivation, self-efficacy, self-reflection

Time: 1 hour to 3 hours

Materials: worksheet, or any audio or visual material as appropriate/needed

Aims

- To develop motivation to make positive changes in the client's lifestyle and attitudes.

- To make the next step towards change.

- To develop the client's sense of self-efficacy – 'I can do it.'

- To develop an optimistic outlook.

- To reflect on myself and whether I think I deserve to live a better life.

Method

Use the worksheet *Do I Want to Change?* or any other appropriate means to focus discussion on the client's reasons for wanting or not wanting to change. Use Socratic questions and motivational interviewing principles to help motivate the client to make positive changes.

It is important to acknowledge that making changes may involve ending contact with some people or giving up ways of living which have been associated with criminal behaviour. These connections may have, at one time, represented a source of belonging and identity to the client. It is important to acknowledge and accept that making changes may well involve some losses as well, and that the client may have mixed feelings about this.

Note with the client: *Lasting change generally comes only from within – as opposed to being imposed by external controls. It is important that your reasons for wanting to change have genuine meaning for you, and are not just about behaving well to avoid arrest.*

Positive change is best linked with positive goals rather than avoidance goals (i.e. things you want to avoid).

Variations

Where needed, use objects, drawings, collage, images, music or empty chairs to represent the reasons for and against change, and the consequences. Skills practice can be used at any time that is appropriate.

It may be useful to first do the exercise using the example of a hypothetical person, with the client filling in the detail.

An advanced version of this exercise would have the client speak as themselves in the future, as if they had already made the positive changes they want to make. Ask how they managed to make the changes, and how their life has improved as a result. Try to keep the client in realistic mode as opposed to fantasy lifestyles, etc. If handled properly, this technique can be a highly motivational way of working. A similar approach would be to interview the client at a point in the future, having *not* made the changes they are contemplating. Have they been re-arrested? Are they lonely and without friends? Have they hurt someone else? Still in custody? This can then be contrasted with the interview where they spoke as if they *had* made the changes and are living a positive lifestyle. The intention here is again to be motivational; by speaking as if they have made positive changes, the client may more firmly believe that change is possible.

Worksheet: Do I Want to Change?

Name: _____ **Date:** _____

Areas of life to consider: family; social life/friends; health/fitness; finance/wealth; work/studies; self-image; spirituality/the big picture; personal growth; making a contribution to society/'giving back'; fun/recreation; love/intimacy; any other areas of life.

I AM THINKING ABOUT CHANGING...	POSITIVES OF CHANGING	NEGATIVES OF CHANGING	GOALS I CAN ACHIEVE IF I CHANGE	WHAT EVIDENCE DO I HAVE THAT I CAN MAKE THIS CHANGE?

The motivational cycle of change

Motivation, self-efficacy, making positive changes

Time: 1 hour to 2 hours

Materials: worksheet or any audio or visual material as appropriate/needed

Aims

- To understand how people change and how to make changes.

- To understand what a lapse is and what a relapse is, so the client can prepare to handle setbacks along the way.

- To help the client to develop motivation to make positive changes in their lifestyle and attitudes.

- To make the next step towards change.

Method

Using the illustrated version provided or your own illustration, discuss with the client the parts of the motivational cycle of change. The version that we offer here is a combination of two models described in Prochaska *et al.* (1992) and O'Reilly *et al.* (2001). Following this, use the worksheet *Where Am I on the Cycle of Change?* or another means to focus discussion on areas that the client would like to change. Use Socratic questions and motivational interviewing principles to help motivate the client to make positive changes.

Discuss with the client: *If we are unhappy with something about our life or one of our habits or behaviours, this is the first important step towards changing it. Change can be difficult, especially when we are trying to change long-term habits. But it is possible to make permanent changes in the way we live our lives. What it takes is motivation, a clear plan, focused attention and good support.*

The process of change can involve lapses (e.g. a return to pro-offending thoughts). It is crucial to understand that the occasional lapse does not mean it is 'all for nothing'. You can, if you are firm with yourself, get quickly back on track. The important thing is not to let the lapse slide any further towards relapse – a relapse would be a return to the old behaviour. Stop the lapse as soon as you become aware of it.

Think about some changes that you have made in the past, and changes that you want to make. For each of these types of change, consider where you are on the cycle of change. You can record your reflections on the worksheet.

Variations

It is often useful to set out the cycle of change on the floor and ask the client to 'walk through' the motivational cycle of change, to see where they are now on the cycle, and to set goals.

Where needed, use objects, drawings, collage, images, music or empty chairs to represent the parts of the cycle of change. Skills practice can be used at any time to practise change-promoting skills.

It may be useful to first do the exercise using the example of a hypothetical person making an important change, with the client filling in the detail.

An advanced version of this exercise would have the client speak as themselves in the future, as if they had *already* made the positive changes they want to make. Ask how they managed to make the changes, and how their life has improved as a result. The client should speak in the present tense, as if they are being interviewed in the future.

The motivational cycle of change

PRE-CONTEMPLATION

I don't have a problem. There's nothing to change.

CONTEMPLATION

- I can see that this behaviour is a problem and that I have some responsibility for this behaviour.

- I have some discomfort about the problem and my part in it.

- I believe things must change.

- I have some responsibility for my own process of change. I can be part of the solution.

DETERMINATION

- I can make a choice. I choose to be part of the solution to my problem.

- I can see the first step in making change. I know I can ask for help now and in the future when I need help with this change.

- I want to make a change. I am making a plan and writing it down.

ACTION

I am making changes and paying constant attention to the change to keep it going.

POSSIBLE LAPSE/RELAPSE

MAINTENANCE

I am maintaining change over the long term and remaining vigilant in case I slide back to old habits. I have a good support network and call on my supports when I need them.

POSSIBLE LAPSE/RELAPSE

INTEGRATION

This change is now so long-lasting that it is deeply a part of my identity. The old behaviour is a part of my history but does not dominate my present.

Worksheet: Where Am I on the Cycle of Change?

Name: _____ **Date:** _____

Think about some changes that you have made in the past, and changes that you want to make. For each of these types of change, consider where you are on the cycle of change. You can record your reflections here.

TYPE OF CHANGE	WHERE I AM ON THE CYCLE OF CHANGE IN RELATION TO THIS CHANGE	IS THERE ANYTHING HOLDING ME BACK FROM MAKING THIS CHANGE? IF SO, HOW CAN I OVERCOME THIS BARRIER?
Examples: habits; lifestyle; behaviours, including positive behaviour and negative/ offending behaviour; how I treat other people; how I treat myself	Example: contemplation stage – 'I believe things must change.'	Example: thoughts holding me back: I am making excuses like 'it's too much effort' or 'someone else has to help me'. Thoughts that help me move forward: 'I know I will feel better so I want to just do it!'

Pros and cons of offending

Motivation, consequential thinking, self-identity

Time: 1 hour to 2 hours

Materials: worksheet, flipchart paper and other materials as needed

Aims

- To maintain the motivation of the client to engage in the process of positive change.

- To offer the client the opportunity to weigh up the pros and cons of offending.

- To acknowledge and explore any ambivalence which the client may be experiencing.

- To explore the client's perception of their offending, and of the lifestyle they were living at the time of their offending.

Method

When clients start to work with you, they may be at any point on the *Motivational Cycle of Change* (see p.83). Some clients, especially those in the contemplation stage, may feel as though they are at a crossroads, with a big decision to make about whether to continue living the life they have known, or whether to take the brave step to choose to live in a different way. It is important to acknowledge that the life which they were living at the time of their offending may have involved some positive elements, such as comfort, pleasure, familiarity, camaraderie, status, a sense of belonging, money, etc. Leaving behind the familiar can be daunting for any human being, and even more so for people who may lack support or social resources.

It can help clients to think more clearly if we encourage them explore the positives and negatives of their previous way of life, for themselves and others, and in the short term and the long term. This exercise can be particularly useful if the client is still attracted to, or tied to, the lifestyle they were living at the time of their offending.

The exercise begins with a list of questions, designed as prompts to explore the client's perception of their offending, and how it fits with the person they would like to be. We suggest that you have a conversation, using the questions as a starting point, and focusing upon those which seem most relevant. During the conversation, you could capture important points on the chart, which examines the pros and cons of offending, for the client and for others, in the short term and the long term. It is important to note that this exercise is not meant as an attempt to convince the client of the need to change; rather, it is designed to promote genuine dialogue, to facilitate their own thought processes, and to support the client in reaching their own conclusion. Any ideas which we, as workers, impose upon clients, are unlikely to reflect their own lived experiences and will lack credibility or influence.

After filling in the chart, you could ask the client to rate how important each consequence is, from 0 (unimportant) to 10 (very important), and add up the values for each list.

Variations

To make this exercise more interactive, you could create a simple balance in the room (e.g. a ruler placed across a pencil, so it becomes a weighing scale), which you can use to compare the 'weight' of the pros versus the cons. Simple everyday objects, such as buttons or small stones, can be used to represent the various pros and cons, and placed on the scale. This exercise could be repeated to show how the balance looked at different points in time (e.g. *Me when I was offending* versus *Me now*).

A more advanced version of this exercise would be to ask the client to participate in an 'internal dialogue' where the pros and cons have a discussion. You could set out two chairs – the client could sit in one, and take on one role, and you could sit in the other chair and take on the opposing role. Or, the client could alternate between both roles, taking on one followed by another. If you do this, it is best to use two chairs, to make it clear which role the client is in.

Pros and cons of offending:
Questions for discussion
WHO IS IN CONTROL?

- How much are you in control of your actions? (0–100%)

- If you aren't in control of your actions, what is? Or who is?

- Do you have any choice in whether you commit an offence? How much choice?

- At which point in the behaviour leading to your offending could you have acted differently?

DO I WANT TO CHANGE?

- What will be the consequences for you of not making changes in your life?

- What will be the consequences for other people of you not making changes in your life?

- What will be the consequences for you of making changes in your life?

- What will be the consequences for other people of you making changes in your life?

- What things might you have to give up in order to change?

- What things might you lose if you don't change?

CONSEQUENCES OF OFFENDING

- What has resulted from your offending that you don't like?

- Who is worse off as a result of the offence? Why?

- What has been the most difficult consequence for you? Why?

- Were there any 'pros' to offending, like good feelings, or some of your needs being met?

- If you did gain things from your offending, how important are those gains to you now?

- If you hadn't committed this offence, in what ways would you be better off now?

Other people

- In what ways have other people acted differently towards you because of your offence?

- Whose opinion of you matters most to you?

- Who would you like to think well of you?

- What effect has your offending had on the way you have had to deal with other people?

Influences

- What aspects of your life made/make your offending more likely?

- Would you like to change any of these aspects of your life?

- Is there anything that you can do about them?

Sources of support

- Who would encourage you to make positive changes?

- Who could offer you support in living a different way of life?

- Who can give you regular feedback about the progress you are making?

Worksheet: The Pros and Cons of Offending

Name: _____ **Date:** _____

	PROS: WHAT I GAINED	CONS: WHAT I LOST
SHORT TERM At the time of offending, and shortly afterwards		
LONG TERM Now, and in the future		

Think about the other people affected by your offending. They could include your family, children (if you have children), your friends, people you committed offences with, the victim, the victim's family and anyone else who you think is important. How did your offending affect them?

	WHAT OTHER PEOPLE GAINED	WHAT OTHER PEOPLE LOST
SHORT TERM At the time of offending, and shortly afterwards		
LONG TERM Now, and in the future		

CHAPTER 4

Looking Inward

Understanding Myself and My Patterns of Behaviour

This chapter contains ten exercises that help the client to look at some of the significant highs and lows they have experienced in their life, how they have coped, and the strategies they use for regulating and expressing their emotions when they are in stressful or threatening situations. This includes an exercise focusing on the impact of perceived danger upon the brain, and how the limbic system can become activated by real or perceived danger.

The chapter contains several autobiographical exercises aimed at helping the client to understand their patterns of behaviour at key points in their life, and to find meaning in their responses. This includes an exercise designed to promote better understanding of the offence, and alternative decisions they could have made. The client is encouraged to talk through their understanding of why they responded as they did, and how they want things to be different (or similar) in the future. Several exercises specifically look at experiences during childhood, and how these experiences may have influenced the development of their later responses and strategies.

The chapter also contains exercises aimed at promoting improved self-regulation, for example through practising the skills of mindfulness, self-compassion, internal dialogue and reflection and other self-regulation skills.

Understanding my brain
Self-awareness, reflection, self-regulation

Time: 1 hour or more, as needed
Materials: worksheet and other materials as needed

Aims

- To develop an understanding of three major regions of the brain and the role they play in processing our thoughts, feelings and behaviour.

- To learn more about the 'two speed' brain.

- To understand that our fast, 'emotional' brain is very useful for keeping us safe when we are in danger, but can be unhelpful if we do not balance it by using our 'cognitive' brain as well.

- To understand that, to live as an integrated adult, it is important to use both our cognitive and emotional abilities in flexible and strategic ways.

Method

Discuss with your client the worksheet *Understanding My Brain: Part 1*. This worksheet contains a line drawing of the brain, with short descriptions of the functions of three major brain regions: the brainstem, the limbic system and the cortex. These three regions specialise in different jobs. Go through this worksheet with your client, and check their understanding, perhaps by asking them for examples of life situations when they need to use their thinking brain or their feeling brain.

Discuss with your client how all three systems are of vital importance and all contribute to human survival. However, when we are faced with a perceived danger and our fight–flight–freeze response is triggered, we can be overwhelmed by the quick operation of the limbic system. This is sometimes called 'emotional hijack' (Goleman 1996). In addition, people who have lived in situations where they have been exposed to chronic stress or danger, or to trauma, can develop difficulties with regulating their limbic system (Briere and Scott 2006). This can lead to them becoming unable to 'turn off' the body's reaction once the danger has passed. The chemicals associated with our body's reaction to danger (such as adrenalin and cortisol) have a negative impact on our ability to think clearly and to make long-term plans, as they prioritise quick action, without time for considered thinking (Panksepp 2005). Interestingly, living in chronic poverty has recently been shown to have an impact on the functioning of the limbic system and cortex (Blair 2010).

Now move on to the worksheet *Understanding My Brain: Part 2*. Explain to your client the Brain in the Hand model, developed by Dan Siegel. Work through the questions to explore times when your client may have responded emotionally when a more thought-through response would have been appropriate, and also times when your client may have dismissed or ignored their own emotions. In each case, use the questions as a guide to explore these situations more fully. There is a rating scale included, to help your client to consider whether they are, in general, more feelings oriented or more thoughts oriented. You could also ask them to rate these tendencies across their lifespan, to identify whether their strategies of emotional self-regulation have changed over time, or not. You could also help them to identify any situations where their strategies change, for example, do the strategies differ at work, with friends, with parents, with their partner, with their children?

Variations

To make this exercise more active you could set out three chairs to represent the brainstem, the limbic system and the cortex. The client could sit in each chair in turn and describe how it feels to be putting that part of the brain in the driving seat.

You could ask your client to think of different life situations they have faced or might face in the future. You could encourage them to move between the three chairs, and to notice what each part of the brain is 'saying' or signalling for them to do. Encourage the client to:

- notice the signs from my body that I'm preparing for action

- focus on my breathing

- count to 10 slowly

- use positive self-talk.

Having sat in all three chairs, the client can be encouraged to make an 'executive decision' about how they perceive the situation and what they want to do.

This exercise links with *Becoming an Integrated Adult* in Chapter 5, *Practising Mindfulness* in Chapter 4 and the skill of *Relaxing when I am stressed*, see Appendix 3 p.193. If you want to read more about the brain, we recommend www.mindsightinstitute.com, which is Dr Dan Siegel's website.

Worksheet: Understanding My Brain (Part 1)

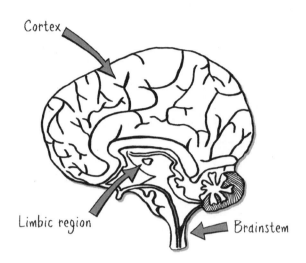

Cortex

Limbic region

Brainstem

The brainstem: our 'doing' brain

The brainstem is the earliest part of the brain to develop, and all types of animal species with a spinal column have a brainstem. It is the part of the brain which links with the central nervous system and through the spinal column, it is connected to all of our body. It controls the body's systems which we need to stay alive, such as breathing, circulation, digestion, temperature regulation, sleeping and waking, etc. These are all things which happen without us having to consciously think about them.

The limbic system: our 'feeling' brain

When we are under threat, or in danger, we need to act quickly to protect ourselves. The limbic system is the part of our brain which works like an alarm, to tell us when something important is happening which we need to respond to urgently. It sets off a chain of events which prepare us to fight, run away or hide. This is sometimes known as the fight–flight–freeze response, and involves the release of chemicals such as adrenaline and cortisol, which flood the brain and the body,

preparing us to respond to danger. It also regulates important emotions such as fear and aggression. The limbic system works much faster than the cortex – up to 40 times faster, often in milliseconds – because we need to be able to respond quickly to danger.

The cortex: our 'thinking' brain

This is the part of the brain that mostly develops after we are born, and is larger in humans than in other mammal species. It specialises in language, thinking about ideas, making decisions, considering other people's point of view, thinking about emotions, and logical reasoning. The pre-frontal cortex (just behind the forehead) is the part of the brain that controls our ability to pay attention and to focus. This part of our brain can only function properly if we feel safe and calm. It operates at a slower speed than the limbic system, so we need to allow time and safe space in order to think clearly, and to use our cortex to the best of our ability.

To discuss: thinking about our 'two speed brain'

Our limbic system needs to be able to operate quickly, because it needs to be able to sound the alarm when we are in danger, so that we can act to protect ourselves. However, sometimes, this speed of response can become a problem if it overwhelms us and stops us from thinking clearly. Some people react emotionally when a thoughtful response is called for (e.g. becoming angry when we perceive that someone is criticising or insulting us, without checking out what they are really saying). One way of looking at this is that the limbic system is in the driving seat at a time when it would be more useful to use the cortex (Kahneman 2011).

Worksheet: Understanding My Brain (Part 2)

There is a simple way to understand how different regions of the brain react in moments of perceived threat or danger, using your hand as a model. This is based on the work of Dr Dan Siegel, and you can watch a clip of him explaining it on the internet, at the following web page: www.youtube.com/watch?v=DD-IfP1FBFk.

First, hold up your hand and forearm with your hand open, like this...

The fleshy part at the base of your palm represents your **brainstem**. Your arm, stretching down from your palm to the elbow, represents your spinal column, which reminds us that the brain is connected to every part of our body through our central nervous system.

Next, fold your thumb across your palm, like this...

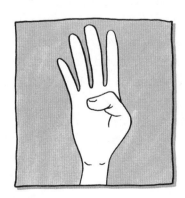

Your thumb represents the **limbic system**. This is the part of the brain which reacts very quickly when we perceive threat or danger. It triggers our fight–flight–freeze response, which helps us to survive in the world. However, the limbic system isn't always able to tell the difference between real danger and imagined danger. So, sometimes, it reacts when we are actually safe.

Next, fold your fingers over your thumb, to form a fist...

The bottom part of your fingers, and your fingernails, represent your **pre-frontal cortex**. This is the part of your brain which is capable of thinking clearly, weighing up ideas and making decisions. It is also capable of recognising what is going on in the other parts of the brain and regulating the limbic response and the brainstem. The cortex works best when we feel safe, and calm. When your limbic system is in charge, because it works so much faster than the cortex, it is more difficult for your cortex to 'interrupt' and take over.

We can illustrate how the limbic system responds to threat by quickly raising up our fingers (representing the cortex) to show that the thumb (representing the limbic system) is now in charge. In the video clip referenced above, Dan Siegel refers to this as 'flipping our lid'. If there is real danger, then this response means we are able to take quick action to protect ourselves. However, if there isn't real danger, this can mean that we act quickly when a more thought-through response would have been helpful.

Exercise

Focus on feelings

Can you think of a time when the action of your limbic system was helpful to you? In other words, a time when the quick emotional reactions of your limbic system helped you to take action in a dangerous situation (e.g. slamming the brakes on in your car if a child runs into the road, moving out of the way of a falling object on a building site). When did this happen? Where were you? Who was with you? What was the situation? What happened? What physical feelings did you have in your body when your emotions were triggered? How did your stomach feel? What happened to your heartbeat? What other physical sensations did you have? What sort of facial expression might you have had?

Now can you think of a time when your limbic system reacted as though there was a threat when you were actually safe? (e.g. thinking that a driver had deliberately cut you up, when it was really just a mistake; feeling jealous about a partner when there was a simple misunderstanding). When did this happen? Where were you? Who was with you? What was the situation? What happened? What physical feelings did you have in your body when your emotions were triggered? How did your stomach feel? What happened to your heartbeat? What other physical sensations did you have? What sort of facial expression might you have had?

We can help ourselves to manage our brains better if we learn what sorts of situations are likely to trigger a 'false alarm'. We can also teach ourselves some basic techniques to help the cortex to regain its executive function.

Focus on thinking

Can you think of a time when you were facing a situation that demanded that you carefully think through a range of options, thinking ahead to weigh up the consequences of different decisions? If you can think of such a situation, then that was certainly a time when you needed to use your cortex. Where were you? When did this happen? Who were you with? What was the situation? What options were you weighing up? What were the possible consequences you were thinking about? How was your cortex useful to you on that occasion?

Now can you think of a time when you were so focused upon thinking about facts and details that you didn't realise that deep down, you had powerful feelings about the situation? Where were you? Who was there? What was the situation? How do you think the situation might have turned out differently if you had been more in touch with your feelings, and able to express them clearly?

Self-rating scale

Healthy adult functioning and mature communication with others involves balancing our thoughts and our feelings, and integrating how we use our cortex and limbic systems. How would you rate yourself at different ages in terms of the integration of thoughts, and emotions? The line below represents completely thoughts oriented on the left, and completely emotions oriented on the right. Mark where you think your general tendencies have been across your life up to the present day. You could also draw a number of different lines, to represent a number of different types of situations (e.g. at work, with friends, with your partner, with your children, with your parents).

THOUGHTS ORIENTED   *FEELINGS ORIENTED*

Practising mindfulness

Emotional regulation, thinking skills, self-management

Time: 30 minutes to 1 hour per session

Materials: worksheet, optional audio CD, optional objects such as pebbles

Aims

- To introduce the idea of mindfulness.

- To encourage clients to consider whether it may be of use to them to practise mindfulness.

- To offer a structure for a mindfulness practice session, with some example exercises.

Method

Read through the worksheet, *Introduction to Mindfulness*. Have a discussion about the client's attitude to exploring mindfulness – do they think it might be of any benefit to them? Remembering that this is work which we do with people, rather than to them, it is important that the client chooses whether to pursue this at this time. Some clients may already have an interest in mindfulness, or have practised using it before.

Start by identifying how the client thinks it might help them. For example, it can help to accept, rather than fight against, difficult emotions such as sadness, anger, jealousy, guilt and shame. It can help us to live in the present moment, rather than ruminating about the past or worrying about the future. It isn't meant to help us learn to be relaxed and serene – rather, just to build up our mental muscles. A client may not fully know how mindfulness could help them. This is ok – all that is needed is a level of curiosity and a willingness to have a go.

Start with the introduction to the mindfulness practice, perhaps using the paragraph below as a starting point. After this, try an exercise from the list. After the exercise, ask the client how they found it. Take some feedback, following the guidelines below. Then, depending on how it has gone, maybe try another exercise, and then take more feedback. It can be a good idea to do one practice which focuses on breathing, and one which focuses on an external source, such as an object or a sound. At the end, you could agree on a mindfulness practice which the client can do in between sessions, to discuss next time.

General introduction to mindfulness practice

This is a suggested outline as a starting point. *'While we are practising mindfulness, I am going to ask you to try to focus on a particular thing. While you are trying to do this, you will probably find that your attention keeps wandering, and you feel distracted. Everybody's mind wanders – it is what minds do! If your mind wanders, just notice where it has drifted to, and gently return your attention to the task. This is what practising mindfulness is all about. Whenever you notice that your mind has wandered, and return it to the task, you are practising mindfulness. Over time, this gets easier, and you can feel more in control of your mind, rather than your mind being in control of you.'*

Taking feedback from practices

After a couple of moments of silence, ask the client how they experienced the practice. What thoughts and feelings did they have? What was it like to do it? Reflect on each comment, and be curious about it. Ask whether they were able to bring their mind back to the practice. Use questions like, *'When did you first notice that thought? What did that feel like? Do you feel / think that way at other times? How might it be useful to you if you could develop the skill of returning your mind to what's going on in the present moment?'*

It is important for you to be a neutral observer – help the client to reflect on their experience, without you needing it to be a certain way. It is the process of reflecting which is important, rather than the content of their thoughts. Don't take it personally if the client doesn't enjoy it, or doesn't want to continue.

Further reading and resources

There are many books about mindfulness, some of which come with audio CDs of mindfulness practices. One which we have found accessible and easy to use is *Mindfulness: A Practical Guide to Finding Peace in a Frantic World* (Williams and Penman 2011). Another very practical resource is *Teaching Clients to Use Mindfulness Skills* (Dunkley and Stanton 2013).

Mindfulness-based cognitive therapy (MBCT) is a recognised treatment offered by the NHS for depression and other mental health conditions and if a client wants to pursue this, they could see their GP for a referral.

Worksheet: Introduction to Mindfulness

Mindfulness has its roots in ancient Buddhist principles, but is not restricted to any particular religious or spiritual framework. The key element of mindfulness is to learn to focus the mind on the direct experience of the present moment. Jon Kabat-Zinn offers this definition:

> Mindfulness means paying attention in a particular way: on purpose, in the present moment, and nonjudgementally.

> (Kabat-Zinn 2004, p.4)

The fundamental principle of mindfulness is that thoughts and feelings are internal processes that are experienced, often very vividly, within the self, but *do not necessarily reflect anything that truly exists in the external world in the past, present or future*. A mindful person consciously tunes into their internal processes and observes the thoughts and feelings which they are experiencing, but without passing judgement upon them. By focusing exclusively upon the present moment, and suspending the 'inner censor', a person is more able to control their behaviour, by reducing the prevalence of unconscious or automatic actions, which are most often driven by deep-seated fears and anxieties. Mindfulness is not about achieving a particular aim or outcome. Rather, it invites the individual to know the direct experience of the moment without acting on an urge to fix anything. Kabat-Zinn refers to this as a shift from 'doing' to 'being'. A useful analogy can be that if the mind is a radio, mindfulness can help us to learn how to adjust the volume, or even to change the frequency we are listening to.

For example, a mindful approach to being stuck in a traffic jam would begin with paying conscious attention to the thoughts and feelings that I am experiencing in the present. I might notice that I am feeling frustrated, worrying about being late, thinking unkind thoughts about other drivers and giving myself a hard time for having left the house later than I had planned. I might also notice that I am breathing more shallowly, frowning and tapping my fingers on the steering wheel. By identifying that I am experiencing these thoughts and feelings, and the automatic behaviour which is connected to them, I can limit their power to overwhelm me by becoming more conscious of them, and remembering that they do not define me, and they will pass. The part of me that is aware of my frustration is not itself frustrated. By being more mindful of my thoughts and feelings in the present moment, I can recognise that they are simply thoughts and feelings which are currently strong within me, and that I can choose how to react to them. I can allow uncomfortable thoughts and feelings to exist within me without being overwhelmed by them, and I can exercise judgement in how I react to them.

It seems reasonable to ask how mindfulness can be of relevance to people who have committed offences. There is a growing evidence base that regular mindfulness practice can alter the physical structure of the brain, promoting flexibility and growth in areas that are associated with cognitive and emotional processing and well-being (e.g. the middle regions of the pre-frontal cortex, Siegel 2007). Mindfulness-based cognitive therapy is a recognised treatment for a number of health conditions, such as chronic pain and depression. Also, a recent study of mindful breathing techniques with offenders demonstrated the potential for improved emotional control and self-regulation, which are factors linked with re-offending (Gillespie *et al.* 2012)

Worksheet: Mindfulness Exercises

Changing focus exercise

'I'm going to ask you to pick two objects (e.g. this pencil and the door). First of all, please focus on the door. Really look at it, and pay attention to it. Now, please redirect your attention to the pencil. And after a few moments, back to the door.'

The point of this introductory exercise is to help people to experience the level of effort it takes to switch focus from one thing to another thing. Most people find this short exercise very simple, and it can help them to understand the idea that we can choose what to focus our attention on. It also demonstrates that it doesn't take much effort to redirect our attention.

Mindfulness of sounds (do this for 1 or maximum 2 minutes)

'In this practice, I am going to ask you to listen to the sounds you can hear in this room. Usually, when we hear a sound, our mind automatically gives it a word label, such as "that's a dog barking". This is an automatic process, which is useful to us, because it helps us to understand the world. In this exercise, we are going to focus on just hearing the sound, rather than trying to understand what it is, or giving it a label. If you find yourself labelling the sounds, that's ok, just notice that you are doing it, and bring your mind back to the task of just hearing the sound, rather than thinking about it or evaluating it.'

Mindfulness of objects (e.g. a smooth pebble)

'First, hold the pebble in your hand. Notice how it feels against the palm of your hand. How does it feel against your skin? What is its temperature? What is its weight? Use your eyes to explore its colour, and its shape. Does it have a pattern? Are there any variations, or is it the same colour all over? Does the pebble have a smell? During this exercise, if you find your mind wandering, just gently notice that it's wandered, and bring your focus back to the pebble.'

Mindfulness of breathing

'Sit in a comfortable position, with your eyes either open or closed. As you are sitting, you'll become aware that you're not totally still, because you are breathing. Begin to focus your mind and senses on the physical sensations of breathing. There is no need to control it. Let your attention settle wherever it is drawn to. If your mind wanders, notice where it wanders to, and gently return it to your breath. Try not to focus on thoughts about breathing, but experience the breath itself.'

Mindful walking

(This can be easily adapted for people who have mobility difficulties. You could do this exercise very well with someone who uses a mobility aid – just focus on the sensation of moving forwards.)

'Go for a short walk outside/around the room. After focusing on your breath, begin to direct your attention to the sensation of walking. Notice how your feet feel against your shoes and socks. How do your feet feel when you lift one up and place it back down on the ground? Where does your foot make contact with the ground? How does it feel to be in contact with the ground? Notice how your body knows how to walk – you didn't always have this ability, but now you are able to do it without really thinking about it.'

My life experiences

Self-awareness, understanding my coping strategies, understanding key experiences in my life

Time: 1 hour to several sessions

Materials: paper, pen/markers, other materials to create visual representation of the time line

Aims

- To think and talk about some of the positive, negative and confusing experiences in the client's life.

- To make links between the client's life experiences and their later development.

- To help the client to better understand their life history.

Method

This is an autobiographical exercise, aimed at helping the client to understand themselves better and to make links between how they responded to earlier events in their life and more recent events.

Use the worksheet to help the client consider significant events in their life – good, bad and confusing. As always, clients should be encouraged to discuss events at whatever level of disclosure feels right for them.

With each experience or event, help the client to think about and record their thoughts, feelings and responses at the time. Help the client to make links between current and past strategies they used to protect themselves. Do they still respond in similar ways to strategies they used long ago?

Discuss with the client: *Knowing our patterns of response when under stress – and learning to regulate these patterns – is a key to becoming a fully conscious and aware adult. This is because our patterns of response develop in childhood, so it is a developmental challenge to move beyond these patterns and fully into adulthood. Otherwise we are still, emotionally speaking, a child, because we are responding as we did when we were children.*

Everyone experiences throughout their life a range of experience – good, bad and confusing. By thinking about the experiences that were most significant for you, you can begin to see how strategies you learned in order to survive as a young person may later have influenced your cycle of offending.

Variations

My Life Experiences and the following exercise, *My Life Time Line*, complement each other and significantly overlap. They can be combined in one session if the client is able to work at a sufficient pace to allow this. Or you and the client may think it best to do only one of the exercises.

Where needed, use toys, objects, drawings, collage, images, or empty chairs to represent the elements of *My Life Experiences*. If the client is struggling to understand, it may be useful to do the exercise for a hypothetical person first, with the client filling in the detail.

Where clients struggle to think of experiences, you can offer some examples. Examples of good experiences that clients share might include school, family, any achievements, sporting success, good relationships or good interactions with professionals. Examples of bad experiences that clients share might include suffering abuse, witnessing family violence, offending, family disruption, loss and trauma. Examples of confusing experiences that clients share might include being sexually exploited, seeing parents using drugs or being deceived or blamed by an abusive adult.

Another variation on this idea is to ask the client to write a letter to their younger self at the ages they were when the significant event(s) happened.

Worksheet: My Life Experiences

Name: _____ **Date:** _____

You can use this worksheet to describe the most important good, bad and confusing experiences you can remember over the course of your life. What did you think and feel at the time? How did you respond? How old were you when each of these experiences happened? Use as many sheets of paper as needed.

GOOD EXPERIENCES (MY AGE AT THE TIME)	WHAT I THOUGHT AND FELT ABOUT IT AT THE TIME, AND HOW I RESPONDED. HOW DID THIS AFFECT ME THEN? HOW DOES IT AFFECT ME NOW?	BAD EXPERIENCES (MY AGE AT THE TIME)	WHAT I THOUGHT AND FELT ABOUT IT AT THE TIME, AND HOW I RESPONDED. HOW DID THIS AFFECT ME THEN? HOW DOES IT AFFECT ME NOW?	CONFUSING EXPERIENCES (MY AGE AT THE TIME)	WHAT I THOUGHT AND FELT ABOUT IT AT THE TIME, AND HOW I RESPONDED. HOW DID THIS AFFECT ME THEN? HOW DOES IT AFFECT ME NOW?

My life time line

*Self-awareness, understanding my coping strategies,
understanding patterns in my life*

Time: 1 hour to several sessions

Materials: Paper, pen/markers, other materials to create visual representation of the time line

Aims

- To give the client the opportunity to reflect on events and relationships in their life and to make links with later development.

- To help the client to better integrate past and present experiences, and thoughts and feelings and behaviour.

- To help the client gain insight into their coping patterns.

- To deepen our understanding of the client and what motivates their actions.

Method

This exercise is like creating a visual map of our personal life story (see the example on p.103). To do the exercise, draw a simple horizontal line across the page (or as many pages as are needed). Flip chart paper can be used, if available. This line is meant to represent elapsed time, from birth to the present day. Some clients may be very motivated and curious to go back further in time, before their birth, or to think about their future. The exercise can be used for this, too.

On the time line, the client is encouraged to draw simple pictures or words (cut and paste images can also be used) that describe or illustrate important events or relationships in their life. Good/safe events and relationships are placed above the line, and bad/dangerous events and relationships are placed below the line. Neutral events are placed near or on the line. Key information is written to describe the event.

When the time line is partially or fully completed, you can discuss the following sorts of questions:

KEY EVENTS AND HOW I COPED

- What happened and how did you feel at the time? Did you need to protect yourself at the time?

- How did you meet your needs and survive? What strategies did you use to survive and to meet your basic needs? If you could change some of these strategies or beliefs, what would you change them to? How would these changes help you?

- What are the things you can praise yourself for (e.g. for having survived)?

BELIEFS ABOUT MYSELF AND MY WORLD

- During each experience, what beliefs were you developing about yourself and your place in the world?

- What were the good things you learned about yourself when you were in the best times? What can you learn from that now? Can you still hold onto those views of yourself and others?

- What beliefs about yourself and others do you feel are no longer helpful to you?

FINDING LINKS

- Are there any links you can think of? For example, is there any link between your early coping strategies and your offence? How might the thoughts, feelings and actions shown at stages of your time line be related to thoughts, feelings and actions around the time of your offending?

MAKING SENSE OF IT ALL, AND MOVING FORWARD

- What does the time line tell you about how you have become the person that you are?

- What do you think you practically can do to strengthen your new thinking, feeling and behaviour?

- What questions arise for you regarding 'unfinished business' from the past? What would you like to know more information about? Are there questions that you would like to ask your mother? Your father? Anyone else? If you want to ask them but you can't, try to imagine what their response would be? What does your gut instinct tell you about what they would say (i.e. about the missing information)?

- Is there anyone you would like to thank? There may be one or more key people who have helped you in your life. How could you show your thanks, even if they are no longer alive, or if they are out of contact?

Note: It is important to end the session on a positive note, so time the session in such a way that you finish with a strength or a positive memory/relationship.

Variations

My Life Time Line and the previous exercise, *My Life Experiences*, complement each other and significantly overlap. They can be combined in one session if the client is able to work at a sufficient pace to allow this. Or you and the client may think it best to do only one of the exercises.

If the client finds it too difficult or painful to do the exercise based on their own life, one variation is to do the exercise for a hypothetical person 'like them', or even for a fictional character they are familiar with. After doing this, they may feel more able to do the exercise based on their own life.

An advanced version of this exercise would have the client taking on the role of themselves at the various points in time, using the technique of *interviewing in role*. They would speak in the first-person present tense from one or more of the points in time, in order to fully reflect on their experience at that time, including thoughts, feelings, physical symptoms and behaviours. This can be a profoundly helpful way of discovering patterns within the coping strategies. Another variation on this idea is to ask the client to write a letter from the present day to themselves at the ages they were when the significant event(s) happened.

Reflections and learning points

Understanding the 'story of our life' is an important part of becoming a fully functioning adult. Knowing our patterns of response when under stress – and learning to regulate these patterns – is a key to becoming a fully conscious and aware adult. Otherwise we are still, emotionally speaking, a child, because we are responding as we did when we were children. Many people grow into adulthood with highly distorted memories of – and beliefs about – their early life and how it affected them. Reaching adulthood allows us the opportunity to rethink the early stories we told ourselves, and to think for ourselves about what we understand to be the most accurate story of our life. Through this process we may draw new conclusions about the past, and this can be a painful and difficult process. The benefits can be great, however: by understanding the past, we are better able to see its effects on us, and to release ourselves from 'unfinished business' from the past.

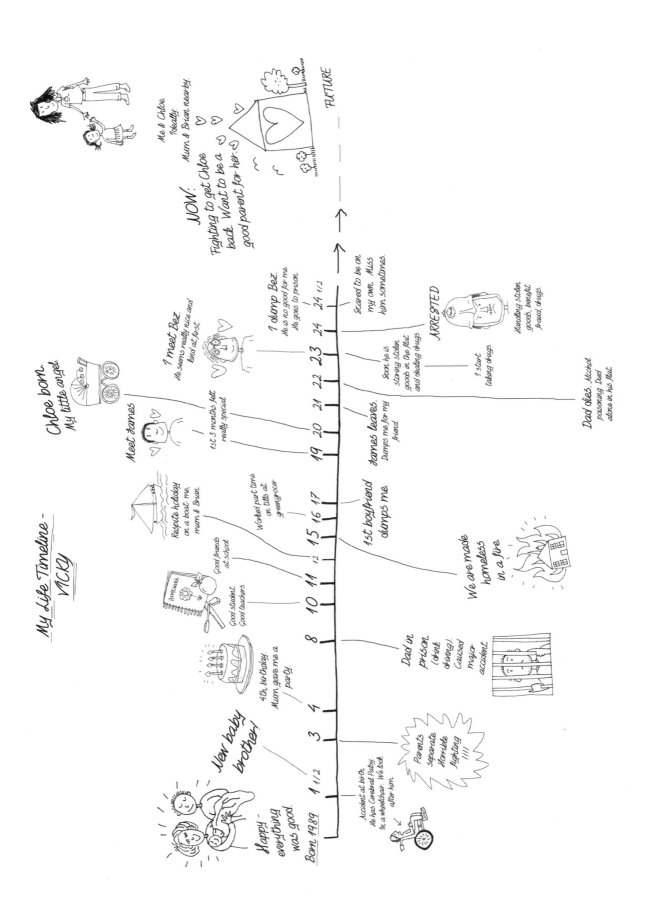

My Life Timeline – VICKY

Born 1989. Happy – everything was good.

New baby brother!

Accident at birth. He has Cerebral Palsy. In a wheelchair. We look after him.

Parents separate. Horrible fighting!!!!

4th birthday. Mum gave me a party.

Dad in prison. (drink driving). Caused major accident.

Good student. Good teachers.

Good friends at school.

Respite holiday on a boat: me, mum & Brian.

Worked part time on tills at greengrocer.

1st boyfriend dumps me.

We are made homeless in a fire.

Meet James. 1st 3 months felt really special.

Chloe born. My little angel.

James leaves. Dumps me for my friend.

I meet Bez. He seems really nice and kind at first.

I dump Bez. He is no good for me. He goes to prison.

Soon he is storing stolen goods in the flat and dealing drugs.

I start taking drugs.

ARRESTED. Handling stolen goods, bought, fraud, drugs.

Dad dies. Alcohol poisoning. Died alone in his flat.

Scared to be on my own. Miss him sometimes.

NOW: Fighting to get Chloe back. Want to be a good parent for her.

Me & Chloe. Ideally: Mum & Brian nearby. ♡♡♡

FUTURE

★

Worksheet: My Life Time Line

Name: _____ **Date:** _____

On the time line, draw simple pictures or words (cut and paste images can also be used) that describe or illustrate important events or relationships in your life. Good/safe events and relationships are placed above the line, and bad/dangerous events and relationships are placed below the line. Neutral events are placed near or on the line. Write key information to describe the event.

Good/safe experiences or relationships

BIRTH

PRESENT DAY

Bad/dangerous experience or relationships

Who am I? The different roles I play

Role theory, motivation, self-knowledge

Time: 1 hour

Materials: worksheet, paper

Introduction

This exercise is based on the concept of role theory, described in Chapter 1. The fundamental idea of role theory is that every individual performs many different roles, both across their lifespan and at any one time in their life. A role is a social category, often described in relationship to another person or group of people. For example, a person could be a mother, a teacher, a daughter, a sister and a hospital patient. The analogy of acting out parts on a stage is often used to illustrate the idea of roles. Once we are familiar with a role, it is part of our 'role repertoire', which means that the role is available for us to use when we need to. The more roles we have in our repertoire, the more flexible we can be at responding to a variety of situations, if we are able to choose from them in a strategic way.

Some roles are derived from family relationships (father, brother, daughter, sister). Others may be connected to social or cultural concepts. Each role carries with it certain assumptions about the kinds of behaviour, responsibilities, rights and duties associated with it. If a person behaves in a way that is contradictory to their roles, then they may face social disapproval, whereas behaving in line with their roles may be rewarded and reinforced by others.

Difficulties lie when either a person has some roles which are under-developed and others which are over-developed, or when their various roles conflict with each other. For example, if a person has a very demanding job, they may have a well-developed role as 'diligent employee' but at the cost of their role as an 'involved parent' or 'caring and present partner'. If this tension goes on for too long, it may result in problems with family relationships, or perhaps the individual concerned may deal with the strain by adopting coping strategies which could be harmful in the long run (e.g. substance misuse, denial, avoidance). It can also be challenging when a person loses a role due to external circumstances (e.g. the end of a relationship, redundancy from a valued job).

Method

Outline the concept of role theory to the client. Using the prompts on the worksheet, ask the client to brainstorm the roles they have in life. Then, using this table as a prompt, help the client to consider these different roles. Which are mainly positive, or mainly negative? Which might be out of date and no longer useful? Which might need some work to develop? For example, a child might need to develop the role of 'vigilant peace keeper' to help parents to resolve conflicts, and this might mean putting their own emotional needs second. However, if this role continues into adulthood, the person may end up feeling very frustrated and unfulfilled. Therefore, the person might benefit from help to find an independent, adult role for themselves.

Use the overlapping circles diagram to explore the idea that some roles may be incompatible with each other. One example would be that a parent may struggle to fulfill the role of 'responsible parent' if they are simultaneously adopting the role of 'problematic drug user'. Role conflict, and the involuntary loss of roles, can be a major cause of distress and psychological suffering.

If your client is able to identify roles which are outdated and no longer helpful, or roles which they would like to develop, you could move on to goal setting. How will your client make this a reality, and what support can you, and others, offer?

This exercise links closely with the exercise *Becoming an Integrated Adult* (p.162), and *Conversations with Myself* (p.122).

Worksheet: Who Am I?
The Different Roles I Play

Name: _____ **Date:** _____

What roles do you play in your life (e.g. parent, child, friend, sibling, worker, patient, carer)? Include roles which are to do with your culture, spiritual beliefs, and anything else which is important to you. Do you also want to include any roles related to committing offences? Why? Or why not?

Redraw this table in a way that is useful to you. Use the questions to prompt some thinking about how you think and feel about your different roles. Which ones were once useful to you, but are now out of date? Which roles are over-developed, and which roles might it be useful to you to develop more?

ROLE	THOUGHTS LINKED WITH THIS ROLE?	FEELINGS LINKED WITH THIS ROLE?	ACTIONS LINKED TO THIS ROLE?	IS THIS ROLE STILL USEFUL FOR ME?	DO I NEED MORE OR LESS OF IT?

Some roles conflict with each other (e.g. a teenager who becomes pregnant has to find a way of being a teenager and a mother, a doctor who has an alcohol problem may struggle to balance her work with her alcohol use). Use this diagram to think about which roles are helpful, unhelpful or need developing more.

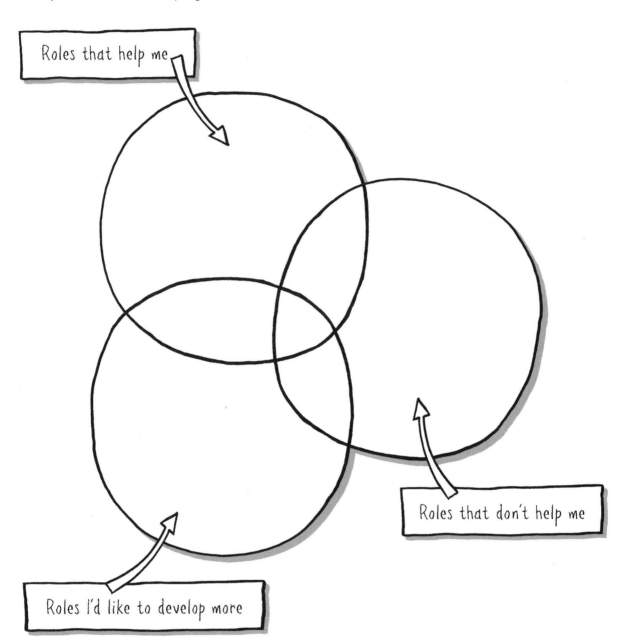

Self-compassion

Emotional regulation, self-identity

Time: 30 minutes to 1 hour per session
Materials: worksheet, paper

Aim

- To introduce the idea of self-compassion.

- To encourage the client to think about developing more compassion for themselves.

- To offer some introductory exercises designed to enhance self-compassion.

Method

Read through the worksheet *An Introduction to Self-Compassion*. Then either give a copy to the client or read through it together. If appropriate, it could be given to the client to read and think about in between sessions. Discuss with the client how they would feel about doing this work together. It can be very helpful for people who experience negative or self-critical thoughts, who feel stuck or who ruminate on difficult emotions or experiences.

Before doing any of the exercises, it can be helpful to focus the mind by doing one of the mindfulness practices from p.98. Or, as an alternative, just encourage the client to sit comfortably, and take a few deep breaths to ground themselves.

Start with some of the introductory exercises, and have a go at them. Self-compassion can be difficult to develop, and it is usually most effective to practise little and often. If your client finds the exercises useful, you could perhaps do one per session over several weeks, to help to develop your client's self-compassionate self.

Once your client is familiar with the concepts of the self-critical self and the self-compassionate self, an advanced version of these exercises would involve setting out two chairs, and labelling one the self-critical self and the other the self-compassionate self. Encourage the client to describe these parts of themselves to make them more vivid, focusing on facial expression, tone of voice and any other qualities they can think of (e.g. 'my self-critic has sharp edges, and a harsh tone of voice, and a frown; my compassionate self is warm, gentle and has a softer voice'). Then, when your client is facing a tricky decision, trying to change a behaviour or feeling stuck, you could encourage them to sit in each chair in turn, and speak from that chair about how they see the problem and what messages they would like to give themselves. Then, they could sit back in their own chair, and think about what the most useful approach would be (Gilbert 2009).

These exercises are useful for most people, so it may well be that you find yourself doing the exercises for yourself as you do them with your client! One of the main principles of self-compassion is of common humanity – we have far more in common with our clients than we have differences, so this seems very appropriate (Neff 2011).

If you or your client would like to learn more about self-compassion, there is a wealth of information and resources available via these websites:

www.self-compassion.org (run by Kristen Neff)

www.compassionatemind.co.uk (associated with Paul Gilbert).

Worksheet: An Introduction to Self-Compassion

The content of these exercises draws upon material from Dr Kristin Neff (Neff 2011), Dr Paul Gilbert (Gilbert 2009), and Dr Dawn Fisher (personal communication).

The exercises in this book are based on a strengths-based approach to building a positive, offence-free life. However, many people who have committed offences do not feel positive about themselves. As a result of remorse and guilt over their offending behaviour, or because of negative experiences in their lives, they may feel they do not deserve anything positive, or have anything to offer the world. Self-compassion involves responding with compassion to yourself for your imperfections and failures of judgement, and during experiences of suffering or difficulty.

There are three parts to self-compassion (Neff 2011)

- *Kindness* – treating the self with care and understanding, rather than with harsh self-judgement or criticism.

- *Common humanity* – seeing one's own experience as part of the larger human experience, rather than feeling separate and isolated.

- *Mindfulness* – being aware of painful thoughts and feelings without being overwhelmed by them.

Self-compassion is linked with increased emotional resilience, optimism and creativity. It has also been shown to improve relationships with other people. Self-compassion differs from self-esteem in that it is not dependent on judging yourself in contrast to others, or on personal success. It is also different from being big headed, or from being arrogant.

People can find it difficult to develop self-compassion, as we are more used to being critical of ourselves, and it can feel awkward to deliberately focus on our positive qualities. So you may need to practise these exercises little and often until self-compassion becomes more natural. Before you practise a self-compassion exercise, it can be a good idea to sit comfortably, take a few deep breaths and find a soothing rhythm of breathing.

Exercises to increase self-compassion
How we judge ourselves

Note down two things that you often judge yourself for, and that are important parts of how you think about yourself (e.g. you might be ashamed of your offending, or might think you aren't a good enough son/daughter or parent). Think about the following questions:

- How often do you display this characteristic – most of the time, sometimes, only occasionally?

- Are there particular circumstances that seem to draw out the characteristic?

- What are the various causes and conditions that have led to your having the characteristic (i.e. early family experiences, life pressures, social circumstances, lack of opportunity, etc.)?

- Did you choose to have this characteristic, and do you have much choice about whether or not you display this characteristic?

- If you did not choose to have this characteristic, how do you now feel about it?

Getting to know the inner critic

- How often are you critical of yourself?

- What aspects of yourself do you typically criticise?

- Why do you think you are so critical of yourself?

- Does the voice of your inner critic remind you of anyone you know (such as a teacher, partner, friend, parent, etc.)?

- Does the inner critic do any good things for you or help you in any way?

- What harmful things does the inner critic do to you?

- Is your inner critic fair, objective, balanced and caring? If not, why should you believe the inner critic?

Giving ourselves compassion

- Think of something you judge and criticise yourself for.

- Write a letter to yourself about this issue from the point of view of an all-compassionate imaginary friend. Pretend this friend knows everything about you, your history, your early family experiences and so on. Also, remember that this friend is completely kind, loving and understanding. This friend wants the best for you and wants you to be happy and healthy.

- What do you think this friend would say regarding this thing you criticise yourself for, what tone of voice would they use, what would their facial expression be like? Imagine your friend reading the letter to you. Focus on their voice, their facial expression and what they are saying to you.

- If this friend thinks you need to change something in your life, how would this friend give you advice about why and how to change?

- Think about your perspective now that you have done the exercise. Think about what the friend said to you, how does that make you feel about yourself now? Can you imagine saying those things to yourself?

Dealing with problems in a self-compassionate way

- When problems arise or you are feeling self-critical or upset about your life in some way, take some time to look at what is going on in a self-compassionate way.

- Identify what the problem is.

- Identify your thoughts and feelings associated with the problem. If this is an experience of suffering, acknowledge it for what it is.

- Imagine what a caring friend would say to you. Try saying that to yourself. Imagine the caring tone of voice and facial expression of your friend, focused on you.

- Try to put the situation into perspective. Do not minimise or exaggerate.

- Think about how the situation could be worse but is not.

- Think about how you are reacting. Is it in proportion to the situation? What else can you do or say to yourself to help. What could you do differently in the future?

- Remember the positive aspects of your situation and your own positive qualities.

- What can you learn from the situation which will be of help to you?

- Remember that no one is perfect and that everyone experiences some level of suffering during their lives.

The self-compassion break (Neff 2011)

This is a quick exercise, which you can do whenever you notice that you are under stress, or experiencing a negative or self-critical emotion:

- Put your hand on your heart.

- Breathe deeply in and out several times and feel your chest rise and fall.

- Say to yourself the following words (or similar):

  'This is a moment of difficulty.'

  'Moments of difficulty are part of life. All human beings experience difficulty.'

  'May I be kind to myself in this moment.'

Understanding my offence and what I can do differently

Self-understanding, motivation to change, alternatives to offending

Time: 2 hours to 3 hours

Materials: worksheet, or any visual/multi-sensory materials as needed

Aims

- To discuss one or more of the client's offences.

- To encourage the client to distribute responsibility for their decisions and actions accurately.

- To help client to clarify 'what I did and why I did it'.

- To identify differences between the client's attitudes now as compared with the time of the offence(s).

- To discuss alternative choices the client could have made at the time and can make in the future.

Method

In the first part of the exercise, use the structure offered on the worksheet to help the client describe their thoughts, feelings and actions in the lead up to, during and after their offence. If you are making notes, it is important to use the client's own words.

Next, help the client identify any places in the description where they have responsibility, and any places where other people have responsibility. Help the client to be alert to ideas that hold victims responsible, for example: 'he needed to be taught a lesson', or 'they were *asking* for me to steal it because they left their car window open', or 'women in short skirts out clubbing deserve what they get'. Encourage the client to challenge their own self-exonerating or victim-blaming ideas, particularly those ideas that, if they stay unchanged, are likely to contribute to further offences.

During the process of discussion and filling in more information, emphasise the points in the sequence of events where the client made choices. This will be crucial in later exercises that emphasise self-management and making better choices. Encourage the client to identify where they would like to reconsider or look more deeply at their process of offending. Help them see the links, for example the links between feeling angry at one person (or their life situation generally) and taking out their feelings of anger on another person. Or feeling sad or helpless, and using this feeling to justify 'getting back at' and feeling powerful over another person. Or feeling powerless in their life in general, and so feeling unable to say 'no' to going along with someone else's plan.

Discuss with the client: *It is important to have a clear understanding of the process of offending, so that in future you are able to take charge of your decisions and make better choices. Taking responsibility for one's offences is an important step in the process of change. It is not uncommon for people to later reflect with deep regret when they consider their past offences and the damage they caused to other people. If this is the case with you, how can you use this feeling of regret to motivate you to live a positive and offence-free life?*

Variations

- Where there are numerous offences, decide with the client on a representative sample.

- Some clients may be able to do some of this work on their own, out of session.

- Where needed, use objects, drawings, chairs, or *interviewing in role* (see Chapter 2) to help the client do the exercise.

- If the client is struggling to understand, or does not admit to committing an offence, it may be useful to do the exercise for a hypothetical person first. Co-create the hypothetical case study with the client, and help them to fill in the worksheet at one step removed. Where appropriate and with the client's consent, move to the personal level and discuss their own offence(s). For more guidance on working with clients who do not admit to committing an offence, see Chapter 2.

Worksheet: Understanding My Offence and What I Can Do Differently

Name: _____ **Date:** _____

MY THOUGHTS AND DECISIONS DURING THAT PERIOD OF TIME	MY FEELINGS DURING THAT PERIOD OF TIME	MY ACTIONS DURING THAT PERIOD OF TIME
Lead-up – weeks before		
Lead-up – hours or days before		
Just before – seconds or minutes before		
During		
A little while after		

★

MY THOUGHTS AND DECISIONS DURING THAT PERIOD OF TIME	MY FEELINGS DURING THAT PERIOD OF TIME	MY ACTIONS DURING THAT PERIOD OF TIME
Days or weeks later		
Now		

Looking back, what do I think and feel about my actions during that period of time? Are there any other choices I could have made? If so, what? How can I meet my needs, solve my problems or express myself in more positive ways?

Moving on from the past: Understanding the connections between my experience of being a victim and my offences

Resolving trauma, expressing difficult and painful emotions, making new choices

Time: 1 hour to 6 hours

Materials: worksheet or any other visual or multi-sensory learning materials, as needed

Aims

- To promote healing and integration, especially in relation to unresolved trauma.

- To help the client to see the connections between the 'victim' and 'offender' aspects of self.

- To give the client an experience of discussing difficult or painful personal experiences within a safe, contained, supportive environment.

- To focus on new choices.

Method

Moving on from the past might be thought of as a series of structured conversations between parts of the self and with other people. The main purpose of the exercise is to promote resolution of trauma while at the same time promoting integration by linking experiences of being harmed with experiences of harming others.

This exercise links with some of the earlier exercises. You may wish to draw on any previous exercises where the client highlighted resolved or unresolved trauma (*My Life Time Line* on p.101 may be one exercise to draw on), and also those exercises where the client focused on their offending behaviour (e.g. *Understanding My Offence and What I Can Do Differently*, p.113).

This exercise also has strong links with the victim empathy exercises in Chapter 5.

This exercise is intended for those clients who have suffered abuse or neglect as children or adolescents. It may be highly emotive; care should be taken, and enough time allowed for discussion, integration of learning and relaxation.

To do the exercise, first reaffirm all of the client's strengths as highlighted in the *Starting from Strength* exercise from Chapter 3 (p.62). Then, use the structure offered on the *Moving on from the Past* worksheet to guide the client through the series of conversations. Encourage the client to enter into the perspective of aspects of self or of themselves speaking to others, as the boxes on the grid indicate. In other words, for each box on the grid, explore with the client what one part would say to the other, and then what the other's response is. Ask open and Socratic questions to help the client find their own way towards integration. An example of becoming more integrated would be if the client hands back responsibility for their own abuse to their abuser, or similarly stops blaming their victims by saying they 'deserved it' or were in some way to blame.

The following is only a suggested sequence for the conversations; elements on the grid can be interchanged and revisited as needed:

1. **Conversation between myself as a victim and the people who hurt me** (i.e. 'You hurt me in these ways…'). Here, the client works towards expressions of (from the victim role) fear, distress, grief, sadness, regret, confusion and ultimately, anger about what happened, and (from the perpetrator role) expressions of the rationale for the 'why' of the abuse, the way

that the abuser objectified them, ignored their feelings, silenced them and/or hurt them. During the process the client works toward an accurate distribution of responsibility for the abuse (e.g. handing back full responsibility for child abuse to the abuser).

2. **Conversation between myself as offender and the people who hurt me** (i.e. 'I am like you in this way...'). Here, the client works towards understanding how their offending echoed or resembled the behaviour of his/her abusers. For example, is there a link between themes of abuse of trust, abandoning responsibility, selfishly ignoring another person's feelings, or getting revenge/feeling justified in hurting someone else?

3. **Conversation between myself as a victim and myself as an offender** (i.e. 'I know what it is like to be hurt by others, and I know that I have hurt others too'). Here, the client is encouraged to challenge their own offender role. The aim is that the 'offender' part of self takes full responsibility and no longer blames victims.

4. **Conversation between myself as a victim and the people I have hurt** (i.e. 'I am like you in these ways...'). Here, the client works towards an understanding of how their own victim experience compares with the experiences of their victims. The aim is to encourage the development of an empathic awareness of the feelings and perceptions of victims of abuse and crime.

5. **Conversation between myself as an offender and the people I have hurt** ('I hurt you in this way...'). The client works towards taking responsibility for their offending behaviour and also the effects on the victims.

6. **Conversation between responsible, integrated self and the people I have hurt** ('I apologise...'). The client offers an apology to the victims, who are represented symbolically in the room by a chair or other object. The apology is clear and simple, with no blame placed on the victim, and delivered with no expectation of forgiveness.

7. **Conversation between responsible, integrated self and the people who hurt me**. Here the client holds their abusers to account and also manages the consequences/effects of the abuse in a healthier way.

8. **Conversation between responsible, integrated self and myself as an offender**. Here, the client works towards integrating this role and taking responsibility for and ownership of their actions and the consequences.

9. **Conversation between responsible, integrated self and myself as a victim** (i.e. forgiving my young, hurt self). Here, the client works towards self-forgiveness. This can take the form of a 'letter to myself', offering forgiveness to the younger self.

At the end of this sequence of conversations, discuss with the client: *As adults, we cannot change the past, but we can make a decision about how we intend to allow our past suffering to affect us in the present.*

Note: This exercise has links with the self-compassion exercise (p.109).

Source: This exercise is adapted from the version described in Baim and Taylor (2004).

Variations

Skip questions that you and the client feel have already been fully covered in earlier sessions.

This exercise can be done in a variety of ways, depending on the needs and learning style of the client. Facilitators are encouraged to use art, story-telling and story-writing, collage, letter-writing, empty chair work, interviewing in role, sculpting or any experiential method that will help the client. An advanced version of this exercise would have the client speaking 'as if' they are in role as the various parts of self, or other people, as represented in the different parts of the grid.

The last element in the sequence is self-forgiveness for being a victim of child abuse or neglect. It is a part of the sequence because it is very common for victims of child abuse to blame themselves and to believe the adults' version of events, which is that they deserved the abuse. The self-forgiveness element can be done in various ways, and is sometimes done in the form of a letter. Here is an example, which can be shared with the client:

LETTER TO MYSELF AS A CHILD

Dear Tony

I know this is going to sound kind of crazy, but I am you, writing to you from the future. You're only young right now – you're only eight. And I want you to know that you are not to blame for what's going on around you and what Mum and Dad are saying about you. They're fighting so much and I know it's terrifying you. But you're only eight and you're in no way to blame. I know you think nobody cares about you, and I can see why. But later on, you'll realise that Mum and Dad are so out of their heads on drink and drugs that they don't really have a clue about how it's affecting you to see them hit each other and wind up in hospital or with the police coming around to the house.

I can see you in my mind, curling up under the bed, hoping he won't come in the room and beat you and tell you he wishes you'd never been born. He is putting so much terror into you, and you can't defend yourself. It's not fair, of course it isn't. No child deserves to be told they are worthless and stupid and nothing but a waste of space, as he is telling you. But don't believe a word of it, because it's not true. You need to be protected and guided, and you never deserved any of this. One day you'll learn that not everybody in the world is out to hurt you, and even that some people can be trusted. I know it seems impossible now, because right now you're shivering and terrified under the bed, wishing your Dad was dead and that your Mum would protect you.

I want you to know that you will get through this, and one day you will become a person who other people think is OK. You'll even have a kid and he'll call you 'Dad'. And you can try to be the best father you can be for him, and show him there's another way to be a father – to be gentle and caring and still strong. So come out when you are ready. There's no need to hide any longer.

Signed,

Your future self

Worksheet: The Connections Between My Experiences of Being a Victim and My Offences

Name: _____ **Date:** _____

Start by revisiting all of the strengths you identified in the *Starting from Strength* exercise. Then, for each box on the grid below, consider and record what one part would say to the other, and then, where appropriate, what the other's response is. Use other sheets of paper as needed or other means to record your thoughts.

   The numbers in the boxes indicate a suggested sequence for the conversations. The order can be adjusted as needed.

	MYSELF AS A VICTIM	MYSELF AS AN OFFENDER	THE PEOPLE WHO HAVE HURT ME	THE PEOPLE I HAVE HURT
MYSELF AS A VICTIM		3. 'I know what it is like to be hurt by others, and I know that I have hurt others too'	1. 'You hurt me in these ways…'	4. 'I am like you in these ways…'
MYSELF AS AN OFFENDER			2. 'I am like you in this way…'	5. 'I hurt you in this way…'
MY RESPONSIBLE, ADULT SELF	9. 'I show self-compassion and forgiveness to my younger self, who is not to blame for being abused or hurt as a child. My message to my younger self is…'	8. 'I take responsibility for this role and its consequences, so I will…'	7. 'I hold you to account for your actions against me, and I take responsibility for managing the effects of the abuse on me by doing the following…'	6. 'I apologise for…'

What is the main learning I can take from each of the following connections

1. The connection between me as a victim and the people who hurt me (telling the people who hurt me how they hurt me).

2. The connection between me as an offender and the people who hurt me (understanding the links between my offending behaviour and the abusive behaviour that was acted out against me in the past).

3. The connection between me as a victim and me as an offender (challenging and confronting the part of me that has hurt other people in the past).

4. The connection between me as a victim and the people I have hurt (understanding the things I have in common with the people I have hurt).

5. The connection between me as an offender and the people I have hurt (apologising to the people I have hurt).

6. The connection between my responsible self and the people I have hurt (taking responsibility for my abusive actions and the hurt I have caused other people).

7. The connection between my responsible self and the people who hurt me (my responsible self holding the right people accountable and responsible for their actions; relieving myself of the load of responsibility they forced on me when I was too young).

8. The connection between my responsible self and me as an offender (how I can take responsibility for the role of offender, and understand and manage that role).

9. The connection between my responsible, adult self and myself as a victim (my responsible adult self giving comfort and forgiveness to myself as a victim). This can be done in various ways, and is sometimes done in the form of a 'letter to myself as a child'.

Conversations with myself

Self-awareness, self-regulation, problem-solving

Time: 1 hour to 2 hours

Materials: worksheet and any other materials to make the work memorable

Aims

- To help the client understand and explore their different internal and external 'roles' or aspects of self.

- To help the client understand that these different aspects can be in or out of balance and can, with awareness and concentrated attention, be brought back into balance.

- To help the client to practise the skills of regulating and conducting these aspects of self.

Method

Ask the client if they have ever been 'of two minds' about something (i.e. with mixed feelings or impulses). A typical example would be a smoker who wants to quit but who feels strong cravings. Or someone who wants to apply for a job but fears being rejected. The point is that this is very normal and most people experience such competing thoughts and feelings. What is important is to become the 'leader of the conversation' rather than allow the impulses, thoughts and feelings to remain ungoverned.

Variations

The various aspects of self and the different perspectives described above can be presented in many different ways. This could include drawings, writing, discussion, using objects or chairs, and also enactment (i.e. 'taking on the role of (X)' and speaking from that perspective or aspect of self). This latter example is a bit like the well-known image of an 'angel' speaking in one ear while a 'devil' speaks in the other.

There is great scope for creativity in this exercise. As ever, find the approach that works for the client.

To learn more about techniques like this, which draws upon psychodrama theory and techniques, see Moreno, Blomkvist and Rutzel (2000), Blatner (2000) and Dayton (2005).

Source: This exercise is adapted from an exercise in Baim and Morrison (2011).

Worksheet: Conversations with Myself

Name: _____ **Date:** _____

Here are some typical examples of internal ideas, impulses, roles and aspects of self that may be explored from one point of view and then the other, in order to find the right balance in a given situation. You may find it useful to set out two chairs to represent the different perspectives, and to sit in each chair as you consider that point of view. Objects or drawings can serve the same purpose. Record your responses in a way that suits you.

Step 1
Think of a situation you are facing currently, or one that you have faced in the past or anticipate facing in the future. It might be in relation to a particular challenge, a troubling event, a habit, a relationship, a choice, a family member, a colleague or anything else that impacts on you and that you are trying to make a decision about.

What is the situation or issue?

_____

_____

_____

Step 2
Choose one or more of the examples below, and think about the situation you are facing from the different points of view. For example, in thinking about how to discipline your child for bad behaviour, you might think about this from your 'logical' self, your 'emotional' self and your 'wise' self. This can then lead you to making a more considered response.

Me in relation to myself

- **Me then** versus **me now.**
- **Me now** versus **me in my rocking chair, as a wise older person, looking back on my life.**
- **My self-critical self** versus **my self-compassionate self.**
- **My live-for-the-moment self** versus **my goal-oriented self.**
- **Me as a helpless victim** versus **me as an empowered, thriving adult.**
- **My optimistic self** versus **my pessimistic self.**
- **Me as a closed mind, fixed forever and unchanging** versus **me as an open mind, capable of learning and growth.**

Me in relation to other people and the world

- **How I see myself** versus **how other people see me.**

- **My point of view** versus **the other person's point of view.**

- **My impulse to do what I want to do, regardless of the effects on other people** versus **me as a person who cares about how my behaviour affects other people.**

- **My demanding, need-to-control self** versus **my easy-going, take-it-as-it-comes self.**

- **Me as a shrinking violet** versus **me as a courageous, self-actualising adult.**

- **Me as someone who takes from others** versus **me as someone who contributes and helps others.**

- **Me as separate from nature** versus **me as a part of nature and in tune with nature.**

Me in relation to life's problems, challenges and dilemmas

- Approaching a dilemma from my '**logical chair**', from my '**emotional chair**', and from my '**wise chair**'.

- **My impulse to 'just do it, don't think'** versus my impulse to '**stop and think of the consequences**'.

- **My impulse to commit an offence** versus **my impulse to solve life's problems in other ways and live a fulfilling and offence-free life.**

- **My tendency to exist on 'autopilot' and just let things happen,** versus **my desire to take charge of my life and live fully and consciously** (i.e. becoming the author of my own story).

Are there any other examples of 'alternative positions' or points of view that I can think of?

_____

_____

_____

Step 3

What are the main learning points I take from this exercise?

_____

_____

_____

Skills practice part 1: Intern... self-management skills

Self-awareness, self-regulation

Time: 3 to 5 sessions

Materials: worksheet, skills outlined in Appendix 3 and any other tools/materials needed

Aims

- To identify self-management skills that need practice.

- To practise emotional self-regulation skills, including high-risk situations and feelings.

- To raise self-awareness, positive self-regard and hope.

Method

The emphasis in these sessions will be on practising the internal self-management skills needed to attain positive goals and also skills needed to avoid high-risk situations and behaviours. While these goals will be an essential part of maintaining an offence-free lifestyle, they are also wider in scope; they are about setting in focus what the client wants to achieve in order to live a fulfilling and offence-free life. While the skills in this section are called internal skills, many of them have an interpersonal component.

In the first part of this exercise, go through the list of self-management skills with the client and identify the ones they would like to practise.

The skills practice can re-enact an actual event or situation in the client's life or can 'fictionalise' matters so that the client is portraying a situation that is close to life but not an exact simulation of their life.

When conducting a skills practice role play, it is best to start with the simplest and easiest version of the skill. The person practising the skill must 'succeed' in each run of the role play. This detail is often overlooked but is absolutely vital. The point of skills practice role plays is, after all, to increase social competence, the sense of self-efficacy and the internal locus of control of the individual. If the individual fails in skills practice, the role play will be counter-productive, as it will tend to reinforce a sense of incompetence. As the client becomes more proficient in ensuing runs of the simulation, the level of challenge can be increased in order to test or 'harden', the skill. As with all skills practice, these role plays should generally be repeated a number of times to improve the likelihood that the skill will be retained and integrated. For some clients, it may take many repetitions. The rule of guidance is that you repeat the skill as much and as often as needed by the individual client (Van Mentz 1983).

The five steps to running a skills practice:

1. Decide on or explain the scenario: What is the situation, where is it set, who is in it?

2. Explain each step of the skill and the level of difficulty that will be used in the role play. Ask the client to plan in advance how they will enact each step of the skill. Include thoughts, feelings and actions in the planning.

3. Run the skills practice at the agreed level of difficulty. Stop the role play when the skill has been completed or if the client is not accomplishing the skill. (In most cases, stop after 30 seconds to 3 minutes maximum.)

4. Discuss how it went. Ask the client in focus what they did well and why. Give feedback using *information feedback and invitational praise*. This means you describe to the client the skills you noticed them using during the skills practice, and you ask the client to offer themselves praise for using the new skill. For example, 'I noticed that this time, you did not raise your voice

when you made the complaint. How did you manage to use that skill so well? How will it be useful for you to be able to complain without showing aggression?'

5. Repeat as needed, and raise or lower the level of difficulty in order to ensure success each time and as the client becomes more skilled, to test and 'harden' the skill, to apply it to more situations and to make the scenarios as close as possible to real-life situations the client faces.

Please see Appendix 3 for a detailed breakdown of many internal self-management skills and the steps or 'micro-skills' needed for each skill. The appendix also offers suggested role play scenarios for practice.

The client can also use the worksheet *Reflecting on a Skill I Practised this Week* (p.128 in order to do just that. The worksheet can be handed in each week and serve as a prompt for discussion and possible further work.

Planning and preparing to facilitate skills practice role plays

Skills-based sessions are devoted to assessing, modelling, practising and testing new behaviours, roles and skills. These demand a carefully controlled structure and detailed preparation and facilitation. Please see the checklist below for guidance during planning sessions.

CHECKLIST FOR PLANNING ROLE PLAYS

- What is the learning aim of the role play?

- Groups: are we mainly focusing on the learning of a main role player or is the learning more broadly focused?

- How many people will be in the role play?

- Will it be a fictional/one-step-removed role play, or will it be a personal level role play? If it is one step removed, will the main role player (if relevant) be in their own role or in the role of a fictional character?

- How detailed a scenario do we need to devise before the session? Alternatively, will we rely on the participant(s) to offer or create a scenario?

- What will be the setting of the role play (e.g. are we imagining that the role play takes place in another setting)?

- How much briefing/induction will we need to give the role players?

- How will we set up the role play? What will we need to explain?

- How long will the role play last? (Usually 30 seconds to 3 minutes is sufficient for skills practice role plays.)

- How will we increase the level of difficulty if the client does the skill very well at an easy level?

A note for facilitators about whether or not to play certain roles in skills practice role plays:

If you are working one-to-one with a client, you can play the other person in the role play, or you can ask the client to alternate between the two roles. Alternatively, you can ask another staff member to take part on these sessions and take the 'other' role in the role plays. If you will be taking roles in the role plays, remember to maintain boundaries and avoid playing the role of sexual partners, victims or offenders. In general, keep to peer, friend, supportive family member, acquaintance, colleague or authority roles. *If in any doubt, ask the client to enact both roles in the role play*, alternating between the two roles.

Variations

There are many variations that can be used to facilitate skills practice. Collaborate with the client to find the modes of working that suit them best. Some clients will work best using the fully enacted version of skills practice. Other clients may benefit from talking through the skill and then rehearsing the skill using objects first, as stand-ins for people. This may lead on to the fully enacted skills practice when the client is ready.

In addition to these variations, some clients may work better at the level of one step removed (e.g. fictional scenarios and characters) and some will work better at the personal level (i.e. close to life simulations).

Worksheet: Which Internal Self-Management Skills Would I Like to Practise?

Name: _____ **Date:** _____

INTERNAL SELF-MANAGEMENT SKILLS	IS THIS A SKILL I WOULD LIKE TO PRACTISE?
Being aware of my feelings and understanding that I have choices about how to act on my feelings	
Having compassion and forgiveness for my past mistakes (and for those of other people)	
Relaxing when I am stressed	
Understanding what other people are thinking and feeling	
Understanding why I think, feel and do what I do	
Understanding why other people think, feel and do what they do	
Managing and controlling my impulses	
Managing my anxiety	
Problem-solving	
Managing my anger	
Reasoning through a moral dilemma	
Dealing with boredom	
Dealing with rejection/failure/disappointment	
Recognising and coping with lapses	
Setting goals and sticking to them	
Any others I can think of?	

Worksheet: Reflecting on a Skill I Practised this Week

Name: _____ **Date:** _____

This is a short report on an opportunity I had to practise a skill over the past week.

What was the skill I practised?

What was the situation?

What I would have thought, felt and done in the past:

What I thought, felt and did this time:

a. Just before

b. During

c. After

How it met my needs:

How did I feel afterwards?

(If relevant) How do I think the other person felt afterwards?

What I have learned:

CHAPTER 5
Looking Outward
Me in Relation to Other People

This chapter contains ten exercises aimed at helping the client to understand how they relate to other people and how their behaviour affects other people. The chapter begins with an autobiographical exercise looking at the person's history of relationships of all types. There are exercises aimed at helping to improve self-esteem and the ability to recognise and communicate about emotions. Other exercises look more broadly at perspective-taking and developing empathy and compassion for other people. One of the exercises encourages the client to understand the impact of their behaviour on the victim(s) of their crime(s) and the people related to the victim. There are also exercise aimed at helping the client to develop their interpersonal/social skills, and becoming more integrated in their emotional, social and psychological functioning.

My relationship history

Self-awareness, relationships and attachments,
coming to terms with my past

Time: 3 hours to 5 hours

Materials: worksheet or any other materials as needed

Aims

- To help the client to understand their childhood experiences and how these experiences have affected them.

- To encourage the client to think about and discuss topics that they may not have thought about before, including topics that may have been 'off limits' in their childhood.

- To give the client an experience of sharing difficult or painful personal experiences within a safe, contained, supportive environment.

- To encourage integration and resolution of past experiences.

Method

This exercise draws from attachment theory (Baim and Morrison 2011; Bowlby 1969; Crittenden and Landini 2011) to help the client understand the effects of early experiences and how they can make new decisions about how to be in relationships. Attachment theory describes the significance of early attachment experiences for later adult relationships. Experiences of positive and/or negative attachments in early childhood affect the way people understand and operate in their adult relationships.

Use the worksheet as the basis for a discussion about the client's relationship history. During the conversation, it may be useful to refer back to themes and events that emerged during exercises such as *My Life Time Line* (p.101). Ask the client to respond only to those questions they feel able to and which are relevant for them. You can always come back later to questions that seem too difficult now for the client.

In the column labelled 'A specific time I remember…' it is important to encourage the client to think of a specific memory rather than a generalised description of combined events. Clients may struggle to find particular events, and this can be an opportunity for further exploration and possibly helping the client reconsider their understanding of what was happening in their early life and how it affected them.

The main aim of this exercise is to improve self-awareness and psychological/emotional integration. The aim is also to help the client make the links between their patterns of emotional expression, their patterns in relationships and their offending behaviour – where this is relevant. The focus can then be on what needs to change.

Discuss with the client: *Our attachment figures have huge significance to us when we are young, and we can often have a highly distorted view that their way of parenting is the only way, or simply 'the way the world is'. As adults, we have the opportunity to re-examine these early assumptions and to consider, from the distance granted by time, our experiences of being parented. This can be highly beneficial to our psychological functioning and our ability to become fully integrated, mature adults.*

Variations

Skip questions that you and the client feel have already been fully covered in earlier exercises.

Some clients may benefit from using drawings, objects or other projective methods to work through the questions on the worksheet.

An advanced version of this exercise would have the client 'speaking to' the various people or aspects of self that are discussed on the worksheet. For example, the client may speak to an empty chair representing their mother/father, talking about how they experienced them as parents and the lessons they took from their parents about how relationships operate. (This could also be done in the form of a 'letter to _____'.) Similarly, the client could speak to their younger self from the present day, offering compassion and understanding to any aspects that suffered and developed self-protective strategies and strategies to meet needs for comfort that later became destructive. These variations may be highly emotive; care should be taken, and enough time allowed.

Worksheet: My Relationship History

Name: _____ **Date:** _____

Think about your responses to the following questions and record your responses on this sheet or another sheet of paper or in another way, for example, electronically, or on an audio recording. Many of the questions address experiences in childhood in order to compare your past and present view of those experiences. For these questions, try to think back as far as you can.

Respond only to those questions you feel able to and which are relevant for you. You can always come back later to questions that seem too difficult now.

Where 'mother/father' are referred to, if you were not raised by your mother or father, include any parental figure who was responsible for you. This can include a key worker at a children's home, a foster parent, a relative, or anyone who had parental responsibility for you. Try to respond to the questions for each significant parental figure, one at a time.

TOPIC	A SPECIFIC TIME I REMEMBER IS...	HOW IT AFFECTED ME THEN, OR WHAT I UNDERSTOOD THEN...	HOW IT AFFECTS ME NOW, OR WHAT I UNDERSTAND NOW...	HOW I WANT TO DO THINGS AS AN ADULT/ PARENT/ PARTNER...
TIME				
How much time did my mother/father spend with me?				
TOUCH				
Did my mother/father and I ever touch or make physical contact? How did I experience their touch?				
EMOTION				
What emotions did my mother/father allow me to see them express?				

TOPIC	A SPECIFIC TIME I REMEMBER IS...	HOW IT AFFECTED ME THEN, OR WHAT I UNDERSTOOD THEN...	HOW IT AFFECTS ME NOW, OR WHAT I UNDERSTAND NOW...	HOW I WANT TO DO THINGS AS AN ADULT/ PARENT/ PARTNER...
What emotions was I allowed to express in front of my mother/ father?				
If I cried, or showed weakness, or needed comfort, how did my mother/father respond?				
If I was happy and feeling good about myself, how did my mother/father respond?				
How did we show love to each other in our family?				
DANGER				
If I was injured, ill, afraid or in danger, how did my mother/father help, protect or comfort me?				
When my mother/father was angry with me or disappointed in me, how did they show it?				
(If relevant) When we experienced a death in the family, how did my mother/father help me to cope with loss and grief?				

TOPIC	A SPECIFIC TIME I REMEMBER IS...	HOW IT AFFECTED ME THEN, OR WHAT I UNDERSTOOD THEN...	HOW IT AFFECTS ME NOW, OR WHAT I UNDERSTAND NOW...	HOW I WANT TO DO THINGS AS AN ADULT/ PARENT/ PARTNER...
SEXUALITY				
What did my mother/ father teach me about sexuality?				
What were the messages I learned about sex and sexual intimacy based on how my mother/father behaved?				
RELATIONSHIPS				
What was my relationship like with my mother/ father when I was a child? (Repeat several times for different qualities of the relationship.)				
What did I do to get attention (or praise or acceptance) from my mother/father?				
When did I really connect in a good way with my mother/father (Or: When did I really feel loved by them)?				
One of my favourite memories of being with my mother/father when I was a child is...				

One of my worst memories of being with my mother/father when I was a child is…				

What didn't happen in our relationship that I really wish had happened?

EFFECTS

How did all of this affect me as a child? What I remember is…

How does all of this affect me now, especially in my close relationships (and – where relevant – my relationships with my children)? What is my general pattern of attachment in intimate relationships/close friendships? Has this changed over time?

How have I behaved when I have felt jealous, when my partner has not met my needs or when they have been angry, refused to have sex or when they have been ill?

(If relevant) What have I done in the past to sabotage my close relationships? How have my past relationships ended? (Address one at a time) How would I like to change in future?

How do I feel about being close to someone emotionally? What feels good about being close to someone? What do I fear most about being close to someone?

How do I meet my needs for: comfort/reassurance/support/understanding/emotional well-being/emotional intimacy/respect and recognition?

Thinking about my responses so far, how do I react *now* when I am experiencing negative emotions?

What was the most common emotion I experienced that triggered or contributed to my offending?

SEEING MY MOTHER/FATHER NOW, AS AN ADULT, NOT A CHILD…

What I understand now about my mother's/father's reasons for treating me as they did…

I think my mother/father misunderstood my intentions in the following ways…

I think I misunderstood my mother's/father's intentions in the following ways…

I think we missed opportunities to connect in the following ways...

What I understand now about the reasons why my mother/father behaved as they did...

In what ways – if at all – is my mother/father different in their behaviour towards me now? What is my understanding about why there is a difference (if there is one)?

INTEGRATION

How I choose to look at these experiences now, as an adult...

As a child, what I most resented about my mother/father was... What I think about that now is...

What I wish we could do over is...

What I do not want to repeat as an adult is...

Instead, I want to actively go forward and achieve my own goals in life, which include...

What happened is now a part of my life history. I am able to see that most people are not all good or all bad, but a mixture. Does this include my mother/father? If so, is there anything I can be positive about? What I appreciate my mother/father for, and what I thank them for, is...

What I have learned from my experiences as a child is...

What have I done in the past to strengthen and deepen my close relationships? What do I intend to do now and in the future?

Add your own questions here. What are you curious to think about?

My sense of self-esteem

Self-efficacy, internal resilience, self-esteem

Time: 30 minutes to 1 hour
Materials: worksheet, paper

Aims

- To increase the client's sense of self-efficacy, locus of control and resilience.

- To encourage the client to recognise that we are all capable of positive growth and change, and that no one needs to be trapped by their past experiences.

- To help the client to recognise that, however hard life may be at times, we are all unique, worth knowing and have the potential to care for other people and to be cared about by them.

Method

Begin by discussing how the client feels about themselves in general. Make the point that we are continually in the process of learning about ourselves and the people around us – facing new challenges all the time. However difficult our life may seem to be sometimes, one of our greatest challenges is to remember that we are unique, worth knowing and that we have the potential to care for other people and to be cared about by them.

Throughout this exercise, use open and Socratic questions to encourage the client to reflect more deeply on their genuinely held beliefs. Some clients may say that they had a more positive self-image when they were offending, or that they are currently feeling low about themselves due to the consequences of their offences. In this case, it can be helpful to encourage the client to reflect upon the difference between short-term and long-term consequences. It may also be worth considering whether there was a difference between how they acted in public, and how they felt when left alone in private (e.g. the gang member who acts like a 'brave warrior' in public, but feels remorse and shame when looking in the mirror).

Ask the client to fill in the table in Part A of the worksheet *My Sense of Self-Esteem*, and use it as the basis of a discussion about their self-esteem. Ask the client whether any patterns emerge, and whether there are any aspects of their self-esteem that they would like to work on.

Ask the client to reflect on how their self-esteem may change over time, using the questions underneath the table. It can be helpful to establish that our self-esteem is not fixed in stone, and is subject to being influenced by external events, and by our own perceptions (either negatively or positively).

Part B of the exercise encourages the client to consider how their own self-belief and perceptions may influence their behaviour and self-esteem. It can be useful to understand the connections between these factors, as outlined in the example. Positive self-beliefs are associated with positive behaviours and positive self-esteem, and vice versa. It may be useful to make links to what you know about the client's early life and their self-beliefs, from exercises such as *My Family Tree* (p.68) and *My Life Time Line* (p.101).

The questions underneath the table offer the client the opportunity to consider specific times in their life when they have thought both positively and negatively about themselves. If a client is feeling particularly low, it may be helpful for them to revisit a time in their life when things were more positive.

Part C of the exercise offers the client the opportunity to reflect upon their self-esteem around the time of their offending. If their offending covered a long period of time, perhaps focus on the first offence they can remember, or an offence which is particularly significant and which they can recall clearly.

For an advanced version of this exercise, set out two chairs and encourage the client to speak about themselves from different points in time (e.g. two years ago/two years from now).

Worksheet: My Sense of Self-Esteem

Name: _____ **Date:** _____

Part A: Statements about my self-esteem

STATEMENT	GENERALLY YES	GENERALLY NO
I am hopeful for my future.		
I trust my intuition.		
I believe in myself.		
I express my feelings easily.		
I think it's OK to be angry in some situations and I know how to manage my anger.		
I can allow myself to feel sad.		
I am good at making decisions.		
I can say 'no' when I want to.		
I can allow myself to form relationships/friendships with other people.		
I can trust and respect other people.		
I can make friends and maintain friendships.		

★

STATEMENT	GENERALLY YES	GENERALLY NO
I can share problems with people who care about me.		
I feel confident with other people most of the time.		
I feel that most other people like me most of the time.		
I feel I know how to be a friend.		
I feel comfortable around women.		
I feel comfortable around men.		
I feel able to establish meaningful intimate sexual relationships with other adults.		
I tell myself I'm good at some things.		
I feel that most people I meet like me at least a little bit.		
I am in control of my own actions and choices.		
I blame other people and hold them responsible for the way my life is.		

Think about the following questions:

- How would I have answered these questions one year ago? Two years ago? Five years ago?

- How would I like to be able to answer these questions one year from now? Two years from now? Five years from now?

- How would you summarise your sense of self-esteem?

Part B: Self-belief and self-esteem

	SELF-BELIEF	EXPECTATIONS	BEHAVIOUR	EFFECT ON SELF-ESTEEM
NEGATIVE	Nobody cares about me and no one is interested in how I am thinking or feeling or what I am doing.	If no one cares about me, then I don't care about anyone else. I'm going to live my life just to please myself.	Offending behaviour. Deterioration of relationships with friends and family.	Committing crimes may make me feel good in the short term, but I feel guilty and ashamed. How can I expect other people to think well of me?
POSITIVE	I am a good person, who cares about other people. Other people care about me too.	Other people will help me when I need support, and I can help others when they need it.	Enjoying being with friends. Showing care and receiving care from others.	I respect myself, and other people respect me too. I can make good choices and resist temptation.

Consider the following questions:

Think of a time when you were feeling positive about yourself. Really focus on it, and allow yourself to remember.

- Where were you? Who was there? What was the situation?
- What were your self-beliefs? What were your expectations?
- How did you behave? How did you feel about yourself afterwards?

Now think of a time when you were feeling negative about yourself. Really focus on it, and allow yourself to remember.

- Where were you? Who was there? What was the situation?
- What were your self-beliefs? What were your expectations?
- How did you behave? How did you feel about yourself afterwards?

Part C – Making links between self-belief, self-esteem and my offences

Think about your self-beliefs and self-esteem when you were offending. Really focus on it, and allow yourself to remember.

- Where were you? Who was there? What was the situation?
- What were your self-beliefs? What were your expectations?
- How did you behave? How did you feel about yourself during your offending? How did you feel about yourself afterwards?
- How are your self-beliefs and sense of self-esteem different now compared to the time you committed your offence(s)?
- What learning do you want to take from this?

The language of emotions

Self-awareness, emotional self-regulation, anger management

Time: 1 hour to 3 hours

Materials: worksheet and any other multi-sensory materials, as needed

Aims

- To help the client learn to recognise, express, tolerate and regulate painful and difficult feelings.

- To help the client name and talk about feelings rather than 'act in' against themselves or 'act out' against others.

- To help the client develop the 'language of emotion' (e.g. naming feelings and understanding the function they serve and where they are in the body).

- To help the client improve their emotional self-regulation.

Method

This exercise addresses a common difficulty among many clients – recognising, expressing, regulating and tolerating painful and difficult feelings, and talking about those feelings. The client may be cut off from and unaware of painful and difficult feelings, and may instead experience vague 'bad' feelings in their body. By contrast, the client may be so overwhelmed by difficult and painful feelings that they cannot gain any sense of distance from them in order to make sense of them and make positive choices.

To do the exercise, take the client through the questions on the worksheet. Select those questions that the client is interested in and wishes to discuss. You can return to the other questions later, if the client wishes to. Record the client's responses yourself, or involve the client in recording them in any way that makes sense to them (e.g. audio, writing, collage, drawing/illustration, etc).

If the client experiences strong emotions during this or any session – for example,

experiencing fear, sadness or anger when discussing their offence or their arrest – this should be treated as an opportunity to discuss 'live' and in the immediate moment the ways that emotions can be recognised and regulated. In other words, the client can 'do things differently' in the here and now of the session, with live material (i.e. their own emotions). This is possibly the best way for the client (and you) to gauge the client's progress in recognising and regulating their emotions.

End the session with a relaxation exercise such as the one on p.193.

Variations

The exercise is typically done through discussion and testing out ideas. However, you can use whatever methods that will have the most meaning and effect for the client. This might include projective methods (using simple objects/toys/stick figure drawings), photographic story-stems (using a photo or other image to start a story, or using several photos or images to prompt a story to be created), hypothetical examples, character creation or story-telling. Sometimes, clients find it helpful to describe emotions by giving them colour, shape and texture (e.g. 'anger is red, hard and spikey', 'joy is yellow, squishy and warm', 'fear is cold and blue and hard').

An advanced version of this exercise would have the client speaking 'as if' they are at different points in time (e.g. two years ago/ two years from now) or 'as if' they are in role as the various topics being discussed. For example, the client could speak 'as if' they are their anger or sadness or fear. From such roles, the client could talk about the characteristics of this emotion (e.g. when they emerge, where they are in the body, the functions they serve (good and bad), how they can be regulated, etc). Similarly, the client could speak to (or write a letter to) their emotions or their emotional self, offering compassion and understanding to any aspects of themselves that suffered and developed self-protective strategies and strategies to meet needs for comfort that later became destructive. A close variation of this is to ask the client to speak 'as if' they are various parts of their own body that are affected by emotion. For example, they may speak in role as their fists: 'I am David's fists, and when he is angry I clench up tightly and hit first, then he asks questions later'. Or as their own feet: 'I am David's feet, and whenever he is afraid – like when anyone offers him kindness or positive feedback – I run away'. The benefit of this type of perspective-taking can be (depending on the interests and capacities of the client) an increased sense of understanding and 'owning' the emotions and the responses they generate. These variations may be highly emotive; care should be taken, and enough time allowed.

FOR CLIENTS WHO HAVE USED PHYSICAL VIOLENCE, INCLUDING VIOLENCE AGAINST THEIR PARTNER

Teach the cycle of violence, sometimes called the wheel of violence (Davies and Frude 1999). The cycle moves through six stages:

1. perceived insult

2. feeling powerless and victimised (regression to fight–flight–freeze)

3. self-righteousness and outrage to feel more powerful ('How dare you!')

4. pumping thoughts ('I'll show you, you @#$%&!')

5. violence and aggression; followed by:

6. self-justification ('he/she deserved it').

Explain the cycle to the client and ask for examples when they have 'travelled around the cycle'. (In some cases, this can happen in seconds.) Discuss options out at each stage of the cycle and strategies for thinking, feeling and behaviour that will help the client to become fully aware of when they are starting the cycle and how they can do things differently. The wheel of violence does not need to spin on 'autopilot'. A key message is that each stage of the cycle allows for a different type of option out or strategy to 'stop the wheel spinning'. For example, at step one (perception) the client could choose to consider other interpretations of the person's behaviour. At step two (fight–flight–freeze), they could use skills of emotional self-regulation, etc.

OTHER TYPES OF OFFENDING

Most types of offending, including property crime, robbery, sexual offences and crimes of deception, can similarly be looked at as a cycle, or a sequence of thoughts, feelings and actions before, during and after the offence. Where it may be useful, work with the client to create a 'wheel' for their particular cycle of offending. Help the client to identify during discussion where they can make different decisions and intervene in the cycle as early as possible. The earlier the better, as once the 'wheel' starts to turn, it gets more and more difficult to stop.

Worksheet: The Language of Emotions

Name: _____ **Date:** _____

This exercise looks at problems in recognising, tolerating, communicating and managing emotions. The first set of questions is meant to be explored in conversation with your facilitator. The second set can be completed on your own and later discussed with your facilitator. Record your responses in writing or through any other means that is useful to you, for example in illustration, collage, audio recording, etc.

Part 1: Questions for discussion

- What is the difference between a feeling (or emotion) and a thought?

- Let's list as many different feelings as we can think of, including positive feelings as well as difficult or painful feelings.

- Are feelings important? If so, why? Or would we be better off without feelings (i.e. more like robots)?

- Where in the body do we feel different feelings? For example, where do we tend to feel fear? Anger? Sadness? Disgust? Happiness? Shame or embarrassment? Longing? For example, fear is very often experienced as 'butterflies in the stomach' and rapid heartbeat. Where in your body do you experience strong feelings?

- What might get in the way of someone being able to realise that they are having feelings?

- What causes people to feel emotions? (Think of different types of events and situations that cause people to feel emotions.)

- Do you think it's possible to have strong negative or painful feelings and to tolerate them and not take them out on other people or oneself? If yes, how do people manage to do that? How do you manage to do that (if you do)? For example, do you ever get angry but not violent? How do you manage to regulate your thoughts, feelings and actions so that you don't use violence or cause violence?

- If you feel a strong emotion like anger, sadness or fear, what do you usually do with that? Do you express it? Bottle it up? Does it depend on the situation? If so, what factors influence how you express or don't express your emotions?

- How do men and women show feelings (e.g. love, sadness, hurt, anger)? Is there a difference between how men and women show these emotions? Why do you think that is? Do you think this is the same in every culture, or do you think it varies?

- How are adults different from children in the way in which they show their feelings?

- If a person were able to be more open and express their feelings more honestly, what effect might this have on them and their relationships with family members/partner/colleagues/friends/etc.?

- Why might a person not express clearly how they feel? (Apply the question to men, women and children.) For example, possible reasons might include not knowing how to express feelings in words, fear of rejection, fear of looking stupid, fear of losing control, fear of hurting others, wanting to please people, wanting to keep things secret, not wishing to 'rock the boat,' not wanting to give in/lose face.

- Think of a number of situations and decide what emotions you are likely to feel in response, then mark on a continuum whether this is a situation to 'contain' or express your emotions, and if so, what would be the best way. Option: Practice this approach using skills practice role play.

Part 2: Questions for self-reflection

Try to answer these questions on your own, and then discuss your responses with your facilitator.

1. Which feelings have I experienced most often in recent months?

2. Which feelings do I find it easy to express? Why might this be?

3. Which feelings do I find it difficult to express? Why might this be?

4. What do I think will happen to me if I express them?

5. In what sorts of situations do I feel these emotions?

6. Who in my life could I talk with about these feelings?

7. Are there people close to me who I think would not want to hear about my feelings? Why do I think they would not want me to share my feelings with them?

8. Can I think of any other constructive and positive ways to talk with other people about my feelings, or tolerate or manage my feelings in a better way?

9. Let me think of a time when I acted on the basis of a strong feeling. What was I thinking, feeling and doing at the time? Looking back and reflecting on that time and situation, what do I now think about the situation and my actions?

10. How do these questions relate to my past offences and my process of change towards positive living?

11. When I experience strong feelings in the future, how do I want to balance my thoughts, feelings and actions?

The relationships ladder

Relationship skills, interpersonal skills, empathy, self-management

Time: 30 minutes to 1 hour or more

Materials: worksheet and any other materials as needed

Aims

- To help the client to explore and understand the process of meeting someone and forming a relationship with them.

- To ensure the client understands the concept of consent.

- To practise the client's self-management and relationship skills.

Method

This exercise focuses on the common ingredients in healthy relationships and the related theme of consent. This exercise can last several sessions and can be revisited where needed.

Begin with an opening question: Can you give an example of a relationship – either based on real life or hypothetical – where both people have equal power and responsibility in the relationship? And now some examples where power and responsibility are unequal?

Examples may include: a couple in a relationship, brother/sister, parent/child, colleagues, friends, managers/supervisees, offender/victim, etc.

Next, ask the client/group to define: What is an adult? What do we mean by describing behaviour as adult? (Bring in the idea of adults having personal responsibility and other responsibilities extending beyond the self.) What defines a child other than simply age? How do their responsibilities differ?

In the next phase of the discussion, explore the definition of 'consent'. Help the client/group reach a definition of 'true consent' (e.g. that 'consent' is not consent if the person fears negative repercussions for saying no, for example, if they are afraid that if they say no they will be hurt, ridiculed or left alone

in a strange place, etc.). Encourage the client/group members to explore the distinction between true consent and 'consent' which is coerced (i.e. not true consent). Encourage the client/group to think about and discuss the ways in which adults may, under certain circumstances, not be able to give informed consent to sexual contact.

Next, introduce the 'relationships ladder': use the worksheet, or create an image of a stepladder on the floor, using string perhaps. Describe the first rung of the ladder as being the very start of a new relationship. Have group members provide all of the details, for example, 'Who is meeting?' 'Two people of the same sex?' 'Man and woman?' 'Teenage boy and girl?' Steer the options so that the relationship will be representative of a consenting sexual relationship in an age group similar to those in the group. Then ask 'Where do they meet?' 'What do they talk about when they first meet?' 'What physical contact is there between them?' etc. Continue the process for each rung up the ladder, the top rung representing the two people forming a lasting commitment to each other. At each rung of the ladder, ask the group to talk about how the move to the next rung is negotiated. Who directs the move? Is it mutual? What would happen if one person tries to force the relationship 'up the ladder'? What would happen if one person wanted it at a different level than the other? Encourage group discussion on the theme 'What are the hallmarks of a healthy relationship?'

Variations

If you choose to focus more intently on the theme of consent: Encourage discussion about the ways in which the behaviour of others can be misinterpreted as consent, and where responsibility lies when one person is unable to give informed consent. If a client raises the issue of how the age of consent differs in various countries around the world and changes over time, encourage discussion about why in this country the age of consent is what it is. Encourage the client/participants to discuss the implications of differences in age (e.g. age gaps of more than three years for teenagers), and similarly differences in levels of maturity, power and authority, and how these affect consent.

Use any audio-visual or other multi-sensory means to conduct the exercise. For example, if an actual stepladder is available, you could bring that into the room in order to demonstrate how the relationship progresses 'up the ladder' and how each step is a mutual negotiation.

Worksheet: The Relationships Ladder

Name: _____ **Date:** _____

Who is meeting? Where do they meet? What do they talk about when they first meet? What physical contact is there between them?

Continue the process for each rung up the ladder, the top rung representing the two people forming a lasting commitment to each other. At each rung of the ladder, consider how the move to the next rung is negotiated. Who directs the move? Is it mutual? What would happen if one person tries to force the relationship 'up the ladder'? What would happen if one person wanted it at a different level than the other? What are the hallmarks of a healthy relationship?

How does this exercise relate to me and my experiences of relationships in the past? How can I use this concept in my current or future relationships?

STOP-MAP: A strengths-based approach to problem-solving

Problem-solving, self-awareness, strengths-focused work, integration

Time: 1 hour, with further work as needed

Materials: worksheet and any other audio-visual material as needed

Aims

- Understanding the STOP-MAP approach to problem-solving.

- Finding examples where the method would apply for the client.

- Practising and applying the STOP-MAP approach in the client's own life.

- Helping the client to become psychologically integrated when facing dangerous or uncertain situations.

Method

STOP-MAP is a strengths-based approach to problem-solving. The acronym stands for *Strengths, Troubling Occurrence, Pattern, Meaning, Alternatives* and *Plan*. The worksheet explains each step of the process. Using the worksheet as a guide, take the client through the process in a collaborative way. With practice, the client can assimilate the approach into their own problem-solving tool kit.

STOP-MAP often leads to skills practice. What makes this perhaps a little different from other approaches is the means by which the client decides the skills he or she wishes to develop. Rather than moving directly from problem to solution, the STOP-MAP approach encourages the client to reflect on their response, their pattern of response, and its historical function in their younger life. This allows the client to practise the skill with a full awareness of the purpose it serves, and

therefore much greater motivation to integrate the new skill as part of a new way of being.

Discuss with the client: *Working through the steps of the STOP-MAP is a way of looking for solutions that do not just answer the demands of the moment. Using the STOP-MAP process encourages us to look deeply into the issue we are facing and to reflect on the pattern and the function of our responses. This way, we are not just coming up with short-term fixes to our daily problems; we are seeking out and developing long-term strategies for personal growth.*

Variations

You can suggest using the STOP-MAP approach any time the client raises a problem or dilemma they are facing,

Use any visual, auditory, sensory or kinaesthetic activities to make the exercise more meaningful and memorable for the client. For example, the client may wish to create a visual map of their STOP-MAP process.

Alternatively, it can be useful to encourage the client to speak from the various roles and points in time that arise during the discussion.

In many cases, clients will benefit from practising essential skills in their 'plan of action'. For example, if the client says that their plan of action is to ask a friend for advice, this may naturally lead to a skills practice.

Source: This exercise is adapted from Baim and Morrison (2011).

Worksheet: The STOP-MAP Approach to Problem-Solving

Name: _____ **Date:** _____

If you are facing a problem, decision, dilemma or troubling situation, whether this is happening now or you anticipate it happening in the near future, it might help you to think about it using the STOP-MAP approach. The process starts with an affirmation of your strengths and skills. Work through the steps of the process several times with help from your facilitator. If it seems useful to you, you can then use the process any time you need it.

Strengths

- First, I will remind myself of my various *strengths*, including my internal, interpersonal and transpersonal strengths. (For this, you may want to refer back to the *Starting from Strength* exercise, p.62.)

Troubling Occurrence

- What is the problem, decision, dilemma or *troubling occurrence* that I am facing?

- Double-checking: is this definitely a problem or troubling situation, or can it be looked at in another way?

Pattern

- How am I responding to this issue now? What are my thoughts and feelings? What reactions am I experiencing in my body?

- How have I responded to this issue, or issues like it, in the past?

- Is there a *pattern* to my responses? What does this response, or this feeling, remind me of?

- Can I remember when I have felt similarly and responded either similarly or differently in the past?

- Where did this pattern start?

- How far back can I remember?

Meaning

- What is the *meaning*, or function, of my past responses? For example, have my responses been to avoid or confront the issue, or to meet my needs for safety, comfort or predictability?

- Can I offer understanding to my younger self for using these strategies at the time?

- Do I want to decide to do things differently now?

Alternatives

- What successful responses/solutions have I used in the past in this sort of situation?

- If none of my solutions have worked in the past, what *alternatives* can I think of that will help me to manage or solve this issue in a productive way?

- Do I need help? Who can help me?

Plan

- My plan of action is...

Note for facilitator: If needed, take time to practise any skills you need to develop in order to carry out your plan of action. See *Internal Self-Management Skills* (p.125) and *Interpersonal Skills* (p.167) for ideas and structures for practising skills. Appendices 3 and 4 offer many examples of self-management and interpersonal skills, divided into micro-skills for the purposes of step-by-step practice.

Perspective-taking

Perspective-taking, relationships, self-reflection

Time: 1 hour

Materials: worksheet, interesting object, paper

Aims

- To understand the importance of recognising and respecting other peoples' perspectives.

- To understand that we may need to shift perspective in order to see 'the whole picture'.

- To understand that the truest version of an event and its impact may be gained by considering and balancing the multiple points of view about that event.

- To encourage your client to recognise that being able to understand other people's perspectives may help when dealing with difficult situations or conflicts.

Method

This exercise focuses on encouraging the client to develop the view that other people's experiences and perspectives might be different from their own, but are still valid, important and worthy of respect. The skill of perspective-taking has links with the concept of empathy, for victims and for people in general, which is the subject of the next two exercises. Being better able to appreciate the perspective of others has a widely applicable benefit for all human beings, beyond simply being applicable to those who have committed offences.

The perspective-taking exercise can be done in a number of ways. One way is to bring in any three dimensional object such as a Rubik's Cube, a paperweight or a human figure such as an artist's wooden model. Place the object in between you and the client, and take it in turns to say out loud some of the distinctive features you see, such as colour, shape, markings, etc.

As an alternative, you can use the diagram of a large number 3 on the worksheet, and place it on a table between you and the client, and call out what you see, rotating the diagram so that you each see each side in turn. Or you could place it on the floor and walk around it. From the sides, it looks like either the letter M or the letter W, from below it looks like a number 3 and from above, it looks like a letter E.

Facilitate a discussion along the lines of 'How is this possible? We are looking at the same object but we see such different things?' Help the client to consider the importance of 'seeing the fullest picture' or gathering multiple perspectives, in order to achieve the truest sense of what is happening. You could change chairs, or the object may be pivoted, to make the point that we can, if we are willing to, change our point of view and gain a fuller understanding of what the other person is experiencing.

Encourage the client to make connections with their life by thinking about the different ways that people perceive events. Encourage the client to identify a recent situation where they were in a conflict with another person, where they both saw the same situation differently. Use the questions on the worksheet to explore the situation. (NB: please screen the example for any concerns about ongoing risk – it may not be useful or safe to pick a very emotionally charged situation or one which involves potential victimisation.)

Encourage discussion around the difficulty of insisting that one point of view is correct, for example, 'If you tell me that I am wrong, then it feels like an attack, and I will be less willing to listen and defensive. If, however, you suggest to me that I have not seen "the full picture", I am more likely to remain open and try to see other possibilities and other points of view.' Encourage the client to recognise that they are likely to make good decisions if they take into account all available information. This is only possible if they are open to other people's perspectives.

Variations

An advanced version of this exercise would involve the client taking on the role of the other person involved in the conflict situation, and you using the technique of interviewing in role to question them about their perspective. Or you could set out two chairs; in one, ask your client to speak as themselves about the situation. In the other, ask them to speak from the point of view of the other person. Please use your judgement about whether this is appropriate for the example chosen by your client.

If your client is unable to identify a conflict in their life, you could use a hypothetical example of people having different points of view. For example, you can create a case study where all of the people in a court room have different perspectives. The case being tried can be any type of crime that the client will have an interest in exploring; it does not necessarily need to match with their own offending. Or, you could choose a story from a newspaper involving some sort of dispute. Or, if it is relevant, you could think about any time when you and the client have disagreed about a situation which has arisen during your work together.

If you notice that your client may benefit from developing interpersonal skills for resolving conflict, it may be useful to facilitate skills practice sessions.

Worksheet: Perspective-Taking

Look at this shape from each of the 4 different angles. What do you see?

Questions to think about:

- "If we see different things, am I allowed to say that your point of view is WRONG?"

- "Why don't you give the same answer as I gave?"

- "What would you think of me if I insisted that my way is the only way?"

- "What must I do in order to shift my perspective and see what you see?"

Applying this to your own life

- Think about a time when you had a conflict or a disagreement with another person. This could be a person in authority, a friend, a partner or a family member.

- Who was the person? Where were you? What had just happened? What did you disagree about?

- What was your point of view? What was their point of view?

- Why did you see things differently?

- How did you feel about them during the conflict? After the conflict?

- How do you think they may have felt about you?

- How might it have helped the situation if you had been able to see things from their point of view?

- What are the obstacles which get in the way of taking another person's perspective (they may include things like drugs, alcohol, strong emotions such as anger or fear, not liking the person, etc.)?

- Are there some people whose perspectives you are more likely or less likely to be able to take on?

Developing empathy and writing an apology letter

Empathy, perspective-taking, integration

Time: 1 hour to 2 hours

Materials: worksheet, small objects (optional), paper

Aims

- To encourage the client to think widely about who may have been negatively impacted by their offending.

- To help the client to learn more about what it means to develop empathy for others.

- To encourage the client to develop active empathy for the victims of their offending.

- To support the client in realising that they cannot change the past, but they can take responsibility for leading an offence-free life in the future.

- To encourage the client to write a letter to the victim (which will not be sent).

Introduction

Recent academic thinking about empathy has raised important questions about whether offenders suffer from a lack of empathy for other people. It seems that many offenders do not lack the capacity to experience empathy for people in general, but rather they might find it more difficult to empathise with particular individuals or groups of people, which may include the victims of their offences. A paper written after a thorough review of the literature on empathy concludes that the most accurate and comprehensive definition of empathy is:

> a cognitive and emotional understanding of another's experience, resulting in an emotional response that is congruent with a view that others are worthy of compassion and respect and have intrinsic worth.
>
> *(Barnett and Mann 2013, p.230)*

It is important to note that many clients may have had experiences of being victims themselves, either during their childhoods or as adults, and that these experiences need to be responded to with compassion. This is not the same as making excuses or justifying offending behaviour; most victims of crime do not go on to perpetrate crimes themselves. However, if we are encouraging clients to develop compassion and respect for others, we need to meet them halfway and extend a compassionate response to their own victim experiences. It is equally important to note that these exercises are not meant to increase the client's sense of shame or to promote harsh self-judgement. Rather, the aim is to empower the client to develop a more rounded understanding of the impact of their offending, to enhance their motivation not to reoffend. It may be helpful to revisit the *Starting from Strength* exercise (p.62) in order to increase the client's resilience for this important work.

Method

Ask your client, 'What is empathy?' Refer to the See/Think/Feel/Do model of empathy (Marshall *et al.* 1995) which is outlined on the worksheet below. Use this to help to deepen your client's understanding of empathy. Encourage the view that it is not sufficient to understand the other person's feelings or how our behaviour will affect the other person. Active empathy requires that we act in a way that attempts to meet the needs of the other person or reduce their distress. (Note that this is not always possible – we may feel empathy for someone but be unable to intervene to help them.)

Ask your client to offer everyday examples of having experienced empathy for others, and having received empathy from others, for example, in intimate or personal relationships at home, at work, in social interactions. How does it feel to be treated empathically by others? How has your client felt after having behaved empathically towards others?

The next step is the Victim Ripple exercise. Use the series of concentric circles (representing the 'ripples in a pond') which are printed on the worksheet. Ask your client to work outward from the centre, identifying everyone they can think of who was affected by one of their offences. This is described as the 'ripple effect', and the aim is to illustrate how many people are impacted by a single offence. If names are known, use first names only, and if they aren't known, then use the person's role as a description (e.g. parents of the victim). Alternatively, use objects or another visual prompt to represent people identified in the ripple effect.

Encourage your client to include not only the direct victims and those around the victim, but also people in his own family/extended family/circle of friends/neighbours/friends, etc. who have been affected by the offending. These are known as indirect victims. Some clients include themselves; it is ok to acknowledge that they have experienced negative consequences as a result of the offence, but this should not become the main focus of the exercise.

The next stage is to encourage your client to think about the type of impact on the direct and indirect victims, in the short and long term. You could draw a simple table, such as the one below, and ask your client to fill it in. Or you could have a discussion and note down the main points.

FIRST NAME	WHO ARE THEY?	SHORT-TERM EFFECTS	LONG-TERM EFFECTS

The final stage is to encourage your client to write a letter of apology to one of the victims. It is very important to emphasise that this letter should not be sent, under any circumstances. Rather, it is an exercise designed to increase the client's ability to empathise with the victim. Another note of caution is that there are some offences where this exercise might not be appropriate, such as hate crimes. Please use your judgement as to whether to include this exercise. It is also important to acknowledge how challenging this exercise may be for your client, who may need support from you.

Ask your client to choose a person to write the letter to (again, emphasising that it is not going to be sent). Then, encourage your client to think about what they might say, using open and Socratic questions. Areas to think about include:

- How might this person have been affected by the offence?

- How might they think about you, or feel towards you?

- What do you want to say to them?

- What sorts of things do you think it might help them to hear from you?

- What sorts of things might not be helpful to write?

- How might it help you to express this apology, even though it's not going to be sent?

- How can this piece of work motivate you to remain offence free and to build a life you can be proud of?

Once the letter is complete, ask the client to read it out, and then discuss it. A variation is for the client to speak the letter out loud, and for you to write it down, using their exact words. An advanced variation is to ask the client to imagine that they were receiving the letter and ask them to comment about how they might perceive it. Then you could offer them the opportunity to make any alterations, based upon this insight. The processing of this exercise needs to remain positive and motivational, so as not to induce shame (which can impact motivation to change in a negative way).

Worksheet: Developing Empathy for Others

Name: _____   **Date:** _____

Part 1: Stages of empathy

a. SEE: Identify the body language of emotions, so that we can tell generally what a person might be feeling.

b. THINK: Predict what emotion a person might feel if something happens to them.

c. FEEL: 'Put ourselves in the other person's shoes' and imagine the thoughts and feelings of the other person.

d. DO: Put this understanding into practice in attempting to meet the needs of the other person.

Part 2: Ripple effect: the lines represent the ripples in a pond after a stone has been thrown into the water.

Who are the people who have been affected by your offending? Think as widely as you can, about the victim, the victim's family and friends, and about your family, friends and other people you know.

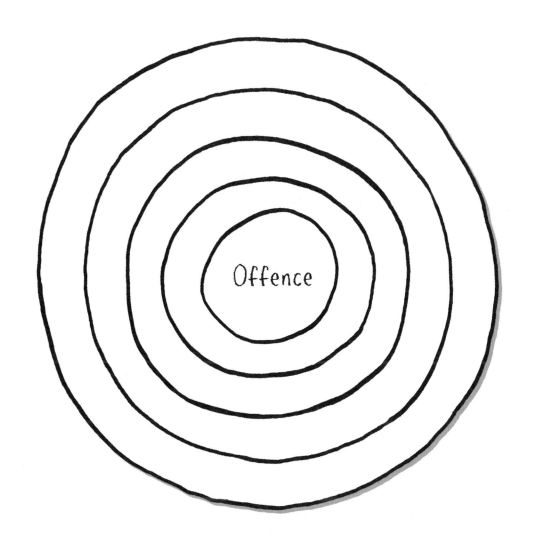

Thinking report, including the victim's perspective

Victim empathy, perspective-taking, motivation

> **Time:** 1 hour or more
>
> **Materials:** worksheet and other paper and materials, as needed

Aims

- To develop a deeper appreciation of the impact of the offence on the victim.

- To encourage the client to develop the capacity for active empathy.

- To reinforce the client's motivation to live an offence-free life by increasing awareness of the negative consequences for victims.

- To help the client to understand that, at the time of the offence, they may have had a very different perspective on the offence, as compared with the victim.

- To encourage the client to recognise the difference between their attitudes and behaviour at the time of offending and in the present day.

Method

This exercise can be a helpful way of offering the client the opportunity to talk meaningfully about the offence itself in more detail. Sometimes, clients have a partial and incomplete narrative of the offence, which has become complicated with layers of self-protective denial. It can be important for clients to fully explore the offence, and to be able to talk about aspects of their behaviour and its consequences which have been troubling them. It can also be useful to offer a client the chance to fully explore the likely impact of the offence upon the victim.

Note: Please be careful if you are considering this exercise for use with a client who is still in contact with the victim (e.g. sexual abuse within the family, or domestic abuse), as it may impact the way in which the client relates to them.

In this exercise, the client is helped to complete a thinking report for themselves, and one from the point of view of one of the victims. Whichever offence is chosen, it is useful if the facilitator has some objective corroborating information (e.g. witness statements, or summaries of evidence) in order to be able to assess the appropriateness/accuracy of the information offered by the client.

To do this exercise, the facilitator helps the client to complete the table, which looks at the thoughts, feelings and behaviours of the offender and the victim at four specific points in time (just before, during, just after and long-term after the offence). These points in time are negotiated and agreed with the client before the exercise begins. Alternatively, the facilitator may decide to ask the client to do this thinking report as homework and then to feed it back afterwards, where the work may be deepened.

Recommended sequence: Complete the thinking reports for the offender and the victim for the same point in time, and only then move on to the next point in time (e.g. complete both halves of the table for the 'just before' point, then move onto the 'during' point).

The points in time are:

- **Just before:** 10 minutes to 1 hour before the offence.

- **During:** This is the time period during which the offence took place. Usually, a moment is chosen just after the offence begins. (Note: This should *not* be a moment of graphic violence or abuse.)

- **Just after:** This is the time period from immediately after the offence to 4 hours after.

- **Long-term after:** This could be several weeks, months or even many years after the abuse. (The appropriate time lapse can be negotiated with the client.) It could even be the present time.

Note: The thinking report does not involve the re-enactment of any of the actions or speech described. The reason for this is to minimise the need for the client to use self-protective defence mechanisms, and out of respect for the victim. Nor should it involve highly graphic sexual or violent detail, which is likely to distract from the main focus.

This exercise can be done in a variety of ways, depending on the needs and learning style of the client. Facilitators are encouraged to use art, story-telling and story-writing, collage, letter-writing, empty chair work, interviewing in role, sculpting or any experiential method that will help the client. An advanced version of this exercise would have the client speaking 'as if' they are in role as themselves, or the other person, as represented in the different parts of the grid.

The facilitator should note that the strong emphasis in this exercise should be on encouraging the client to give an appropriate and accurate (as best empathic awareness would suggest) account of what the victim was 'more likely' to be thinking, feeling and doing before, during and after the abuse.

Processing the exercise

After exploring both of the thinking reports at each of the points in time, the client is then asked to come back to the present time and make observations about how the exercise felt. Ask the client to consider whether there have been any new learning points about their 'old me' behaviour, thinking and feeling, and how they want to make use of this learning. It is very important to re-emphasise the 'new me',

pro-social thinking. In stressing the 'new me' thinking, feeling and behaviours that the client aspires to, we are lessening the likelihood that the client will feel stuck in role as a perpetrator.

To sum up, in doing this exercise, we must support the client to minimise shame or negative affect as a result of undertaking this work (which could, paradoxically, raise risk). We can do this by focusing on how much they have moved on since the time of the offending. We can also invite specific positive self-feedback about having undertaken the work.

Learning points

Genuine perspective-taking demands a good deal of thought, because active empathy is called for. This will involve focused thinking – using all of one's empathic imagination – about the other person's perspective on the thinking, feeling and behavioural levels.

Even actions that we feel very guilty about, and full of remorse about, can be useful to think about and reflect upon, because we can learn 'how not to do things' next time. This is an essential skill of 'new me' thinking – the ability to re-frame events to draw positive learning from them, even when they seem only to carry the weight of regret or shame.

Responsivity variations

The main focus of this exercise is for the client to use their empathic imagination to contrast their own experience and perspective with that of the victim. As with all of the exercises in this book, facilitators should use the appropriate amount of explanation, examples, one-step-removed and projective methods as necessary to adjust for responsivity. Use story-telling, hypothetical character creation, objects, stick figure drawings and other means to help the client learn experientially.

For clients who have not yet admitted their offending behaviour, try doing this exercise using a hypothetical, fictional offence which you create together.

★

Worksheet: Thinking Report for Self and the Victim

(adapted from Baim *et al.* 2002 and Bush 1993)

Name: _____ **Date:** _____

Responses should be written in the first-person present tense, for both people (e.g. I am driving, I am sitting in the living room, etc.).

    Use additional sheets to write on. This page is to be used only as a template, as the boxes are too small to write in.

Brief description of the offence:		
	ME	**VICTIM**
Just before	Thoughts: Feelings: Actions:	Thoughts: Feelings: Actions:
During	Thoughts: Feelings: Actions:	Thoughts: Feelings: Actions:
Just after	Thoughts: Feelings: Actions:	Thoughts: Feelings: Actions:

Long-term after	Thoughts:	Thoughts:
	Feelings:	Feelings:
	Actions:	Actions:

Main learning points:

Becoming an integrated adult

Self-awareness, goal-setting, self-identity, integration, motivation

Time: 1 hour to 3 hours

Materials: worksheet or any other multi-sensory materials, as needed

Aims

- To promote psychological and emotional integration.

- To encourage the client to see 'the big picture' of what the process of change can achieve, that is, what it means to be a self-actualising adult who can achieve long-term fulfilling goals and a happy, non-offending lifestyle.

- To encourage the client to move towards a sense of self-identity that does not include offending behaviour.

Method

This is an exercise that is very broad in scope. It takes the approach of working from the core of existence, (i.e. our basic functioning as an organic being) to the widest possible circle of existence (i.e. living with an awareness of our place in the universe). The exercise is aimed at helping the client to become more integrated in each domain of existence, in order to become as fully functioning as possible. This is not something that should be thought of as a single exercise to be 'completed', but instead should be seen as a reference point for lifelong growth and development. Additionally, there are many different ways to be integrated; integration does not look the same in every person. Indeed, some of the hallmarks of integration are individuality, originality and spontaneity.

Using the worksheet as a guide, discuss with the client the different topics related to the domains of integration. You can also use creative methods such as drawing, using objects and story-telling, collage, sculpting with clay, etc. The different forms of integration can also be illustrated or presented using personal stories, enactments and skills practice (i.e. practising skills of being more integrated in a particular way, in a given situation).

For each of the domains of integration, the worksheet offers three questions for reflection. Work with the client to complete their responses to these questions. Encourage the client to be realistic in their self-assessment and help them to formulate plans and practise skills as appropriate. Again, this is a lifelong process, so taking 'first steps' is fine if that is what is called for.

Source: This exercise is adapted from Baim and Morrison (2011).

Worksheet: The Six Domains of Becoming an Integrated Adult

Name: _____ **Date:** _____

For each of the six domains of integration, think about what the domain means to you and how integrated you are in that particular area. Use the questions to prompt reflection and goal-setting.

1. _____

2. _____

3. _____

1. Integrating my brain and my body
Key features:

- I am aware of what is happening in my body and I do not ignore bodily signals. I am aware that when these bodily signals are ignored, they have a tendency to escalate and become symptoms (anxiety, injury, ulcers, heartburn, gastric problems, heart problems, breathing difficulties, extreme fatigue, headache, backache, injury, etc.).

- I use as many of my senses as I can, including hearing, sight, touch, taste, smell, and orientation in space and time.

- I think of myself not as 'having a body' but instead as 'being a body'. I live fully within my own skin and do not just treat my body as a separate 'thing' that is apart from me.

Questions for reflection:

- How integrated am I in this area? (rate 1–10)

- What is one example of something I do that gives me evidence that I am integrated in this area of my life? (This can include sport and physical activity.)

- What do I need to do to become more integrated in this area of my life? (List three things.)

2. Integrating my mind and my brain
Key features:

- I use my mind to focus on what is happening in my brain, my emotions and in my physical being. I think about my thoughts and why I am having certain thoughts. I do the same for my emotions.

- I understand that what I do with my mind forms new connections in the brain. This is why repeated tasks can become habits, because neuronal connections are forming and strengthening over time and with repeated practice.

- I use my mind with an understanding that my 'higher brain' functions (e.g. abstract thinking) can have a profound effect on my mid-brain (emotional) and lower brain (bodily/physiological processes) functions. For example, if I am stressed, I know that deliberately looking at the situation in a different way (reframing the problem) and taking several deep breaths can change the way I feel and also my physiological anxiety.

- I understand the various emotional 'states' that I can be in, for example, when I am excited, contemplative, interested or bored. I understanding that these are all states of being, and they each have their purpose.

- I understand that just because I feel very powerful emotions and physical feelings about something does not mean that my perception is 'true'. For example, just because I feel afraid does not mean that there is a current threat or just because I feel offended doesn't mean that someone else has intended to insult me.

Questions for reflection:

- How integrated am I in this area? (rate 1–10)

- What is one example of something I do that gives me evidence that I am integrated in this area of my life?

- What do I need to do to become more integrated in this area of my life? (List three things.)

1. _____

2. _____

3. _____

3. Integrating the various 'parts' of myself into a functioning whole
Key features:

- I can 'have a conversation with myself'. I am in tune with my sense of myself and who I am.

- I can step back from immediate experience and observe what is happening in my mind, my brain and my relationships, and I can also be totally involved in experiencing the moment.

- I can integrate the various 'parts of myself', even if they have competing demands. Sometimes this role is called the executive self or the internal manager. I can integrate these various parts of myself and orient myself towards growth, development and positive change.

- I can integrate my creative, intuitive brain with my rational, logical brain.

- I attune to all aspects of my inner and outer experiences, with openness and curiosity.

Questions for reflection:

- How integrated am I in this area? (rate 1–10)

- What is one example of something I do that gives me evidence that I am integrated in this area of my life?

- What do I need to do to become more integrated in this area of my life? (List three things.)

1. _____

2. _____

3. _____

4. Integrating my memories and orienting them in time and place with a continuous narrative
Key features:

- I can think about pleasant memories as well as painful or difficult memories. No memories are 'off limits' or forbidden from my consciousness. I recognise that this is an important type of integration because the parts that are 'forbidden' or 'blocked from view' have a habit of emerging in covert ways if they remain split off or defended against. 'What we resist persists.'

- I integrate my different types of memory so that the stories I tell myself about the past make full use of all of my integrative skills. For example, if I recall an event from long ago, I think about it carefully to give it the right kind of interpretation.

- I integrate the past, present and future, and know where events and relationships happen in time.

- I understand that some information may never be available, so I may have gaps in memory and knowledge about my life.

- I integrate my perspective now with my perceptions in the past. I can trace my evolving understanding to make distinctions about how my perception has changed over time. I understand that at different ages I have had different capacities. I can 'forgive' and show compassion to my younger self, and make use of the lessons learned.

Questions for reflection:

- How integrated am I in this area? (rate 1–10)

- What is one example of something I do that gives me evidence that I am integrated in this area of my life?

- What do I need to do to become more integrated in this area of my life? (List three things.)

1. _____

2. _____

3. _____

5. Integrating my mind and brain in relation to other people
Key features:

- I integrate my perspective, needs, interests, feelings and goals with those of other people. I adjust my actions so that I can work cooperatively with other people, accomplish mutually desired goals and form and sustain loving relationships.

- I integrate knowledge I have discovered for myself with knowledge I have gained from other people. I can decide for myself whether something is true or if someone is telling me something that is false or distorted.

- I understand that my needs, interests and abilities are different now compared to when I was a child, and that the same is true for other people, including (if I have children) my children. Similarly, I recognise that my parent(s) may have changed over time, and also the nature of my relationship with them and their power and authority over me.

- I am integrating all of these factors into a developing sense of my identity as a person. I understand that the identity I have now and that I am developing may have some important differences compared to the identity I had when I was committing offences. Example: The identity of being a criminal versus being a responsible citizen with adult responsibilities.

Questions for reflection:

- How integrated am I in this area? (rate 1–10)

- What is one example of something I do that gives me evidence that I am integrated in this area of my life?

- What do I need to do to become more integrated in this area of my life? (List three things.)

1. _____

2. _____

3. _____

6. Integrating me in relation to the rest of my world/higher consciousness
Key features:

- I can do a reality check and think about the way the world 'is' versus how I think it 'ought' to be. I can accept the way the world is, although this does not necessarily mean passively adjusting to the status quo. I fully recognise and accept the world as it is in order to best orient myself to reality, which may include working to change the status quo.

- I adjust the way I live my life to work with my surroundings. This means I carry out roles suited to my situation, relationships and goals.

- I orient my life towards making a contribution and encouraging growth and well-being in myself and other people, especially the next generation.

- I think about myself as being a part of existence as a whole. I understand my place in the long chain of human history, the cycle of life and death, the evolution of life on Earth, and the ever-expanding cosmos. I am aware of the connection between everything.

Questions for reflection:

- How integrated am I in this area? (rate 1–10)

- What is one example of something I do that gives me evidence that I am integrated in this area of my life?

- What do I need to do to become more integrated in this area of my life? (List three things.)

1. _____

2. _____

3. _____

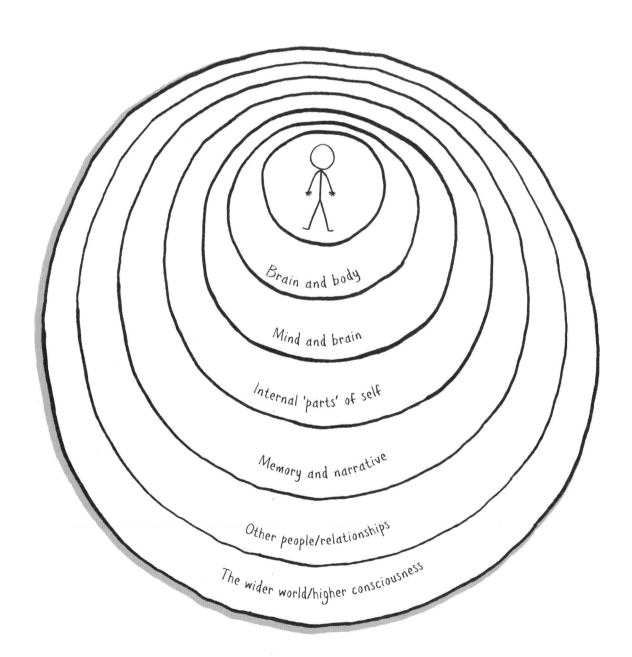

Skills practice part 2: Interpersonal skills

Interpersonal and social skills, communication, self-awareness

Time: 3 to 5 sessions

Materials: worksheet, skills outline in Appendix 4 and any other tools/materials needed

Aims

- To identify interpersonal skills that need practice.

- To practise interpersonal skills, including high-risk situations.

- To put into practice one or more new skills in everyday life.

- To get feedback about how new skills are being practised in everyday life.

- To raise self-awareness, positive self-regard and hope.

Method

The next series of skills focus on interpersonal skills as opposed to the skills of internal self-regulation. Even so, they have important ramifications as far as internal self-regulation is concerned, because what is happening internally will be reflected in the client's interpersonal behaviour. It is important to help the client understand that there is never a clear distinction between what is internal and what is external, as each process is interconnected with the other.

Go through the social skills survey with the client, asking them to choose and prioritise the skills they would like to practise. Emphasise that these are skills that can be learnt or developed, and that most of them apply to most people (not just to people who have committed offences). Where the client seems to have a blind spot (i.e. you disagree with their choices or you think they may have missed something important), offer your own suggestions. Through discussion and collaborative enquiry, arrive at mutually agreed targets/goals.

As with the internal self-management skills practice role plays, the interpersonal skills practice role plays can re-enact an actual event or situation in the client's life or can 'fictionalise' matters so that the client is portraying a situation that is close to life but not an exact simulation of their life.

To facilitate the interpersonal skills practices, use the same general method and approach used for the self-management role plays (see pp.125–126). Use Appendix 4 as a reference point for teaching and practising interpersonal skills.

After several practices of a skill, as a form of debrief, include a discussion where you ask the client to describe one opportunity they will have to practice the skill in the next seven days. (This can be practised too, if needed.) The client can also use the worksheet *Reflecting on a Skill I Practised this Week* (p.128) in order to do just that. The worksheet can be handed in each week and serve as a prompt for discussion and possible further work.

Reminder

If you are working one-to-one with a client, you can play the other person in the role play, or you can ask the client to alternate between the two roles. Alternatively, you can ask another staff member to take part on these sessions and take the 'other' role in the role plays. If you will be taking roles in the role plays, remember to maintain boundaries and avoid playing the role of sexual partners, victims or offenders. In general, keep to peer, friend, supportive family member, acquaintance, colleague or authority roles. *If in any doubt, ask the client to enact both roles in the role play*, alternating between the two roles.

Some suggested discussion points

- New learning and skills can replace unhelpful styles and skills which are no longer appropriate.

- While the skills in this section are called interpersonal skills, many of them have an internal component. Typically, the interpersonal part of the skill is meant to occur after the internal process of reflection and self-management has occurred.

- When, as adults, we think about replacing old habits and coping strategies (including responses linked to 'fight or flight' instincts), it is important to recognise that these responses may once have been crucial to survival – for example, as survival strategies to cope with a violent childhood family setting. The problem is not the strategy in itself, but rather the contexts in which it is now being used. In other words, we 'praise the survival strategy' while at the same time readjusting it to make it more suited to adulthood and current contexts.

- The emphasis in these sessions will be on practising the skills needed to attain positive goals and also skills needed to avoid high-risk situations and behaviours. Whilst these goals will be an essential part of maintaining an offence-free lifestyle, they are also wider in scope; they are about setting in focus what you want to achieve in your life, what vision you have for yourself, and what will give you fulfilment.

Variations

Skills practice can be used at any point of the programme, in any session, as needed.

- During the skills practice sessions, try to make links with all of the client's previous work to help them see the relevance of these skills for everyday living and long-term goals.

- Each description of a skill includes suggested scenarios. You can also work with the client to construct a scenario which arises from their personal experience.

- Some clients may need more sessions or more intense support to help these skills 'stick'. The rule of guidance is that you repeat the skill as much and as often as needed by the individual client. If the client is also seen by other professionals during the week, such as workers at a hostel or institutional staff, you may wish to liaise with them in order to support the client in practising new life skills. Equally, if the client is living with family or in another setting where there are people around them, it may in some circumstances be beneficial to involve these people in assisting and promoting the client's use of new interpersonal skills.

- There are many variations that be used to facilitate skills practice. Facilitators can use their creativity to collaborate with the client to find the modes of working that best suit them. For example, some clients may work better at the level of one step removed (e.g. fictional scenarios and characters) and some will work better at the personal level (i.e. close to life simulations).

Worksheet: Which Interpersonal Skills Would I Like to Practise?

Name: _____ **Date:** _____

INTERPERSONAL SKILLS SURVEY	IS THIS A SKILL I WOULD LIKE TO PRACTISE?
Talking with people in authority	
Disclosing my offence to a friend/family member/employer/new partner	
Asking for help/Talking about my problems	
Resisting pressure from others/Resisting temptation to offend	
Saying 'No'	
Apologising	
Showing empathy	
Dealing with someone else's anger or provocation	
Asking for feedback	
Managing my feelings and stating my views when I feel insulted or ignored	
Starting and continuing a conversation	
Conflict resolution: Negotiating and compromising with others	
Communicating with my child(ren) when they need guidance/boundary setting	
Talking about jealous feelings	
Communicating about sensitive topics with my partner	
Communicating warm feelings to someone close to me	
Applying for a job/talking positively about myself	
Managing sexual feelings in a responsible way	
Having a difficult conversation with someone	
Any others I can think of?	

CHAPTER 6
Looking Forward

Setting Goals, Preparing for Challenges Ahead and Moving Forward with My Life

This chapter contains four exercises that help the client to think about important life goals and aspirations, and then to anticipate, plan and prepare for their future life. An important aim in these sessions will be to look ahead to possible high risk scenarios and situations that can elicit old responses. This can then lead to skills practice of positive ways to deal with challenging situations. During these sessions the client is encouraged to develop more links with the community and to develop more of a stake in society. The exercises encourage the client to link with other people in their support network, for example family, friends, people in the community, volunteers, para-professionals and professionals. This will reflect the important notion of 'social capital', which is a cornerstone of contemporary desistance theory. The exercises are aimed at helping the client to become more confident so that they can maintain changes and also ask for help when they need it. The last exercise encourages the client to look back over their progress and look to the future.

What am I good at and what do I love to do?

Goal-setting, identifying strengths, building social capital, employment/work

Time: 1 hour to 3 hours

Materials: worksheet and any other multi-sensory material, as needed

Aims

- To help the client identify skills and qualities about themselves that are strengths.

- To help the client identify work and leisure-related activities that they really enjoy doing.

- To set goals and plans in place to help the client do more of what they enjoy doing, and to connect this with positive life goals for work, leisure, relationships, etc.

- To set targets for growth where needed, for example, if further education is required, or job skills.

Method

Using the worksheet as a guide, discuss with the client any skills that they have in different aspects of life, for example, work, family, social and other contexts. The client may need some help with this, and perhaps reassurance that it is ok to say what they are good at. Some clients may have experienced extreme criticism or emotional/verbal abuse if they ever tried to say something good about themselves at school, at home or among peers. In such cases you may need to help them to overcome the fear of self-praise and to reassure them that it is not boasting to acknowledge that they have certain skills.

Next, discuss with the client activities that they love to do – or really like to do. Again, these can be broken into categories such as work, family, hobbies/recreation/leisure, social.

Next, consider with the client any overlap between these two areas of their life. Are any of the activities they love to do also ones they are good at? Use the overlapping circles to capture the idea that some activities they love to do are also ones they are good at.

Next, and where appropriate and needed, consider whether any of the activities they like to do and are good at are also activities/skills needed in the job market. Again, you can use the overlapping circles to capture the idea that some activities may meet all three criteria, in which case this would point very strongly towards seeking employment where the client can use those skills.

For example: the client may love to cook and they may also be good at it. By contacting the local job centre or looking in local job advertisements, it would be possible to discover whether or not this is also a skill or trade where there are jobs available and skills needed in your area.

Variations

This exercise can lead into skills practice of situations in the home, in relationships, at work, among friends or in the community. It may also lead into skills practice around applying for work and workplace skills such as time management, task management and getting along with colleagues.

★

Worksheet: What Am I Good at and What Do I Love to Do?

Name: _____ **Date:** _____

It has often been observed that if you can work doing something you love to do, it does not really feel like work at all because you enjoy doing the work so much. Would you like to be in this position? If you are not quite there yet, it may mean giving some thought to the skills you have, what you like/love to do, and whether these skills overlap with jobs and job skills needed in your vicinity. This might also lead you to form goals about training or developing certain skills so you are more 'marketable' in the area where you live.

What am I good at? Here I can list the skills and roles I am good at in different aspects of my life:

Job skills and roles:

Social/friendship/life skills and roles:

Family and relationship skills and roles:

Self-management skills and roles:

What do I love to do?

Work-related activities and skills:

Social/friendship/life skills and activities:

Family and relationship skills and activities:

Self-management and self-care activities (example: looking after my health and/or appearance):

What skills, activities or roles listed in the two sections above are also needed in the workforce/job market?

Skills and roles listed above that are also needed by local employers:

Skills and roles listed above that are also needed by employers further away:

Skills and roles listed above that are also needed in the local economy, where there may not be enough employers (i.e. where I may need to become self-employed/start my own business):

Fill in the diagram below to see clearly where there is an overlap between what you are good at, what you love to do, and what skills are needed in the job market. Where are the overlaps? Are there any three-way overlaps? Does this diagram suggest any goal-setting that may be needed? For example, do you need to train or get further education or job skills in order to make your skills more marketable? Or is there already something you love to do and you never considered that it could be done as paid work? In general, what does this diagram lead you to think about how you live your life and apportion your time and effort?

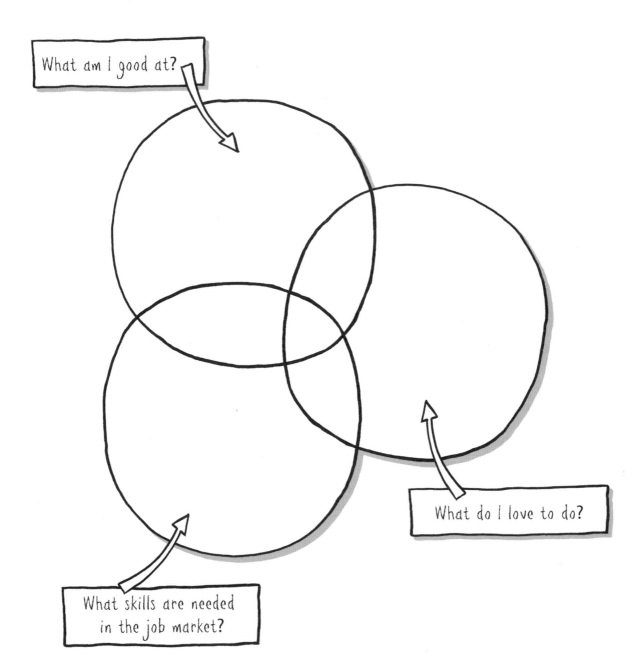

The road ahead: My new way of living plan

Motivation, relapse prevention, asking for help

Time: 2 hours

Materials: worksheet, paper

Aims

- To help the client develop a full and comprehensive *New Way of Living Plan*.

- To build a comprehensive and varied support network of people.

- To practise with the client appropriate cognitive, affective and behavioural coping strategies that work, including strategies for positively managing distressing feelings and situations.

- To understand risk factors for the client and discuss what to do in risky situations; to prepare strategies for coping with lapses and high-risk situations.

Method

Start by taking time to review work completed so far, including exercises from this book and other programmes or activities. The purpose is to review, reflect on learning, identify progress and consider areas that need further work. This is an opportunity to recognise and to celebrate any progress which has been made. Don't forget to include in this review a discussion about your relationship with the client and the process between you. Has this changed during the course of your work? Have you developed a greater trust and rapport? How have you dealt with 'bumps in the road' or miscommunications? What lessons can the client learn from this about whether it is possible to trust professionals? How might this help the client in forming future relationships?

When this process is completed, work through the worksheet *My New Way of Living Plan*. Use the questions as prompts to help the client to explore their motivation to build a new life and the pros and cons of re-offending.

A good plan for relapse prevention needs to balance a strengths-based approach with a realistic appraisal of potential risks and coping strategies. Use the table on the handout to prompt a discussion about likely risk factors. The table suggests the categories of risky thoughts, feelings, behaviours and risky people. Encourage the client to add any other ideas which seem relevant to them, such as risky places, activities, etc. Discuss with the client the idea that, by identifying potential risk factors for offending, he or she can then develop a range of strategies to deal with them if they arise in the future. Clients need to be aware of their own personal risk factors, understand why those factors are risky for them and have as many effective ways of dealing with them as possible.

Discuss coping strategies and how there can be many ways to deal with any given troubling situation. Explain that some coping strategies work in some situations and not in others, so it is essential to have a range of options. Some different types of coping could include things to focus the mind on other things (reading, television, radio, getting involved in a project), listening to music, meditation or simply thinking about things that bring pleasure, like the people who matter most to you.

If appropriate, you could use the skills practice technique to practice any *interpersonal or intrapersonal skills* which are linked to relapse prevention (e.g. dealing with authority, asking for help).

Use the questions on the worksheet to prompt discussion and reflection about the client's plans for the future.

Variations

Where appropriate and needed, facilitators can use projective methods, images or stick figure drawings and/or character creation in order to help the client understand the concepts in this exercise. For example, some clients will benefit from doing this exercise in a much more visual way, such as by drawing a 'Road Map of My Past, Present and Future'. This road map could include a very wide variety of visual metaphors, as many as the imagination can create. For example, a motorway exit could represent leaving the positive life plan (i.e. by lapsing). A 'Danger, Men at Work' sign could represent a risky situation. A destination sign could point to a positive life goal. A 'Stop' sign could represent a coping strategy. A bridge could represent asking for help to get past a difficult obstacle. A car crash could represent re-offending. The list could go on and on.

Worksheet: My New Way of Living Plan

Name: _____ **Date:** _____

1. Motivation

How motivated am I to live the rest of my life in a fulfilling way that does not involve committing crimes? (Mark the line below with an 'X' where your motivation is.)

⟵⟶

Low motivation   **High motivation**

- What are my reasons for placing the mark where I have?

- What are my beliefs about whether I deserve to be living a fulfilling life? Is there anything which holds me back from this? If so, what? Can I change it? If I can't change it, how can I cope with it?

2. Consequences

- If I reoffend, what will the consequences be for me? And for others?

- If I don't reoffend, what will the consequences be for me? And for others?

3. Risk factors and coping strategies

Please redraw this table, and personalise it.

	RISKY THOUGHTS	RISKY FEELINGS	RISKY BEHAVIOUR	RISKY PEOPLE
Brief description				
Why are they risky?				
Past coping strategies?				
Future coping strategies?				
Anything else?				

4. New Way of Living Plan: The basics

	NOW	FUTURE PLANS
My accommodation: Where? Who with?		
My money		
My education, training, or employment		
My leisure activities		
Any statutory supervision requirements or restrictions?		
Anything else?		

5. My personal needs and wants

- The personal needs or wants I met through my offending were...
- In the future, I plan to meet these needs by...
- I will check that my New Life is satisfying me by...
- If I find that I'm becoming dissatisfied, then I will...

6. Coping if I'm struggling

	THOUGHTS	FEELINGS	BEHAVIOURS	ATTITUDES	SITUATIONS
Old patterns when I was struggling					
Signs that I might be slipping					
Things I can do if I notice I'm struggling					
What would other people notice if I was struggling?					

7. Relationships

- What have I learned that I need to continue to develop in my relationships, with family, friends, colleagues, my children (if I have any)?

8. Other obstacles

- What other problems am I aware of, which I want to keep working on? (e.g. substance misuse, smoking, issues of unresolved loss or trauma?) What do I plan to do about them?

9. Support network

- Who are the people who know about my offending, and want to help me to build my New Life?

- Which organisations are there to help me (e.g. voluntary sector, probation, GP, housing provider)?

- How will I make sure that their contact details are on hand should I need them?

10. Keeping busy

- How do I plan to spend my time, during the day, in the evenings, at the weekends, during public holidays?

- If I have spare time, how can I use it to build up my relationship with the community (e.g. volunteering, keeping in touch with my support network)?

11. Anything else important to me?

The *Wheel of Life* revisited, and reminder cards

Values, self-identity, reinforcing New Me, validating change

Time: 1 hour to 2 hours

Materials: first version of *Wheel of Life*, worksheet, paper

Aims

- To help the client to revisit the *Wheel of Life* (see p.78), paying attention to any progress made, and any areas which still need to be worked on.

- To help the client to set new goals in relevant segments of the Wheel.

- To help the client create reminder cards (or similar tools) to serve as prompts and memory aids.

- To better understand how motivated and able the client is to make positive changes, and how much they can promote the achievement of hopes and goals with realistic and actionable plans and life skills.

Method

This exercise should be completed in tandem with the *New Way of Living Plan* (p.175). They complement each other, and they can be done in either order.

If the client filled in the *Wheel of Life* in a previous session, it will help to have the original copy available. If the client has not done this exercise, then the first step is to support them to complete it from the point of view of themselves at the time they were just starting this programme of sessions with you.

Having established what the *Wheel of Life* looked like in the past, you can now encourage the client to fill it in again, from the point of view of the present day. You can either offer the client a new blank worksheet to fill in, or you could ask the client to use a different coloured pen to write on the original sheet, with the colours representing the different points in time.

Having filled in the Wheel from the point of view of the present day, use open and Socratic questions to encourage the client to speak about areas where there has been progress. You could use the *invitational approach* (see Chapter 2) to invite the client to offer themselves praise for the progress made.

For an advanced version of this exercise, put out two chairs, one to represent the past and one to represent the present. Ask the client to sit in each chair in turn, and speak from those different points of view about their satisfaction with the different segments of the Wheel. It can be very powerful for a client to hear themselves speak from the present-day chair about the progress they have made, and how it was achieved.

Now explain the idea of reminder cards using the worksheet about reminder cards. If available, give the client three or four cards of each colour – red, yellow and green – to use as reminder cards. They should be small enough to fit in an average wallet or purse. Generate some ideas of what they could write or draw on the cards that would be helpful, and note with the client that they can revise these cards in future.

Worksheet: The Wheel of Life Revisited

Name: _____ **Date:** _____

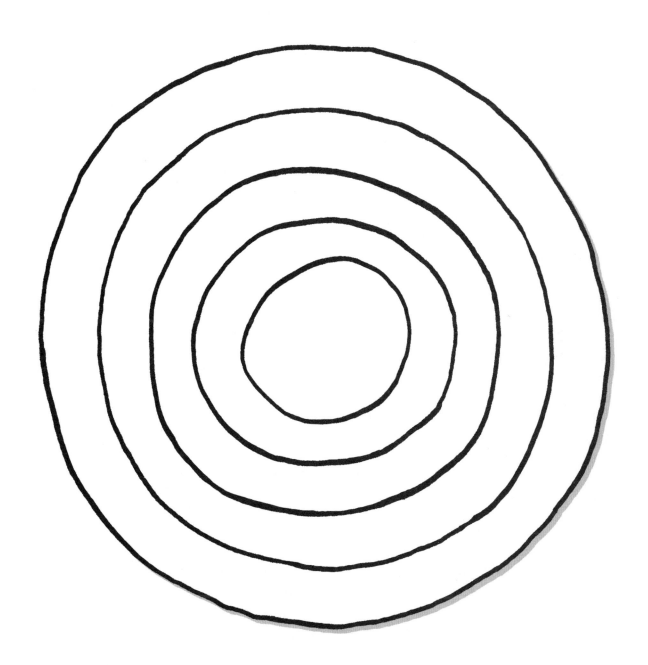

Worksheet: Reminder Cards

Name: _____ **Date:** _____

Reminder cards can be useful to sum up the progress you have made, and the things you have learned about what it important for you, in order to keep living a safe life you can be proud of.

Some people use these cards as 'In Case of Emergency' reminders, for example, who to call and under what circumstances to call them. Some people find it useful to discuss these cards with people from their support network. If you do this, it may be helpful to add the category of 'things you might notice if I am beginning to struggle'.

Try to summarise the key points from your *New Way of Living Plan*. Use different colours and use words, images, symbols that have a powerful meaning for you. If you use words, use your own, not those of other people. Try to use the following categories, and add any others which you think are meaningful for you.

	OLD ME (RED)	WARNING SIGN (YELLOW)	NEW ME (GREEN)
Thoughts			
Feelings/Moods			
Behaviours			
Strategies for coping			
Friends			
Intimate relationships			
Situations			

It is very important to keep reviewing your reminder cards. First of all, it can be very motivating to remind yourself of the progress you have made. If you refresh them from time to time, it will help to keep them relevant and at the forefront of your mind.

It might be of help to you to find somewhere to keep your reminder cards which is meaningful for you. For example, one person, whose offence had involved drink-driving, kept the cards in the glove box of her car (once she got her driving licence back!) to reinforce her determination never to commit a drink-drive offence again.

What has changed? Closing session

Self-reflection, positive ending, review, goal-setting

Time: 1 hour

Materials: worksheets from previous sessions, worksheet

Aims

- To help the client to complete this work in a positive way, and to focus on next steps.

- To help the client to plan how to use their reminder cards/*New Way of Living Plan* in practical ways.

- To reinforce the importance of the client's support network.

- To offer the client and the facilitator an opportunity to give feedback to each other about how they have experienced their working relationship.

Method

This exercise can be used either at the end of your period of working with the client, or after having completing a number of exercises from this book. Endings are as important as beginnings, and it is important to acknowledge the thoughts and feelings which might be experienced at this time. The client may have been through many moments of reflection during your work together, and may have experienced strong emotions and vulnerability. Sometimes, there can be feelings of loss, sadness, abandonment, fear or anger when a particular relationship ends, including professional relationships. This is partly because some types of ending can echo previous endings or separations that occurred earlier in our lives. Many clients will have experienced abrupt and unattuned endings of relationships in the past, so this is a chance to offer them a different experience. It is important to take time and acknowledge a potentially difficult or painful experience of ending, if it is there. Therefore, it is important to offer the client the chance to experience a compassionate and meaningful ending to the relationship.

The first part of this exercise is to review the content of your work together. Collect together the worksheets which have been completed during the sessions. Help the client review the work, noticing important points of progress, and reflecting on moments of challenge or insight. If available, and relevant, you could also review reports from other programmes or pieces of work. It will be very important for the client to have tangible objects/reminder cards/journals/portfolios to take away from your work together. It is important for the client to have some of the material in a form that they can review and keep safe. Use the questions from the *Reviewing the content of our work* section in the worksheet to guide this part of the exercise.

If at all possible, it is helpful to obtain feedback from the client's support network. For example, if it is safe and appropriate, it may be very motivational to be able to pass on positive feedback from the client's family and friends, as well as other professional contacts. The client would need to have given consent to you making contact, and do exercise caution in cases where the offences have occurred within the family (e.g. sexual abuse or domestic abuse).

The second part of the exercise is to reflect on your professional relationship, and how that has developed during your time working together. Many of the exercises in this book focus on the importance of expressing emotions within relationships, and it is good modelling to put that into practice. Of course, your relationship is a professional one, so certain emotions are inappropriate and off limits, but it remains useful to discuss how you worked together, as well as what you did.

Use the questions in *Reviewing the process of our work* and *Reviewing the emotions I have felt during this work* from the worksheet as the basis for this conversation. Choose the questions which seem relevant and appropriate for you and your client.

Variation

An alternative ending exercise is for you and the client can both take a piece of paper and draw around the outline of your hands. Write your name on the sheet, and then swop pieces of paper. Take a few minutes to write five comments, one in each finger space, to reflect things about each other which you have appreciated during your time working together. This exercise could be done out loud, or with you doing the writing, if that is more appropriate. If the client responds well to active exercises, there are a number of experiential ending exercises in Baim *et al.* (2002).

Letter-writing can be a powerful motivational tool at this point. For example, it can be useful if you write a letter to the client. This can summarise the progress you have observed, and serve as a further motivating tool. If the worker has been able to make contact with members of the client's support network, then their positive comments could be included as well. Feedback from other professionals and workers could be included as well. The letter can be read during the session and kept by the client.

Similarly, it may be useful to ask the client to write a letter to their future self, in one year's time, focusing on their progress so far and what they hope to achieve in the next year. The facilitators can ensure that they get this letter in 12 months. An advanced version of this exercise would be asking the client to speak as though they were themselves in 12 months' time. Use the technique of interviewing in role to ask questions about how they overcame challenges in the 'previous' 12 months, what their main achievements have been, plus positive feedback they would like to offer to themselves. You can write this down, and give a copy to the client to keep.

Worksheet: What Have I Learned?

Name: _____ Date: _____

Reviewing the content of our work

- What has been most useful during this work together?

- What has been most challenging about this work?

- What are three important things which I have learned?

- What are three things which I need to continue to work on?

- What are my goals for this week? This month? This year?

- What would I have liked to spend more time on?

- Which topics would I have liked to explore which weren't included in our work together?

Reviewing the process of our work

- What have I most appreciated about the way we have worked together?

- What positive praise can I offer you?

- What could I encourage you to think about doing more of, or doing differently?

- What analogy would best describe our working relationship (e.g. pulling teeth, climbing up a mountain and enjoying the view from the top, co-piloting a plane)?

Reviewing the emotions I have felt during this work

- What positive feelings have I experienced during our work together?

- What negative feelings have I experienced during our work together?

- How do I feel about the end of this work?

- Is there any unfinished business? Are there any conversations which I'd like to have?

APPENDIX 1
Learning and Reflections Journal

Below is a reflections journal form that can be duplicated and used after every session. This is meant to assist integration of the material and to promote maximum learning.

For clients who cannot read or write, you can go through the form together or find a colleague or someone in the client's support or professional network who could help them.

There is much scope for adapting the mode of recording, depending on what suits the client. Some clients use audio recording, collage, drawings and other means to create a meaningful journal.

Facilitators may wish to assemble these journal sheets into a portfolio, folder or a binding in order to preserve the journals as a user-friendly reminder of the client's work.

Worksheet: Learning and Reflections Journal

Name: _____ **Date:** _____

Adapt the questions as you see fit. Record your thoughts and reflections in a way that suits you and that you can share with your facilitator.

What did we do in today's session? What was it about?	
What is one main thing I learned from this session?	
How can I use what I have learned?	
What do I need help with?	
What do I want to learn next?	
Anything else I need to say or record?	

APPENDIX 2
Templates for End-of-Session Recording and Progress Report/Final Report

This appendix offers two templates for you to use and adapt as needed.

The first template is a form you can use at the end of each session in order to track progress, highlight areas that need to be addressed further with the client and identify immediate needs and risks. The form is also a useful tool for supporting the supervision of your practice and it can inform the development and modification of the way you deliver your sessions.

The second template is a report form that can be used as an interim report of the client's progress, or as a report at the end of your work with the client. This report is meant to be informed by some or all of the following:

- session records
- out-of-session work
- assessments and other information from professionals and volunteers who are familiar with the client and have a significant role in relation to the client
- information from family, friends and associates
- other assessment tools, such as psychometric measures, as used.

Please see the opening pages of Chapter 2 for more discussion of assessment, planning, recording and report writing.

End of Session Record Form

This is a suggested format for the end-of-session record for facilitators to use at the end of each session.

Unless there are exceptional reasons, this form should be written so that it can be shared with the client.

END OF SESSION RECORD FORM			
Client's name			
Date of session		Session length	
Conducted by		Are these notes written to be shared with client? Yes/No	
Purpose/theme of session			
Client's participation/interest/behaviour during session			
Level of participation/cooperation (rate 1–10)			
Understanding of learning points (rate 1–10)			
Session content			
Progress evidenced or general observations about the process during the session			
Action needed/out-of-session assignment given			
Any immediate risk issues to be communicated immediately to appropriate staff/agencies, followed by written confirmation			
Date of next session			

Progress Report/Final Report

This report template can be used for progress reports and final reports.

Name: _____ **Date:** _____

Person(s) completing this report:

Is this a *progress report* or a *final report*? (Circle one)

Part 1

Rate on a scale of 1 to 10 the client's progress/participation in relation to the following themes or exercises:

EXERCISE AND/ OR THEME	DATE(S) ON WHICH THE EXERCISE WAS UNDERTAKEN	RATING 1–10 (1 IS LOW/ POOR, 10 IS HIGH/ EXCELLENT)	COMMENTS ON PROGRESS MADE, STRENGTHS, LIMITATIONS, RESPONSIVITY ADJUSTMENTS, WORK STILL NEEDED, CHANGES NEEDED TO MAKE THE WORK MORE EFFECTIVE AND LASTING, ETC.
Name of exercise:			
Name of exercise:			
Name of exercise:			
Name of exercise:			
Name of exercise:			
Name of exercise:			
Name of exercise:			
Name of exercise:			
Name of exercise:			
Name of exercise:			
Name of exercise:			

Overall cooperation with treatment/ rapport with facilitators demonstrated			
Overall ability to make use of and integrate the work undertaken on the programme so far			

Part 2: Progress or otherwise in relation to dynamic risk

Progress evidenced (include motivation, strengths, progress, concerns, risk issues, gaps in learning)

PSYCHOLOGICAL AND MENTAL HEALTH ASPECTS

- Extreme minimisation or denial
- Attitudes that support or condone offending
- Problems with self-awareness
- Problems with stress or coping

- Problems related to unresolved trauma or loss
- Personality disorder
- Major mental illness
- Problems with substance abuse
- Violent or suicidal ideation

SOCIAL ASPECTS

- Problems with intimate relationships
- Problems with non-intimate relationships

- Problems with employment
- Criminal lifestyle

ENGAGING IN THE PROCESS

- Problems with planning
- Problems with participation in sessions

- Problems with supervision

Part 3: Plan of action

Acute risk

RISK FACTORS EMERGING, AND/OR ACUTE RISK FACTORS THAT NEED MANAGEMENT NOW

(Include action that will be taken, when and by whom.)

RECOMMENDED ADJUSTMENTS

(Examples: extra sessions to help client complete out-of-session work, responsivity adjustments, moving to one-to-one work if in a group, or vice versa; liaison with other staff.)

APPENDIX 3
Internal Self-Regulation Skills and Suggested Scenarios for Practice

The skills and strategies outlined here are inspired by Goldstein (1988) and McGuire and Priestley (1981, 1987).

Skill: Being aware of my feelings and understanding that I have choices about how I act on my feelings

1. Stop and think: What is happening inside my body and mind? Where are the feelings and sensations? Am I experiencing a strong emotion, positive or negative? I notice the feelings but do not act on them. I use them as information that can inform but not dictate my actions.

2. Ask: Why am I feeling this way? Consider my options about how to deal with my feelings in a positive way. How can I challenge any of my automatic thoughts that could take me backwards, for example, 'This is hopeless, I give up'.

3. Which option can I use now? Check: Is this an option I will enjoy and/or one that will lead in a positive direction?

4. Act on my decision.

5. Give myself praise: I have made a positive decision and it has changed my mood and thinking. I value the choice, the activity and/or the benefits to me and other people.

Suggested skills practice scenarios

- You are alone in your room, and something happens that causes you to feel strong feelings. What is the 'something' that happens, and how will you respond?

- You are around other people and something causes you to feel difficult or painful feelings such as fear, anger, sadness, shock, grief, jealousy or resentment. What is the 'something' that happens, and how will you respond?

- You feel provoked by another person and begin to get agitated by their behaviour towards you or a person you care about, such as a friend.

- You do not receive the phone call/letter/ visit you have been expecting for several weeks. You have wanted the contact very strongly.

- You are alone in your room and feel funny, weird and generally bad and unsettling feelings and sensations from inside your body. Where are these sensations in your body? What are these sensations telling you?

Skill: Having compassion and forgiveness for my past mistakes (and for those of other people)

1. I recognise that I am having thoughts and feelings of shame, regret, remorse, self-hatred, self-doubt or other feelings related to having committed offences or other actions. If I really feel like I am suffering, I notice this and treat this seriously.

2. I consider why such thoughts and feelings are useful or not useful. I do not judge the thoughts and feelings, but try to see the value of them. For example, how can regret lead me to make better decisions in the future?

3. Decide if I can forgive myself for past mistakes and make a new start. Imagine what a caring friend would say to me. How would they give me support? Would they help me to put it in perspective? Would they empathise with me?

4. Decide if I can make a new start.

5. Act on my decision.

6. Give myself praise, and think about whether or not I can be as forgiving to other people for their mistakes.

Suggested skills practice scenarios

- You are alone in your room, and you remember your offence(s). You feel embarrassed and ashamed, and other feelings. You are troubled by these difficult and painful feelings.

- You are alone in your room, and feeling hopeless because your criminal record seems to make it impossible to ever clear your name and live a good life. It all seems rather pointless.

- You hear that another inmate is being released because they have made good progress. You have thoughts and feelings of self-hatred that you are not seen to have progressed as much.

- You hear a story on the TV news about a crime similar to yours, where the victim says 'these people are a menace to society' about the criminals. You feel a jolt of shame, and begin to spiral downwards emotionally.

Skill: Relaxing when I am stressed

1. Decide if you need to relax.

2. Do the exercise when you're not in a rush:

- Loosen tight clothing and remove glasses.

- Make sure your body is completely supported by a chair, bed or the floor.

- Take three slow, deep breaths.

- Close your eyes.

- Pay attention to the difference in sensations between relaxed and tense muscles.

- Breathe in when you tense a muscle and out when you relax. When you tighten one part of your body, count to three, and relax.

Legs and feet

- Tighten your leg muscles, then relax.

- Press your heels into the floor, then relax.

- Point your foot away from your face, then relax.

- Point your foot towards your face, then relax.

Torso

- Tighten your stomach and buttocks, then relax.

- Tighten the muscles in your back and upper torso, then relax.

- Shrug your shoulders, then relax.

Arms

- Clench your hands into fists, then relax.

- Bend your hands at the wrist pointing your fingers straight up, then relax.

- Try to touch your shoulders with your fists, then relax.

Head

- Press your chin as close to your chest as possible, then relax.

- Roll your neck to the right and then to the left, then relax.

- Press your head back as far as it will go, then relax.

- Wrinkle up your forehead and raise your eyebrows, then relax.
- Screw your eyes up tightly, then relax.
- Wrinkle your nose tightly, then relax.
- Clench your jaw, then relax.
- Purse your lips together tightly, then relax.

All over your body

- Tighten every muscle you can at the same time, then relax. Do this several times.
- Ask yourself how you feel. Finish by spending a few minutes breathing deeply and notice how relaxed you have become.

Suggested skills practice scenarios

- You feel nervous prior to seeing someone important and close to you. You practise relaxing.
- You are angry or upset with a friend/ partner/family member/someone else, and you want to relax to give you some peace.
- You are about to do something scary, for example, giving a talk, doing a job interview or having a difficult conversation. You do some relaxation beforehand.
- You have had a very bad day. You are tired and irritable. You decide to intervene before you risk being abusive to someone else (e.g. by snapping at them). You find some time to relax using the above suggestions.

Skill: Understanding what other people are thinking and feeling

1. I recognise that, while I have thoughts and feelings and priorities, so does the other person/the other people, and these thoughts, feelings and priorities may be very different from my own. I recognise their right to have different thoughts, feelings and priorities.

2. I try to see the value of the other person's point of view.

3. I think about and decide how I will respond, based on my deeper understanding of other people and their point of view.

4. I act on my decision.

5. I give myself praise for making my best effort to understand other people's point of view.

Suggested skills practice scenarios

- You are alone in your room and recall memories from long ago, when you were hurt by someone else. The incidents were upsetting events and left you confused. You try to understand the thoughts and feelings that must have been driving the other person's/people's behaviour.
- You feel provoked by something another person says.
- You do not receive the phone call/letter/ visit you have been expecting for several weeks. You have wanted the contact very strongly.
- You are very keen to start a friendship/ relationship with someone, but they make it clear they are not interested in a friendship/relationship with you.
- A friend says they will meet you 'one day soon', but cancels on three separate occasions at short notice. They explain this is due to family or work crises, or being ill.
- You are afraid to go into work today because – through an unfortunate coincidence – some of your colleagues have become aware of your criminal record.
- You have kept your past offences hidden from certain people in your extended family. You become aware that they have discovered your offence history, and you are going to see them later today at a family gathering. You know they will be very upset with you, but you do not fear physical violence (as long as no one is drinking alcohol).

Skill: Understanding why I think, feel and do what I do

1. Recognise that I am experiencing powerful thoughts and/or feelings. Or, recognise that I have behaved in a way that was self-defeating or harmful, abusive or insensitive to others.

2. Ask myself why I may be experiencing these thoughts and feelings, or why I acted as I did. Look to the recent, middle and distant past for clues.

3. Decide if my current thoughts, feelings and actions are being influenced too much by similar situations in the past, and whether or not I need to generate a new, more adequate response in these new circumstances.

4. Act on my decision.

5. Give myself praise for making my best effort to understand why I think, feel and act the way I do.

Suggested skills practice scenarios

- You shout at another person in anger, and later you think about why you did that, because it just ended up getting you into trouble.

- You take part in a series of practical jokes with other people, and the jokes are all played on one person. In the end, the person complains, and you take time to think about why you continued to do the practical jokes even after the person looked very upset by them.

- You keep making promises to yourself to save money each week, but then you break your promise each week and spend your money on 'junk' as you put it. You take time to think about why you do this.

- You do not receive the phone call/letter/visit you have expected for several weeks. You have wanted the contact very strongly. You write a very angry letter, full of blame, to the other person. Just before you post it, you pause to think about what you have written and why you think and feel the way you do. This also gives you time to think about the thoughts, feelings and priorities of the other person.

- You feel a need to be near a certain person. You pause and ask yourself why.

- You recognise that you have a very strong 'inner critic' and ask yourself these questions: How often are you critical of yourself? What do you typically criticise in yourself? Why do you think you are so critical of yourself? Does the voice of your inner critic remind you of someone (such as a teacher, partner, friend, parent, etc.)? Does the inner critic do any good things for you or help you in any way? What harmful things does the inner critic do to you? Is your inner critic fair, objective, balanced and caring? If not, why should you believe the inner critic?

Skill: Understanding why other people think, feel and do what they do

1. I recognise that while I sometimes experience powerful thoughts and feelings, or behave in ways that are not always 'perfect,' other people are the same (i.e. 'nobody's perfect').

2. I ask what I would think and feel in that person's shoes, so to speak. I really think it through.

3. Based on my reflection, I decide on a response.

4. I act on this decision.

5. I give myself praise for making my best effort to understand why other people think, feel and act the way they do.

Suggested skills practice scenarios

- Another person is acting in a way that angers you and other people. You try to understand why they are doing this and the thoughts and feelings behind their actions.

- You discover that another person has been saying things about you behind your back. You consider why they may be doing this and the thoughts and feelings behind their actions.

- A family member does not come to visit you when they keep saying they will. You try to figure out the reasons behind this.

- A person you have met via the internet stops emailing as soon as they learn you have a criminal record. You think about their possible reasons for doing this and the thoughts and feelings behind their actions.

- A certain person seems to want to be your friend, and they do not take your hints that you do not want to be their friend. You stop to think about why they are doing this and the thoughts and feelings behind their actions.

- You offer friendship to another person, and they turn their back on you. You stop to think about why they might be acting in this way and the thoughts and feelings behind their actions.

- During a very rushed and stressful day, a person in authority briefly shows insensitivity towards you. You take a moment to consider why they may have acted in this way and the thoughts and feelings behind their actions.

Skill: Managing and controlling my impulses

1. Recognise that I am feeling a strong impulse to do something. What is the impulse?

2. Ask myself what is behind the impulse. Is it a feeling? A thought? A physical urge or need or discomfort? Why do I think I have this impulse?

3. I weigh up the pros and cons of acting on that impulse.

4. I make a decision and act on that decision.

5. I praise myself for not just acting on impulse, but considering options and consequences before acting.

Suggested skills practice scenarios

- During a sporting match, a player from the other team insults you. You feel the impulse to attack them, and you take a moment to think about this impulse.

- You discover that another person has been saying things about you behind your back. You want to go and get revenge, but first you pause to consider what is behind the impulse.

- A family member does not come to visit you when they keep saying they will. You have an impulse to call them and shout down the phone at them. You pause to consider your impulse calmly and carefully.

- You receive disappointing news. Your impulse is get angry and protest, and blame other people. You pause to consider your impulse and to identify the best strategy.

Skill: Managing my anxiety

1. I recognise that I feel anxious and am experiencing physical symptoms.

2. I ask myself what is behind the anxiety. Is there a reason? Or is it mysterious? What is my best guess about what this connects to? I realise that it might be a random association such as a voice, a TV programme, something overheard, a shape, a movement, an image, a smell, a taste, etc.

3. I use a prepared strategy to decrease my physiological arousal and anxiety. (Facilitator note: The client may benefit from practising simple behavioural techniques and self-talk that will help them to regain control and become calmer. Sometimes, this may include graduated exposure using timed hyperventilation and talk-down/verbalised self-soothing, e.g. 15 seconds, then 30, then 45 seconds of

hyperventilation, to simulate the effects of anxiety/panic attack.)

4. I give myself praise for managing my anxiety in a positive way.

Suggested skills practice scenarios

- Someone insults you and it makes you furious. You pause to use one of your anxiety management strategies.

- You feel very anxious just before an important staff meeting which is about you.

- A family member does not come to visit you when they said they would. You feel anxious that they will never come to see you.

- You are watching television and are suddenly struck by a wave of anxiety. It takes you by surprise, and you feel afraid. You use a strategy to calm yourself and gain some perspective on the anxiety and what triggered it.

Skill: Problem-solving

1. I recognise that there is a problem and it needs solving.

2. I try to look at the problem from all sides. I consider what I am certain about, what may be completely guess work and what I need more information about in order to form a complete picture.

3. I consider strategies for addressing the problem, including what the short and long-term consequences would be of varying solutions. I consider the consequences for me and the other person/people. I consider if doing nothing – or taking a 'wait and see' approach – may be the best solution.

4. I make a decision and act on that decision.

5. I give myself praise for not just acting on impulse, but considering options and consequences before acting.

Suggested skills practice scenarios

- You are on unescorted leave and have five minutes to get back to the prison/hostel/hospital. You are too far away to walk there in time and you have no money for a taxi. Your mobile phone has no battery charge left.

- A friend of yours has become a scapegoat. People make hurtful comments and it is beginning to take its toll on your friend. You decide to express your point of view and try to solve the problem, which you see as unfair.

- Several people are trying to provoke you into an outburst by throwing stones against your window. You consider your options to solve the problem.

- You are given £10 too much change by a busy and distracted shopkeeper. You go into this shop regularly.

Note: This problem-solving skill is recommended for non-recurring situations. With recurring problems, it may be more useful to use the more comprehensive STOP-MAP approach to problem-solving (see p.149).

Skill: Managing my anger

1. I stop and count to 10. What is making me angry? Is there another way to see this situation? Am I perceiving it accurately?

2. I think about my options in the situation. What are different ways I can manage or express my anger?

3. I tell the person why I am angry, or, I walk away for now in order to give myself time to think. I find a way to express my anger in an appropriate way. If needed, I do a relaxation exercise.

4. I give myself praise for dealing appropriately with my anger. When I am calm, I think over the situation and ask if I can do anything better next time.

Suggested skills practice scenarios

- You discover that your partner has spent more money than the two of you can afford. When you challenge them about this, they call you 'Scrooge'.

- Your friend was supposed to meet you but did not turn up. You are very disappointed because it meant you missed an important event that you really wanted to attend.

- Your child has been playing in the street and has deliberately scratched the paint on your car.

- At work, a colleague has attributed blame for someone else's error to you, and the boss gives you a verbal warning because of this.

Skill: Reasoning through a moral dilemma

1. I recognise that there is a dilemma. For example, I want this but B wants that. Or, when paying attention only to my immediate needs and desires, I want to do X, but my best values tell me to do Y.

2. I think about the situation from all sides. I get the full facts and think about my choices. I think about the short- and long-term consequences for me and the other person/people (and society as a whole) based on the choices I generate.

3. I ask for help or advice if I need to.

4. I make a decision and act on it.

5. I give myself praise for dealing with the dilemma in the best way I could.

Suggested skills practice scenarios

- You have begun to form a relationship with someone and sexually, it has not yet progressed beyond kissing. You both have very good feelings towards each other and you both want to progress the relationship. You feel that you should tell the person about your criminal record, but you are afraid of the consequences, that is, they may want to end the relationship.

- You want to play in/attend an important sporting match, but this conflicts with a very important family event.

- You accidentally scratch your neighbour's car and then walk away. Later, the neighbour asks you if you saw anything. (Would it make a difference if you knew there was CCTV footage?)

- Your friend is feeling suicidal and asks you not to tell anyone. You are worried about them.

- You become aware that a friend/family member is bringing stolen goods back to where you are renting a room in their house. If you leave you will have nowhere to stay.

- You find a wallet in the street with £250 cash in it, and there is plenty of ID for the owner of the wallet.

- You are working as a mechanic and are desperate to keep the job. You are working with another mechanic who accidentally cracks the exhaust manifold while working on the engine. (It is expensive to replace.) Your colleague pleads with you to back him up when he tells the customer that the manifold was already cracked and that they (the customer) will have to pay for it. The boss asks you if that is true. (Or, think of any similar workplace scenario that fits a work environment relevant to you.)

- You are living in a hostel, and your roommate has smuggled alcohol into the room. This is a serious violation and could get you both excluded from the hostel. You try to get them to remove the alcohol but they tell you to mind your own business.

Skill: Dealing with boredom

1. I recognise that I feel bored.

2. I think of things I have enjoyed doing in the past that are legal and pro-social. Or, I think of something new that I would like

to learn how to do. I focus on pro-social alternatives and I include other people if appropriate. I consider community/further/adult education classes, hobby clubs, work training, ramblers associations, art classes, etc. I look at resources in the community, including libraries, local government resources, volunteer groups, etc.

3. I decide which one I might be able to do now that would be a good decision for me and other people in the short and long term. I make sure that this is an activity that I will really enjoy and (where relevant) I clear the activity with my probation officer/key worker.

4. I start the activity.

5. I give myself praise that I have made a positive decision, and I recognise the change in my mood and thinking. I value the positive activity.

Suggested skills practice scenarios

- You are unemployed and sitting alone in your flat. You have very little money, and no friends. You are bored.

- You are very bored and lonely and feel tempted to go back to an offending behaviour or a behaviour that was a part of your offending pattern.

- You are working in a factory doing a mundane and repetitive job which gives you little satisfaction and does not challenge your mind. You do not have workmates around you that you feel you can have a laugh and a joke with.

- You are sitting alone in a pub. Everyone around you seems to be in groups of friends. No one is talking to you. You have nothing else to do.

Skill: Dealing with rejection/failure/disappointment

1. I recognise that I feel this way because of rejection/failure/disappointment. I think about what has happened to cause me to feel rejected/like a failure/disappointed. I try hard to get the facts straight and to understand my role in the sequence of events.

2. I tell myself: 'Everyone feels rejected sometimes. It's not the end of the world.' I decide if my feelings of rejection are warranted. I ask myself if this is more about me or more about the other person.

3. Do I leave well enough alone? Build bridges? Change my behaviour? I decide how to best deal with this rejection/failure/disappointment. For example, I consider whether I will try to improve my interactions with the other person, talk with the other person about their behaviour and mine, or leave the other person alone and manage my feelings on my own or with the help of other people. An option: I do an activity that I know will help me feel more positive. I make a decision and act on it.

4. I give myself praise for handling rejection/failure/disappointment in a mature manner.

Suggested skills practice scenarios

- You receive a rejection letter from a job you have applied for. You have been interviewed and were told at the interview that you did have the appropriate qualifications.

- You have asked a man/woman that you know out for a drink. They have turned you down politely but firmly.

- You try to join a conversation among some people in the pub. They turn away and continue their conversation, ignoring you.

- A man/woman you have been seeing for several months tells you that they no longer want to be in a relationship with you.

- You are in the common room at your hostel. Another resident comes in and asks someone else to play snooker, ignoring you. (If this example is not one you can relate to, think of a similar situation that is closer to one you could face.)

Skill: Recognising and coping with lapses

1. I recognise that I am experiencing a lapse, that is, a thought, a feeling, a response or a behaviour that is part of my offending cycle or that can lead me back into a full relapse (an offence). I am realistic and honest with myself and I try to identify the lapse as soon as I possibly can. I recognise that lapses are common, that many things can trigger them, and that they can be controlled. Having a lapse does not mean that I have not changed – it just means that I am still working on it.

2. I take action at the earliest possible opportunity and I do not let the situation get worse. I recognise that the longer the lapse continues, the harder it is to intervene and stop the full relapse. I take control of the potential lapse, using any of a wide range of self-talk and behavioural strategies. For example, I might say to myself, 'Stop!' and get fully absorbed in a positive and distracting activity.

3. I give myself praise that I was able to control and manage a lapse and a potential relapse.

Suggested skills practice scenarios

- You are watching television and a 'true crime' programme is advertised as coming up next. You know from previous experience that these programmes tend to make you feel bad about yourself. What will you do?

- A person you knew before your arrest attempts to get you to come back to crime. What will you do?

- You are feeling like you deserve more money and possessions and you want to impress others. You have thoughts about committing crime…

- You are living in the community and you are tempted to buy alcohol. You committed your offence while intoxicated with alcohol.

- What situations can you think of that would represent you at the start of a potential re-offending cycle? What locations and situations are potentially risky for you? What are your early warning signs or higher risk situations? Consider them one at a time. How might you deal with them at the earliest possible moment? Why is it dangerous to 'just test' yourself (i.e. to put yourself in a high-risk situation)?

Skill: Setting goals and sticking to them

1. I ask myself: 'What do I want to achieve, and why?' I think about my 'approach goals,' that is, positive goals I want to achieve.

2. I consider what I need to achieve my goal.

3. I check whether the goal is realistic and I break the goal down into mini-steps towards the goal.

4. I put the plan into action.

5. I praise myself when a mini-step is achieved. Then I keep going.

Suggested skills practice scenarios

- You have moved into a new area and are isolated. You decide that you want to take a class in a subject that interests you or that you will find useful.

- You want to lose weight/stop smoking/start exercising/eat a better diet. You begin to think of a plan after you recognise that only you can really effect this change.

- You have been unemployed for a long time and you decide that you want to seek work.

- At work, you decide that you would like to better yourself and go for promotion.

APPENDIX 4
Social and Interpersonal Skills and Suggested Scenarios for Practice

The outlines of the 'micro-skills' for many of these skills are adapted from Goldstein (1988).

Skill: Talking with people in authority

- I listen carefully to the request/demand.

- I ask questions about anything that I do not understand.

- I consider if the instruction is safe and within my ability/job description. If I need to clarify, I repeat the instruction to the other person or to myself.

- I follow the instructions, unless there is a good reason not to. (What are some good reasons not to? What are not good reasons?)

Suggested skills practice scenarios

- Your boss/manager asks you to undertake a task you have not done before.

- Your instructor/teacher asks you to do a homework assignment, and you need clarification.

- A police officer stops you in your car and asks you to take a breath test because they suspect you are intoxicated. Or, the police stop you because your car has a broken brake light.

- The benefits agency asks you to come to their office to explain your claim form which they are querying.

- The assistant warden at your hostel asks you to complete a diary to account for your whereabouts at 15-minute intervals throughout your waking hours.

- A police officer visits your home unannounced and asks to look through your personal possessions. You have previously signed an agreement that the police can do this from time to time as part of your license/court-imposed restrictions. Or, the police have a warrant to do this.

- You are on a train and the conductor tells you your ticket is not valid on this train. (You have made an honest mistake and thought it was the right train.) You must either get off the train or pay the full fare again. You are on a tight schedule and need to get to your destination on time.

Skill: Disclosing my offence to a friend/family member/ employer/new partner

- I think about and decide the reasons why I should share this information with the other person. I consider the potential consequences of making this disclosure (both positive and negative).

- I consider what to say.

- I rehearse how to say what I need to say. I rehearse what to say and do if there is a negative reaction. I rehearse how to give the other person time and space to consider their response.

- I find an appropriate time and place, and tell the other person what I intended to tell them about my past.

- I listen to the other person's response. Where appropriate, I give the other person time to think about what I have told them. I agree when I will next talk with them.

- I give myself praise for being honest and strong enough to face my fear. I feel good that I have respected the other person. If I experience rejection as a result, I will cope with that and see the other person's point of view.

Suggested skills practice scenarios

- You are being interviewed for a job for which you are qualified and for which there are no special restrictions. The interviewer asks you if you have a criminal record.

- You have recently begun a relationship, which has not yet involved full sexual intercourse. But you have both reached the stage where a full sexual relationship is being wished for. You have both shared a range of experiences together. You are considering whether or not to disclose your previous offending.

- You are with a friend and you are aware that this friend knows something about your offending history. You decide to bring it up in conversation, in order to clear the air and move on.

Skill: Asking for help/Talking about my problems

1. I ask myself, 'Can I do this alone?' If not:

2. I consider who I could ask for help. I choose a person who I think will offer constructive feedback and assistance.

3. I consider what I will say and how I will ask for help.

4. I ask for help in a clear and polite way.

5. I listen to the response. If the person agrees to help and their help is acceptable to me, I act upon the advice/assistance. If the requested help is not offered, I decide if I can or should ask someone else for help.

6. I give myself praise for being able to ask for and accept help.

Suggested skills practice scenarios

- You have formed a relationship with a person who does not know of your offences. You want help in deciding how to tell them.

- A good friend of yours has suffered a setback/bereavement, and you are not sure what to say to them. You decide to ask your partner/friend/counsellor for advice on what to say.

- At work, you have been given a task to do that you do not quite understand. You decide to ask for help.

- You are feeling very low, or you are getting into a high-risk mood. You decide to ask for help.

- You want to apply for a job but need help putting together a CV. You are at the job centre and there is someone there who can help.

Skill: Resisting pressure from others/temptation to offend

1. I recognise that I am in a high-risk situation. I stop and think of what the consequences of an action might be.

2. I remind myself that I do not want to commit any offences. I consider my options, for example to avoid the situation, control my thoughts, feelings and actions in the situation, or escape the situation if the offence could be committed right now.

3. I decide on an option and put it into practice. If this involves explaining to another person what my decision is, I do that using clear and direct language.

4. I give myself praise for recognising the high-risk situation and intervening appropriately.

Suggested skills practice scenarios

- You are in the pub and someone offers to sell you what are clearly stolen goods.

- You walk past a parked car that has a window down. Someone has left their wallet on the seat in clear view.

- You bump into some people you used to commit crimes with, and they pressure you to get involved in a crime again with them.

- You are out late at night and you see a house with the window left open. You can see valuables within easy reach of the window.

- You are in a situation very much like other situations where you have committed crimes in the past. What is the situation? What will you do?

Skill: Saying 'no'

1. I listen to the other person's request politely and attentively. I ask for further information to help me decide: 'Can you say more about what this will involve?'

2. I decide whether I want to say yes or no to the request.

3. If I decide to say no to their request, I think of my reason for saying no.

4. I explain to the other person in a friendly and confident way that I cannot do what they are asking. I do not have to make excuses or invent lies (e.g. 'I will be out', or 'I have an appointment'). Nor do I need to apologise or give reasons for saying no. I am caring in the way I say 'no' – a refusal does not have to be expressed aggressively or in a blunt or hurtful way.

5. If the person persists in their request, I explain in a clear and friendly way that I have made my decision and would appreciate if they would not ask again. I stick to my decision.

6. I give myself credit for sticking to my decision. I pay attention to my self-talk about saying no, and the feelings I am left with.

Suggested skills practice scenarios

- A friend asks to borrow 10 pounds. You are not short of money, but this friend has not repaid money in the past.

- Your neighbour has asked you to give her a lift to pick up her clothes from her ex-boyfriend's flat. Your car is not taxed or insured so you cannot give her a lift.

- You are out at a pub after work with workmates. You are drinking soft drinks only, and someone who is buying a round of drinks insists you have a lager as it is the famous local brew. You no longer drink alcohol, and you want to stick to your policy.

- You are in any situation where you cannot, should not or do not want to say yes to a request or demand. Practise saying 'no'.

Commentary: Saying 'no' sounds easy. It is such a short word, so what could be difficult about it? Yet people frequently do feel anxious about saying 'no'. As we all know, there are situations where the prospect of saying 'no' makes us feel anxious, guilty and uncertain. It is often so much easier to say 'yes'. You may feel guilt at first about saying 'no'. And people may well not make it easy for you, particularly if they know which buttons to press to get you 'hooked'. But with practice it becomes easier to make an assertive refusal. You will survive the guilt and enjoy the reward of making a clear, honest decision. Staying assertive means staying in control.

Skill: Apologising

1. I think about and focus on what I want to apologise about.

2. I ask to speak with the other person. I make sure I have their attention and it is an appropriate time and place, free of distractions.

3. I apologise in a clear and friendly way.

4. I listen to the other person's response. I do not pressure them to accept my apology. I am prepared for them to respond in a variety of ways, some positive, some neutral or some negative.

5. I respond to any comments or questions they have in a clear, friendly and non-defensive way.

Suggested skills practice scenarios

• You arranged to meet a friend yesterday, and you forgot. You decide to talk to them directly in order to apologise.

• You forgot your partner's birthday and they have been very silent since then.

• Last night you said something very rude about your partner's friend/mother/father, and your partner was angry about your comment. You decide to apologise to your partner.

• You wrongly accuse your adolescent son/daughter of possessing a half-full bottle of alcohol you found under their bed. You later learn that an adult house guest of yours had left the bottle there. You decide to apologise.

• You did not do an important task at work that you had promised your boss you would do. (You simply forgot to do it.) You decide to apologise before your boss comes to you (they already know you did not do it).

• You spoke rudely to a friend/colleague yesterday, and it was clear from their reaction that they were offended. You decide to apologise.

• You are offered the opportunity, through a mediation and restorative justice project, to apologise to a victim of one of your crimes.

Commentary: Be prepared for the other person to respond in any number of ways to your apology. Be aware of your self-talk. Do you expect the apology to be accepted? Are you in any way pressuring the other person to accept your apology? If so, it is not a genuine apology.

Skill: Showing empathy

1. I think about how I feel about the situation. Am I shocked or scared of what has happened to the other person? Am I angry on their behalf? Do I feel helpless about the situation, or very sad?

2. I think about what I want to say to the person and I decide how and when I can talk to the person when they will have the time to talk with me.

3. I ask to talk with the person in a friendly and polite way.

4. I tell the person about my feelings/concerns in a friendly and polite way. I leave a space for them to respond if they wish to. I do not offer them advice and I do not in any way minimise what has happened by encouraging them to 'look at the bright side'. I let them know that I can see it is a painful or difficult time for them and that I am available if they ever need to talk about it.

5. I listen to the other person's reply and think of an appropriate response. I think about what the other person has said and try to see things from their point of view.

6. I continue to listen and respond, and end the conversation at an appropriate time, in an open way that allows for future communication.

Suggested skills practice scenarios

• Your friend was made redundant from his job recently, and he appears quiet and withdrawn, not his usual self. You want to communicate with him and help him.

- Your partner seems to be tired, stressed and irritable. You decide that you would like to talk with them about this.

- Your child has failed a test or exam that they were very much hoping to pass.

- Your friend has been very ill for several months, with no sign of improvement. You go to visit them.

- Your teenage child has just broken up with their boyfriend/girlfriend, and is heartbroken. You decide it is best to talk with them about it. Or, same scenario but it is your good friend, not your child.

- Your friend has suffered a bereavement of someone very close to them. You attended the funeral, and you go to visit them a week/several weeks later.

- Empathic communication about good news (not about a problem): your best friend has recently become engaged to be married. This is the first time you have seen them since they told you the news. Or, same scenario, except this time the 'news' is that your friend has got a job they were really hoping for after a long period of unemployment.

Skill: Dealing with someone else's anger or provocation

1. I listen to what the person has to say. I consider how I feel as they speak. Am I feeling challenged, angry, afraid, shocked, confused, etc?

2. I think about my choices. Some of my options include: walk away, keep listening, acknowledge and validate the other person's anger, particularly if they are angry because of something I have done, ask why they are angry, give them an idea to fix the problem, tell the other person in a friendly, polite and assertive way that I am leaving now/taking some time to think on my own, walk away for now, give it at least 20 minutes and return when I am confident that I can handle the situation.

3. I put into action my best choice.

4. I try to relax.

5. I give myself praise for handling the situation with careful thought and in the best way I could.

Suggested skills practice scenarios

- Your neighbour shouts abuse at you (e.g. regarding your behaviour/your appearance/your past offending/your race/your sexual orientation).

- You are in the pub and some people start to shout angrily at each other. Someone shouts at you, 'What are YOU looking at?!' And then they insult you and swear at you.

- You have driven into the back of the car in front. The driver of the other car is fuming.

- Your child has kicked their football through the neighbour's window. Your neighbour is shouting at your child and you.

- You have come home late. Your partner is very angry because you promised to be home early. They have cooked a special meal for you – your favourite – and it is now spoiled.

- A colleague at work is angry about the fact that you did not complete a task on time, meaning they had to stay late three nights in a row, costing them extra money for child care.

- Your supervisor is angry with you for missing an important deadline which has cost the company significantly. You had tried your best but could not meet the deadline. You recognise in hindsight that you could have asked for help to meet the deadline but did not.

Skill: Asking for feedback

1. I decide what I would like feedback about and why. What are my reasons for asking?

2. I decide who I would like the feedback from and in what form I would like the feedback.

3. I decide how I will ask for the feedback. Will it be by phone, letter, email, direct contact? I decide how I will respond whether the feedback is negative or positive.

4. I choose an appropriate time and ask for the feedback.

5. I listen carefully to the feedback. I respond to the feedback in a friendly and respectful way. If I need to, I ask for time to think about the feedback before responding.

6. I thank the person who gave the feedback. I think about and decide what I will do differently based on the feedback.

Suggested skills practice scenarios

- You have recently started a new job and would like feedback from your supervisor.

- You have agreed to be more considerate in your relationship. You want to know if your partner can see a difference in your behaviour and attitude.

- You are living in an institutional setting (prison, hospital, hostel, etc.) and you would like some feedback from the staff about your progress.

- In your group therapy programme, you have been more verbally active in the sessions and you would like some feedback from the facilitator(s) and/or the other members of the group.

Skill: Managing my feelings and stating my views when I feel insulted or ignored

1. I consider what I am feeling in the situation and what my options are.

2. I decide the best time and place to make my views known, if that is my decision.

3. I state my concerns or point of view in a friendly, polite and assertive way.

4. I listen carefully to the person's reply, and I respond to them respectfully.

5. If I need to, I ask for time to think about the feedback before responding.

6. I thank the person, if appropriate. I give myself praise for handling the situation in a mature way.

Suggested skills practice scenario

- You are applying for a job, and the person receiving your application makes an unwarranted assumption about you that you perceive as an insult.

- You are among friends who have known you a long time, and someone makes an unthinking remark that 'a leopard never changes their spots', implying that you are bound to commit crimes again. You perceive this as an insult and it makes you angry.

- You are out with a group of friends and your partner puts you down in front of the others. You decide to talk about it after you have had time to think it through.

- Your supervisor keeps calling you by the wrong name even though you have corrected them several times.

- In a busy fish and chip shop in a neighbourhood that is unfamiliar to you, you are waiting to be served. When it is your turn the staff member says 'just a moment' and then takes another person's order, even though it is clear that you were there first. This happens several more times and it gradually occurs to you that they do not want to serve you. You ask very clearly to be served, and again the person says, 'just a moment', and serves someone else. You realise very clearly now that they will not serve you, and you consider how to respond. Could they have mistaken you for someone else? Is this blatant racism or prejudice? What could be behind this?

Skill: Starting and continuing a conversation

1. I see a person I want to talk with.

2. I think about what I want to say.

3. I choose a good time and place.

4. I start talking in a friendly way. I ask the person how they are and show interest in them and what is happening in their life. I maintain appropriate personal space and boundaries. I take turns in listening and responding and continue to show interest in what they have to say, picking up their points as appropriate. I respect the other person's right to decide what to talk about and what not to talk about.

5. I end the conversation when it feels right, in a friendly and polite way.

Suggested skills practice scenarios

- You are out shopping and you see a former school friend.

- You are in the canteen at work and you want to talk to your line manager to get to know them a little better and let them get to know you a little better, too.

- You have a new neighbour and see them in the street while you are outside your front door. You would like to meet them and introduce yourself.

- You begin a conversation with a work colleague during a break.

- You have a conversation with your partner/a trusted friend about their childhood, and you share things about your childhood, too.

- You begin a conversation with your child about their day at school.

- You have a conversation with a fellow passenger on the train/bus.

Skill: Resolving conflict: Negotiating and compromising with others

1. I think about whether we have a difference of opinion or a conflict, and I decide if I need to say something to the person.

2. I tell the other person what I think about the situation. I state my own position and ask them what their perception is. I listen openly to their answer and I do not interrupt.

3. I think about their reply and try to see their point of view. I check that I understand and I am prepared to be wrong. (We all make mistakes.)

4. I suggest a compromise that takes into account the opinions and feelings of us both. I try to find a win–win solution and I encourage the other person to join me in finding a win–win solution.

Suggested skills practice scenarios

- You and your partner want to watch two different programmes on the television at the same time. You do not have a TV recorder or second TV.

- Your daughter/son (age 15) asks if they can stay out until midnight at a disco.

- Your boss has given you a deadline for an urgent piece of work, on top of your other work.

- Your neighbour is consistently staying up late into the night with other people and making a lot of noise. You need to sleep in order to get up for work each morning. You go to speak with him.

- Your neighbour asks you not to park your car in front of his house because his mother-in-law lives with them and because she is very frail, they need to park in front of their house so she can get to and from the car when they take her out. There are no disabled parking markings in the street in front of their house.

- You have recently purchased a radio/CD player/electronic device, and it is not working properly. You return it to the shop where you purchased it.

- You have planned to have an evening out with your friends. Your partner asks you to stay in because you do not spend enough time together.

- You and your partner discuss budgeting, and they ask you if you are willing to stop spending money on non-essentials in order to make ends meet. You realise this means giving up one or more expensive habits or hobbies.

Skill: Communicating with my child(ren) when they need guidance/boundary setting

1. I think about what my child has done and I decide what level of intervention the behaviour merits.

2. I check my own feelings and ask myself if I need to take a time out before proceeding.

3. I explain to my child what behaviour was unacceptable and why, and what I intend to do about it (if this is needed). I label the behaviour and *not* my child (e.g. 'I don't want you to mark the wall with your pen' rather than 'You are a bad girl/boy'). If I use discipline, it is clear, proportional, timely and appropriate to their age and understanding.

4. When the disciplining is over, I find a positive activity to engage in with my child in order to reassure them that there is still a supportive, secure relationship and I love them.

Suggested skills practice scenarios

- Your seven-year-old refuses to do something you are asking them to do.

- Your nine-year-old child has taken their bicycle out into the street without your permission or supervision.

- You discover your son/daughter (age 12) has been taking money from your wallet.

- Your 14-year-old child has stayed out three hours beyond curfew. Their mobile phone was switched off.

- You see your 13-year-old son/daughter smoking with friends on their way home from school.

- You hear from a friend that your 14-year-old son/daughter has been having sex with a boy/girlfriend.

- You find a near-empty bottle of vodka under your 16-year-old son/daughter's bed.

Skill: Talking about jealous feelings

1. I ask myself why I am feeling jealous. Is the jealousy based on real or imagined circumstances? What is my evidence?

2. I look at the other person's perspective to assess whether my feelings are based on facts or assumptions.

3. When I have thought through the situation, I may decide to share my feelings and concerns with the other person. I discuss the matter clearly and make my point of view and my feelings clear, but I do not give ultimatums or use threats, manipulation or emotional coercion.

4. I listen to their response and discuss with the other person a way that we can both help to resolve the situation (e.g. through compromise, clearer communication in future, changing the way in which contact is made with the third party).

Suggested skills practice scenarios

- You are at a party and your partner is talking with someone for what you perceive to be a long time. You are becoming jealous.

- From the phone bill, you discover that your partner has been having telephone conversations with their former partner.

- Your partner has become quite friendly with a colleague from their work, and has been going out lately for a drink after work. You have not met this colleague yet. You are becoming jealous.

- Your partner starts to dress up more, wear perfume/aftershave, and finds reasons to go out without you. You are becoming jealous.

- Your partner has to travel away from home for work, and is often away overnight. Sometimes you cannot reach them on their mobile phone. When this happens, you feel jealous and hurt.

Skill: Communicating about sensitive topics with my partner

1. I ask myself what I feel and why.

2. I try to see things from my partner's perspective, and decide whether or not I want to raise the subject with them. I think about how I can communicate my needs and my point of view while also respecting my partner.

3. When I have thought through the situation, I share my feelings and concerns with my partner in a gentle and respectful way.

4. I listen to their response, and respond in a respectful way, trying to find a win–win solution together.

Suggested skills practice scenarios

- You return home from work after a hard day and you ask your partner for a comforting, non-sexual hug. Or, your partner returns home from work after a hard day and does the same.

- You feel resentful because your partner has been uninterested in sex for the past month. You suspect their feelings towards you may be changing.

- You want to talk with your partner about their recent behaviour and how it is affecting you. You have noticed that they have been particularly distant from you in the past few weeks, and you are not sure if it is because you have done something to annoy or disappoint them.

- You want to take on more work in order to make more money, and your partner says no, they would like you to spend more time at home.

- You have been in a relationship for several years, and you continue to have a lifelong, deep and painful feeling of being emotionally lonely and isolated. You feel stuck, and unable to communicate with your partner about your true feelings. The only closeness there has been in the relationship has been sexualised, and both of you are left feeling dissatisfied after such contact. You decide to broach the subject with your partner, as you have realised that you have used sex as a compensatory behaviour for comfort, support or to give comfort and support to your partner. You recognise that you would both like things to be better and more fulfilling in the relationship. You open the conversation.

- Your partner is neglecting themselves and not taking care of their appearance and well-being in the way they usually do. You are concerned about them and wonder if there is something wrong that they are not telling you about.

- You are in a long-term relationship, and would like to talk with your partner about trying new things, sexually.

- You are concerned that you are not satisfying your sexual partner. You have been avoiding sex. Your partner feels hurt, confused, rejected and unattractive. You decide to ask them how they feel, and to talk about your insecurities.

Skill: Communicating warm feelings to someone close to me

1. I decide if I have good feelings about the other person.

2. I consider whether or not the other person would like to know about my feelings. I consider how I might feel and respond if they give me a negative, neutral or positive response.

3. I think of the best way to express my feelings.

4. I choose the right time and place to express my feelings, and I express my feelings in a friendly, non-threatening way.

Suggested skills practice scenarios

- You have very warm and caring feelings toward your partner, and you want to let them know.

- You love your partner/son/daughter/parent/sibling/etc. and you want to tell them.

- Your friend has recently helped you through some hard times and you want to tell them how much you appreciate their friendship and support.

- You have been out on several dates with someone you really like and you would like to tell them how you feel about them.

- Your teenage son/daughter has been spending a lot of time with you during a very difficult time in their life. You feel very supportive of them and love them very much, and want to let them know this.

Skill: Managing and communicating about sexual feelings in a mature way

1. I can have sexual feelings and when I do, I recognise and am aware of this. I consider sex and sexual feelings to be a normal and natural part of being an adult, and I am not ashamed of my sexuality or sexual feelings.

2. I am aware of the various choices I have about how to manage my sexual feelings.

3. If I choose to masturbate, I stay aware of what is positive and appropriate for me to

think about. I am also aware of what is unhelpful for me to think about.

4. If I am with a partner, it is fine to let them know I am in the mood. I am aware that they may also be in the mood but they also may not be. I am very aware of what the boundaries are around consent, and I respect those boundaries.

5. I can and do manage my sexual feelings in a mature and empathic way, taking into account the other person's feelings. I am proud that I handle my sexual feelings in a mature way.

Suggested skills practice scenarios

- You are with your partner and they say they are not interested in having sex. You are. How will you manage your sexual feelings?

- You are living in the community and you do not have a sexual partner. You are feeling very lonely and sexually frustrated. How do you manage your sexual feelings?

- You meet someone at a social event/club and they make it clear they are open to having unprotected sex. You have never met them before. You are feeling sexually aroused and interested. What will you do?

Skill: Having a difficult conversation with someone

There are many situations in life where we need to have a conversation that feels difficult to start because the issue feels scary or we feel angry, frustrated, sad or powerless about the situation. Very often, such conversations are not about facts, but instead they are about feelings, perspectives, misunderstandings or people having different motives and not understanding each other. We give more space and detail to the description of this skill, because it is so crucial and because it can be applied in many different life situations.

There are some very well-established principles to follow before and during difficult conversations:

1. **Prepare first** by thinking about the purpose of the conversation. What would be an ideal outcome for you and the other person? What assumptions are you making about what you know and what the other person knows? What assumptions are you making about your intentions and the other person's intentions? (Example: just because you are annoyed or insulted does not mean that this was the other person's intention.)

   Crucially, what did you contribute to the situation developing? This is an extremely important question and is often overlooked. Too often, we focus only on what the other person has done, and blame them entirely. But, before we go into a difficult conversation, we need to be very honest with ourselves about our actions, motivations and contributions to a situation. And sometimes this means we have to face some uncomfortable truths! Maybe we were sloppy, or ignored the other person's feelings. Maybe we had motives that were a little selfish (or a lot). Maybe we were just not thinking, or avoiding the issue, or denying that we knew the situation would only get worse but we did not want to deal with it – so it did get worse. Only after we fully own up to our role in contributing to the situation should we then move on to think about what the other person contributed.

   What are your feelings about the situation? Is any 'old stuff' getting triggered? Does this situation remind you of situations from earlier in life? If so, how can you think about these old 'triggers' in a way that allows you to see this situation for what it is, clearly and cleanly.

   Are you catastrophising and making this situation far worse than it really is? Try to gain some perspective. Try to think about the other person not as an opponent but instead as a partner in the conversation, where you will both be looking for a solution together. What is the other person's perspective likely to be? What emotions are they likely to feel about the situation? How are they likely to view their role and contribution to the situation? What solution do you think they would propose? Do the two of you have any common concerns? Can you think of any possible common concerns?

   Think about how a neutral third party (like a referee, or an arbitrator) would see and describe this situation. Be willing to move away from I-am-right-and-you-are-wrong type thinking.

2. **Ask to speak with the person and find an appropriate time and place** where you can talk. Stay centred, calm and firm in your stance. Be prepared for the other person to have strong views or have powerful feelings. Be clear in your mind that you do not want the conversation to degenerate into a battle over who said what or who knew what when or who intended what. Instead, stay focused on trying to find a solution that you can both live with and which avoids blaming or shaming.

3. **Begin the conversation.** Here are some suggestions for ways to start the conversation (crucially, all of these openers have one thing in common: they are openers that demonstrate respect, invite dialogue and recognise the importance of the other person's perspective and feelings):

   ○ *'I think we have different points of view about _____. I'd like to understand your point of view and discuss the situation.'*

   ○ *'I'd like to talk about what just happened. Do you have time to talk? I'd like to see if we can find a solution that works for both of us.'*

   ○ *'I am interested to hear your point of view about _____ and see if we can find a better understanding about what happened. I want to understand your point of view and your feelings and I'd also like to explain my perspective as well.'*

○ *'I would like to discuss something with you that I think will help us to work better together.'*

○ *'I'd like to talk with you about _____. It feels important to discuss this now, so that we can sort it out. I have a feeling that we both might have strong feelings about this, so I'd like to share some of my perspective and hear what your perspective is too.'*

4. **Enquire and acknowledge**. Show genuine curiosity and a willingness to learn about the other person's perspective, feelings and intentions. This must be absolutely genuine, otherwise there is no point. After all, you don't know what is or was in the other person's mind. This is the opportunity to learn. Listen fully until the person is finished. Respond only to understand and to fully hear what they are saying. What does this person really want? What do they really think? Whatever you hear, don't get defensive or take it personally (if you take it personally, as in a personal attack, you are very likely to get defensive). If they have had a strong emotional reaction, listen to and respect their point of view and their feelings. Acknowledge the other person's position, validate their feelings and show genuine respect. If there is this form of respect shown to the other person, the other person is more likely to show similar respect to you, and there may be some hope of shifting, compromise and a mutually satisfactory outcome.

5. **State your own position:** Recognise the other person's point of view, and explain your own. Be clear about the feelings you have about the situation, just as you invited the other person to be clear about theirs. Example: 'From what you have explained, I can see how and why you came to that conclusion and why you felt angry at me for missing that important deadline. I thought that we had agreed (x) and I can see that you thought it was (y). I assumed we were using the old system to slot in deadlines, and did not realise we had moved to the new system. Maybe we can talk about this issue so that the situation does not happen again. I'd also like to say that I was surprised that you yelled at me in front of the whole team, and I felt embarrassed and pretty angry about that, even though I know it is very unusual for you to take that approach and that's not your usual style. I hope we can discuss how, if you are angry about something I have done in the future, you can talk with me one-to-one rather than shout in front of the whole team.'

6. **Focus on problem-solving**. Build solutions. Keep enquiring. Ask the other person for ideas about solutions. Whatever they say, find something to build on. If the other person becomes defensive and gets into a blaming, I-am-right-and-you-are-wrong stance, go back to asking questions to understand the situation and find a solution. Encourage the person to engage in the conversation, be supportive to them and stay constructive and focused on a solution that works over the long term.

Suggested skills practice scenarios

- Your child has been getting into fights at school, and you want to discuss this with them. You received a phone call from the teacher that seems to suggest that your child has been provoking the fights.

- A friend has said something to a third person that you told them in confidence. You are angry and upset about this.

- Your partner has criticised you in front of friends, and you are feeling hurt and angry about this.

- Your partner does things round the house that make you very annoyed.

- Your brother or sister has not helped with a family situation that you think is the equal responsibility of all of the siblings. You decide you need to talk about it.

- Your parent criticises you a lot and it hurts. You decide you want to talk it through with them and find a solution.

- Your teenage child stays shut away in their room after school and never speaks to you. You decide to talk with them about this.

- Your child reports to you that their teacher teases them and embarrasses them in the classroom. It is so serious that your child does not want to go to school. You decide to speak with the teacher and the head teacher.

- At work, your supervisor has overlooked you three times for promotion, in favour of colleagues who you think are less able than you. You decide to raise this with the supervisor.

- You want to ask your boss for a pay rise.

- You are a supervisor at work and an employee has been under-performing or has done something wrong.

- You decide, after careful consideration, to end a relationship of several years.

- An old friend is being released from jail and wants to meet up with you. You know that the conversation is very likely to be about committing a crime. This is a friend who you committed crimes with in the past, and you have decided it is important for you to move on with your life and not to have friends who are still committing crimes. You decide to tell the person that you have decided to move on with your life and not commit crimes. This may mean the end of your friendship.

See Stone, Patton and Heen (1999) for more guidance about how to have a difficult conversation.

About the Authors

Clark Baim has 25 years of experience working internationally as a trainer, group facilitator, supervisor and psychotherapist. He has facilitated groups and workshops in more than 200 prisons, probation centres and forensic hospitals across Europe, North America, Australia and South Africa, and conducted staff training in 15 countries. He is a registered psychotherapist and senior trainer with the British Psychodrama Association, and he is co-director – with Lydia Guthrie – of Change Point Learning and Development, providing staff training and development in the criminal justice, social work, mental health, voluntary and private sectors. Between 2000 and 2012, Clark was contracted as the co-lead national trainer for the UK's community-based sexual offending treatment programmes, run by the Probation Service for England and Wales. He is also co-director of the Birmingham Institute for Psychodrama. He has authored and co-authored numerous manuals for offending behaviour programmes, and has published widely on topics related to offender rehabilitation, supervision, groupwork methods, psychotherapy, attachment-informed practice and applied theatre. He is a Fellow of the Berry Street Childhood Institute in Melbourne, Australia. Early in his career, Clark was the founding Director of Geese Theatre UK, a company focusing on offender rehabilitation. A native of Chicago and graduate of Williams College, Massachusetts, Clark now lives in the UK.

Lydia Guthrie is a trainer, group facilitator and supervisor, working in criminal justice, mental health and social work settings. She spent ten years working for the Probation Service in a range of specialisms, including work with long term prisoners and groupwork with men who have committed sexual abuse and domestic abuse. She worked as a supervisor and team manager and also developed and delivered programmes for victims and survivors of abuse. From 2008–2012, she was contracted as co-lead national trainer for the UK's community-based sexual offending treatment programmes, run by the Probation Service for England and Wales. Since 2009, Lydia and Clark have been Co-Directors of Change Point Learning and Development, providing training, consultancy, groupwork programmes, and supervision across the criminal justice, mental health, social work and voluntary sector settings in the UK and internationally. Before qualifying as a social worker, she gained an undergraduate degree (PPE) and an MSc in Social Work from Oxford University and worked in the voluntary sector with adults with learning disabilities, adults with physical disabilities and with teenagers in the 'looked after' system. Lydia is passionate about attachment theory, reflective supervision, mindfulness and self-compassion. She is currently an MSc candidate at Roehampton University in Attachment Studies.

If you have found this book useful, and would like to learn more, please contact the authors for more information about training and consultancy: www.changepointlearning.com

References

Ainsworth, M., Blehar, M., Waters, E. and Wall, S. (1978) *Patterns of Attachment*. Hillsdale, NJ: Erlbaum.

Andrews, D. A. and Bonta, J. (2006) *The Psychology of Criminal Conduct* (4th edn). Newark, NJ: LexisNexis.

Andrews, D. A., Bonta, J. and Wormwith, J. S. (2006) 'The recent past and near future of risk and/or need assessment.' *Crime and Delinquency 52*, 1, 7–27.

Andrews, D. and Dowden, C. (2007) 'The Risk-Needs-Responsivity Model of assessment in human service and prevention and corrections: Crime prevention jurisprudence.' *Canadian Journal of Criminology and Criminal Justice 49*, 4, 439–464.

Baim, C., Brookes, S. and Mountford, A. (2002) *The Geese Theatre Handbook: Drama with Offenders and People at Risk*. Winchester: Waterside.

Baim, C., Burmeister, J. and Maciel, M. (eds) (2007) *Psychodrama: Advances in Theory and Practice*. London: Routledge.

Baim, C. and Morrison, T. (2011) *Attachment-Based Practice with Adults: Understanding Strategies and Promoting Positive Change*. Brighton: Pavilion.

Baim, C. and Taylor, S. (2004) 'The perpetrator and the victim: Using psychodrama with perpetrators who are also survivors of childhood abuse.' Handouts accompanying the workshop at the International Psychodrama Conference, Oxford, England, 9–15 August.

Bandura, A. (1977) *Social Learning Theory*. Englewood Cliffs, NJ: Prentice-Hall.

Barnett, G. and Mann, R. E. (2013) 'Empathy deficits and sexual offending: A model of obstacles to empathy.' *Aggression and Violent Behaviour 18*, 228–239.

Bateman, A., Brown, D. and Pedder, J. (2010) *Introduction to Psychotherapy: An Outline of Psychodynamic Principles and Practice* (4th edn). Hove: Routledge.

Bateson, G. (1972) *Steps to an Ecology of Mind: Collected Essays in Anthropology, Psychiatry, Evolution, and Epistemology*. Chicago: University of Chicago Press.

Bateson, G. (1979) *Mind and Nature: A Necessary Unity*. New York: Hampton Press.

Beck, A.T., Freeman, A. and Davis, D.D. (2003) *Cognitive Therapy of Personality Disorders*. New York: Guilford Press.

Beck, A. T. (1976) *Cognitive Therapy and the Emotional Disorders*. New York: International Universities Press.

Becker, H. (1963) *Outsiders*. New York: Free Press.

Blagden, N. J., Winder, B., Thorne, K. and Gregson, M. (2011) '"No-one in the world would ever wanna speak to me again": an interpretative phenomenological analysis into convicted sexual offenders' accounts and experiences of maintaining and leaving denial.' *Psychology, Crime and Law 17*, 7, 563–585.

Blair, C. (2010) 'Stress and the development of self-regulation in context.' *Child Development Perspectives 4*, 3, 181–188.

Blatner, A. (1997) *Acting in: Practical Applications of Psychodramatic Methods* (3rd edn). London: Free Association Books.

Blatner, A. (2000) *Foundations of Psychodrama: History, Theory and Practice* (4th edn). New York: Springer.

Bloom, B. (1956) *Taxonomy of Educational Objectives: Handbook One: Cognitive Domain*. New York: David McKay.

Bowlby, J. (1969) *Attachment and Loss. Vol.1. Attachment*. New York: Basic Books.

Brandon, M., Belderson, P., Warren, C., Howe, D. *et al.* (2008) *Analysing Child Deaths and Serious Injury Through Abuse and Neglect: What Can We Learn?* London: Department for Children, Families and Schools.

Briere, J. and Scott, C. (2006) *Principles of Trauma Therapy: A Guide to Symptoms, Evaluation and Treatment*. London: Sage.

Browne, K. D., Beech, A. R. and Craig, L. A. (2013) *Assessments in Forensic Practice: A Handbook*. Chichester: Wiley-Blackwell.

Bush, J. (1993) 'Cognitive self-change.' Workshop presented at *What Works* conference on effective practice, Salford, England.

Buzan, T. and Buzan, B. (2010) *The Mind Map Book: Unlock Your Creativity, Boost Your Memory, Change Your Life*. Harlow: Educational Publishers.

Calder, M. (2008) *The Carrot or the Stick? Towards Effective Practice with Involuntary Clients in Safeguarding Children Work*. Lyme Regis: Russell House.

Cicchetti, D. and Valentino, K. (2006) 'An Ecological Transactional Perspective on Child Maltreatment: Failure of the Average Expectable Environment and Its Influence upon Child Development.' In D. Cicchetti and D. J. Cohen (eds) *Developmental Psychopathology: Risk, Disorder, and Adaptation* (2nd edn) (Vol. 3). New York: Wiley.

Cooper, M. (2008) *Essential Research Findings in Counselling and Psychotherapy: The Facts Are Friendly*. London: Sage.

Craig, L., Dixon, L. and Gannon, T. (2013) *What Works in Offender Rehabilitation: An Evidence-Based Approach to Assessment and Treatment.* Chichester: Wiley-Blackwell.

Crittenden, P. M. (2008) *Raising Parents: Attachment, Parenting and Child Safety.* Uffculme: Willan Publishing.

Crittenden, P. and Landini, A. (2011) *Assessing Adult Attachment: A Dynamic-Maturational Approach to Discourse Analysis.* New York: Norton.

Dallos, R. (2006) *Attachment Narrative Therapy.* Maidenhead: Open University Press.

Davies, W. and Frude, N. (1999) *Preventing Face-to-Face Violence: Dealing with Anger and Aggression at Work.* Leicester: Association for Psychological Therapies.

Dayton, T. (2005) *The Living Stage: A Step-by-Step Guide to Psychodrama, Sociometry and Experiential Group Therapy.* Deerfield Beach, FL: Health Communications.

Dunkley, C. and Stanton, M. (2013) *Teaching Clients to Use Mindfulness Skills: A Practical Guide.* London: Routledge.

Farrall, S. (2002) *Rethinking What Works with Offenders: Probation, Social Context and Desistance from Crime.* Cullompton: Willan Publishing.

Fonagy, P., Gergely, G., Jurist, E. L. and Target, M. (2004) *Affect Regulation, Mentalisation and the Development of the Self.* London: Karnac.

Gilbert, P. (2009) *The Compassionate Mind.* London: Constable.

Gillespie, S. M., Mitchell, I. J., Fisher, D. and Beech, A. R. (2012) 'Treating disturbed emotional regulation in sexual offenders: The potential applications of mindful self-regulation and controlled breathing techniques.' *Aggression and Violent Behaviour 17,* 333–343.

Goffman, E. (1959) *The Presentation of Self in Everyday Life.* New York: Anchor Books.

Goldstein, A. (1988) *The Prepare Curriculum: Teaching Prosocial Competencies.* Champaign, IL: Research Press.

Goleman, D. (1996) *Emotional Intelligence: Why It Can Matter More than IQ.* London: Bloomsbury.

Gorman, K., Gregory, M., Hayles, M. and Parton, N. (eds) (2006) *Constructive Work with Offenders.* London: Jessica Kingsley Publishers.

Greenberg, G., Ganshorn, K. and Danilkewic, A. (2001) 'Solution-focused therapy: A counseling model for busy family physicians.' *Canadian Family Physician 47* (November), 2289–2295.

Hanson, R. and Bussiere, M. T. (1998) 'Predicting relapse: A meta-analysis of sexual offender recidivism studies.' *Journal of Consulting and Clinical Psychology 66,* 2, 348–362.

Hanson, R. and Morton-Bourgon, K. (2005) 'The characteristics of persistent sexual offenders: A meta-analysis of recidivism studies.' *Journal of Consulting and Clinical Psychology 73,* 1154–1163.

Hudgins, M. K. (2002) *Experiential Therapy for PTSD: The Therapeutic Spiral Model.* New York: Springer.

Jenkins, A. (1997) *Invitations to Responsibility: The Therapeutic Engagement of Men Who Are Violent and Abusive.* Adelaide: Dulwich.

Kabat-Zinn, J. (2004) *Wherever You Go, There You Are: Mindfulness Meditation for Everyday Life.* London: Piatkus.

Kahneman, D. (2011) *Thinking Fast and Slow.* London: Allen Lane.

Kottler, J. (2010) *The Assassin and the Therapist: An Exploration of Truth and its Meaning in Psychotherapy and in Life.* New York: Routledge.

Laub, J. H. and Sampson, R. J. (2001) 'Understanding Desistance from Crime.' In M. Tonry (ed.) *Crime and Justice: A Review of Research, Vol. 28.* Chicago, IL: University of Chicago Press.

Laws, D. R. and Ward, T. (2011) *Desistance from Sex Offending: Alternatives to Throwing Away the Keys.* New York: Guilford Press.

Mann, R. E. (2000) 'Managing Resistance and Rebellion in Relapse Prevention Intervention.' In R. D. Laws, S. M. Hudson and T. Ward (eds) *Remaking Relapse Prevention with Sex Offenders: A Sourcebook.* London: Sage.

Marshall, W. L., Hudson, S. M., Jones, R. and Fernandez, Y. M. (1995) 'Empathy in sex offenders.' *Clinical Psychology Review 15,* 99–113.

Marshall, W., Marshall, L., Serran, G. and Fernandez, Y. (2006) *Treating Sexual Offenders.* London: Routledge.

Marshall, W., Serran, G. and Cortoni, F. A. (2000) 'Childhood attachments and sexual abuse and their relationship to coping in child molesters.' *Sexual Abuse: A Journal of Research and Treatment 12,* 1, 17–26.

Marshall, W. L., Serran, G. A., Fernandez, Y., Mulloy, R., Mann, R. E. and Thornton, D. (2003) 'Therapist characteristics in the treatment of sexual offenders: Tentative data on their relationship with indices of behaviour change.' *Journal of Sexual Aggression 9,* 1, 25–30.

Marshall, W., Thornton, D., Marshall, L., Fernandez, Y. and Mann, R. (2001) 'Treatment of sexual offenders who are in categorical denial: A pilot project.' *Sexual Abuse: A Journal of Research and Treatment 13,* 3, 205–215.

Maruna, S. (2001) *Making Good: How Ex-Convicts Reform and Rebuild Their Lives.* Washington, DC: American Psychological Association.

Maruna, S. and LeBel, T. (2010) 'The Desistance Paradigm in Correctional Practice: From Programmes to Lives.' In F. McNeill, P. Raynor and C. Trotter (eds) *Offender Supervision: New Directions in Theory, Research and Practice.* Cullompton: Willan Publishing.

Maruna, S. and Mann, R.E. (2006) 'A fundamental attribution error? Rethinking cognitive distortions.' *Legal and Criminological Psychology 11,* 155–177.

Maslow, A. H. (1943) 'A theory of human motivation.' *Psychological Review 50,* 4, 370–396.

Maslow, A. (1954) *Motivation and Personality.* New York: Harper.

Masters, R. (1994) *Counselling Criminal Justice Offenders.* London: Sage.

Matza, D. (1969) *On Becoming Deviant.* Englewood Cliffs, NJ: Prentice Hall.

McGuire, J. (2000) *Cognitive-Behavioural Approaches: An Introduction to Theory and Research.* London: HM Inspectorate of Probation.

McGuire, J. and Priestley, P. (1981) *Life After School: A Social Skills Curriculum.* Oxford: Pergamon.

McGuire, J. and Priestley, P. (1987) *Offending Behaviour: Skills and Stratagems for Going Straight.* London: Batsford.

McNeill, F. (2012) 'Counterblast: A Copernican correction for community sentences.' *Howard Journal of Criminal Justice 51,* 1, 94–99.

McNeill, F., Farrall, S., Lightowler, C. and Maruna, S. (2012) *How and Why People Stop Offending: Discovering Desistance.* Insights: Evidence summaries to Support Social Services in Scotland. Glasgow: Institute for Research and Innovation in Social Services.

McNeill, F. and Weaver, B. (2010) *Changing Lives? Desistance Research and Offender Management.* Glasgow: Scottish Centre for Crime and Justice Research.

Mead, G. H. (1934) *Mind, Self, and Society.* Chicago: University of Chicago Press.

Miller, W. R. and Rollnick, S. (2002) *Motivational Interviewing: Preparing People for Change* (2nd edn). New York: Guilford Press.

Moreno, J. L. (1993) *Who Shall Survive? Foundations of Sociometry, Group Psychotherapy and Sociodrama* (student edn). Roanoke, VA: Royal Publishing Company with American Society of Group Psychotherapy and Psychodrama.

Moreno, J. L. (1946) *Psychodrama: Volume One.* New York: Beacon House.

Moreno, Z. T., Blomkvist, L. and Rutzel, T. (2000) *Psychodrama, Surplus Reality and the Art of Healing.* London: Routledge.

Neff, K. (2011) *Self Compassion.* New York: Harper Collins.

Nunes, K., Hanson, K., Firestone, P., Moulden, H., Greenberg, D. and Bradford, J. (2007) 'Denial predicts recidivism for some sexual offenders.' *Sexual Abuse: A Journal of Research and Treatment 19,* 2, 91–105.

O'Reilly, G., Morrison, T., Sheerin, D. and Carr, A. (2001) 'A group-based module for adolescents to improve motivation to change sexually abusive behaviour.' *Child Abuse Review 10,* 150–169.

Panksepp, J. (2005) *Affective Neuroscience: The Foundations of Human and Animal Emotions.* Series in Affective Science. Oxford: Oxford University Press.

Perry, B.D. (2009) 'Examing child maltreatment through a new developmental lens: clinical application of the Neurosequential Model of Therapeutics.' *Journal of Loss and Trauma 14,* 240–255.

Pincus, A. and Minahan, A. (1973) *Social Work Practice: Model and Method.* Itasca, IL: F. E. Peacock.

Porporino, F. (2010) 'Bringing Sense and Sensitivity to Corrections: From Programmes to 'Fix' Offenders to Services to Support Desistance.' In J. Brayford, F. Cowe and J. Deering (eds) *What Else Works? Creative Work with Offenders.* Uffculme: Willan Publishing.

Prochaska, J. and DiClemente, C. (1982) 'Transtheoretical therapy: Towards a more integrative model of change.' *Psychotherapy – Theory, Research and Practice 19,* 3, 276–278.

Prochaska, J., DiClemente, C. and Norcross, J. (1992) 'In search of how people change: Applications to addictive behaviours.' *American Psychologist 47,* 9, 1102–1114.

Roberts, B. and Baim, C. (1999) 'A community-based programme for sex offenders who deny their offending behaviour.' *The Probation Journal 46,* 4, 225–233.

Rogers, C. (1967) *On Becoming a Person: A Therapist's View of Psychotherapy.* London: Constable.

Siegel, D. J. (2007) *The Mindful Brain.* New York: Norton.

Seligman, M. E., Steen, T. A., Park, N. and Peterson, C. (2005) 'Positive psychology progress: Empirical validation of interventions.' *American Psychologist 60,* 5, 410–421.

Senge, P. (1990) *The Fifth Discipline: The Art and Practice of the Learning Organisation.* New York: Doubleday.

Stone, D., Patton, B. and Heen, S. (1999) *Difficult Conversations.* London: Penguin.

Tannenbaum, F. (1938) *Crime and Community.* London and New York: Columbia University Press.

Thornton, D. (2002) 'Constructing and testing a framework for dynamic risk assessment.' *Sexual Abuse: A Journal of Research and Treatment 14,* 2, 139–154.

van der Kolk, B. A. (1994) 'The body keeps the score: Memory and the evolving psychobiology of post-traumatic stress.' *Harvard Review of Psychiatry 1,* 5, 253–265.

Van Mentz, M. (1983) *The Effective Use of Role Play.* London: Kogan Page.

Vennard, J., Hedderman, C. and Sugg, D. (1997) *Changing Offenders' Attitudes and Behaviour: What Works?* Home Office Research Study 171. London: Home Office Research and Statistics Directorate.

Ward, T. and Maruna, S. (2007) *Rehabilitation.* London: Routledge.

Ward, T., Bickley, J., Webster, S. D., Fisher, D., Beech, A. and Eldridge, H. (2004) *The Self-Regulation Model of the Offense and Relapse Process: A Manual. Vol. 1: Assessment.* Victoria, BC: Pacific Psychological Assessment Corporation.

Ward, T. and Gannon, T. A. (2006) 'Rehabilitation, etiology and self-regulation: The comprehensive good lives model of treatment for sexual offenders.' *Aggression and Violent Behaviour 11,* 1, 77–94.

Ware, J. and Mann, R. E. (2012) 'How should "acceptance of responsibility" be addressed in sexual offending treatment programs?' *Aggression and Violent Behaviour 17,* 279–288.

Weiner, R., Adderley, D. and Kirk, K. (2011) *Sociodrama in a Changing World.* Raleigh, NC: Lulu.

White, M. (2007) *Maps of Narrative Practice.* New York: Norton.

White, M. and Epston, D. (1990) *Narrative Means to Therapeutic Ends.* New York: Norton.

Wilber, K. (2000) *A Brief History of Everything.* Boston: Shambhala.

Williams, M. and Penman, D. (2011) *Mindfulness: A Practical Guide to Finding Peace in a Frantic World.* London: Piatkus.

Index